Successful Charity Marketing

Successful Charity Marketing

Meeting Need

Second Edition

Ian Bruce

ICSA Publishing
The Official Publishing Company of
The Institute of Chartered Secretaries and Administrators

With

PRENTICE HALL EUROPE
London   New York   Toronto   Sydney   Tokyo   Singapore
Madrid   Mexico City   Munich   Paris

First published 1994 by
ICSA Publishing Limited

Second edition published 1998
by ICSA Publishing Limited
with Prentice Hall Europe
Campus 400, Marylands Avenue
Hemel Hempstead
Hertfordshire, HP2 7EZ

© Ian Bruce 1998

All rights reserved. No part of this publication may be reproduced,
stored in a retrieval system, or transmitted, in any form, or by any
means, electronic, mechanical, photocopying, recording or otherwise,
without prior permission, in writing, from the publisher.

Typeset in 10/12pt Palatino
by Fakenham Photosetting Limited, Fakenham, Norfolk

Printed and bound in Great Britain
by Biddles Limited, Guildford, Surrey

British Library Cataloguing in Publication Data

A catalogue record for this book is available from
the British Library

ISBN 1–860720–38–2

1 2 3 4 5   02 01 00 99 98

To my parents and the other parent figures in my life:
Tom and Una Bruce, Bob and Lillian Barker, John and Edna Stroud, and
Peter and Margery Rowland

CONTENTS

PREFACE TO THE FIRST EDITION

There is a rising groundswell of interest in charity marketing. Research among the largest 200 charities (Bruce and Raymer 1992) showed that 'understanding customer need' was the third most important managerial attribute rated by charity chief executives. This point of view may also reflect the thinking of middle and junior managers if the over-subscription of recent seminars on marketing run at the National Council for Voluntary Organisations is anything to go by.

Apart from the wide range of people interested in how charities are and should be run, there are three particular target groups for this book: charity managers; undergraduate and postgraduate students; and commercial and statutory sector managers becoming interested in the voluntary sector.

Obviously, like most authors, I hope that readers will start at page 1 and work through until the end. However, it is many years since I read a book like that. With this in mind, I have constructed the book to allow readers to dip into it in different ways. For example, students and business people who know about commercial marketing might want to read Chapter 1, looking at charity marketing, and then move to Chapters 3, 4 and 5 where marketing is applied to the charity sector. Later chapters will be read according to interest in the various subjects, e.g. service provision, fund-raising, etc. Charity managers, especially if they are not familiar with marketing, will probably want to read the first five chapters and then go to whichever later chapter most closely correlates with their own work, e.g. fund-raising, service provision or pressure group work. However, if that seems over-methodical, the structure should accommodate the reader who wishes to turn first to the particular chapter of functional interest, e.g. physical goods marketing or service marketing. Commercial or statutory sector managers less familiar with charities and their work might find the last six chapters the best place to start. There is a further contextual point to make regarding the relative terminology of voluntary organisations and charities. Charities are technically those bodies (in England) registered with the Charity Commission. Voluntary organisations include all of those plus many other bodies which, for one reason or another, are not registered. I have mainly used the term 'charity' but the statements made can in most cases be generalised to include voluntary organisations, except in Chapter 9 in the section on market sources and size.

I have tried to use a marketing approach in over twenty years of working in the voluntary and statutory sectors. Despite the bad press on its superficial interpretation (advertising and selling), I think it provides a philosophy as well as a planning, management and implementation mechanism which is ideally suited to meeting need by the voluntary and statutory sectors. With the existing turbulence in the areas where the commercial, statutory and voluntary sector waters meet, it provides a particularly useful compass to help us steer a sensible, thoughtful course to the benefit of the people and causes we are here to serve. A vital point to stress is that a marketing approach is for *all* charity staff not just fund-raisers and media officers. Staff in service provision, campaigns, human resources, finance, etc., can and need to embrace a marketing philosophy and practice.

If a marketing approach has always been central to one's way of working, it is difficult to know where to stop when acknowledging helpful influences. While there was life before Unilever, there was not much marketing life, and a special tribute must go to that company and colleagues in Lever Bros., especially my fellow marketing trainees from whom I learned so much: Howard Belton, John Howkins, Peter Kirby-Higgs, Irving Kucynski, Jim Maxmin and Charles Murdock.

Translating my marketing into the charity sector proved a positive experience because of the support and encouragement of David Hobman, Age Concern's first director, and because of Patricia Hewitt's help. At the Volunteer Centre UK, Eileen Ware introduced all the marketing experience at her time at Shelter. I learned a great deal in local government, particularly from Tony Allen and John Harwood but then, at least, local government was a marketing desert.

However, it is at RNIB that the scope for applying a charity marketing approach has been greatest and I am particularly indebted to my honorary officers Sir Duncan Watson, John Wall, Colin Low and Jack Dunn for the trust they placed in me. At the level of implementation my thanks go to my colleagues Tony Aston, Paul Ennals and Barry Gifford, and especially to Mike Lancaster, Stephen King, Sanchi Heesom, Steve Cooper, Bob Empson and John Godber for the professional marketing knowledge and experience they bring. We still have considerable progress to make but the achievements of the last few years have been considerable.

Special thanks are due to my new colleagues at City University and its Business School for welcoming me into the world of academia – Raoul Franklin, Adrian Seville, David Kaye, Humphrey Bourne, Leslie de Chernatony, Martin Collins, Alison Dalby, Sarah Finch, Margaret Harvey, Clive

PREFACE TO THE FIRST EDITION • xiii

Holtham and Axel Johne, and to two special mentors, Gerald Goodhardt and Diana Leat.

In terms of the practicality of writing this book, I owe a whole range of people an enormous debt of gratitude: Susan Richards, Pat Lomax and Frances Dedrick from ICSA Publishing; Anne Biggs, Martin Green, Pam Pearse and David Saint from Action Planning; and David Horton Smith, Arnold Hughes, Jim Forward, Hal Neslen, Mary Smith and the Freeth family.

I always wondered why immediate family received such a prominent mention in acknowledgements, that is until Tina, my wife, wrote her first book – so I can fully appreciate all the support that Tina, Hannah and Tom have given me, especially for coping with my seemingly endless dictation into a tape recorder as we all chugged up the River Thames together on what was officially called a summer holiday. (I suppose I should also include lock-keepers who held strange packets of tapes and scripts and kept an eye open for a battered motorboat called *Tarita*.) I particularly appreciate the support that Tina gives – as a liberated and loving person, she somehow manages to combine intellectual stimulation and calm support. I wish I knew how she does it!

I.W.B.
Jan. 1994

PREFACE TO THE SECOND EDITION

I am obviously encouraged that demand for this book is such that the publisher wants a second edition. Existing readers may like guidelines on the major differences. Perhaps the most fundamental has been the opportunity to draw on the recent rich vein of practitioner and academic articles, especially those made available through the new *Journal of Non-profit and Voluntary Sector Marketing*. Also, as a result of reader interest I have expanded coverage of two themes, namely price (Chapter 4) and the reasons why charities undervalue customers (Chapter 5). Lastly, two chapters have had major changes: the ones on fund-raising (Chapter 9) and on whole charity identity (Chapter 10). The latter has been of growing interest to academics and practitioners with several recent articles contributing new ideas. The chapter on fund-raising has had the benefit of the major contributions of the Johns Hopkins Comparative Non-profit Sector Project and the Office of National Statistics Survey of Charitable Organisations.

My thanks to all who helped me on the first edition remains undiminished but for help with the second edition I would like to add Clare Grist-Taylor, Catriona Gordon, Laura Miller and David Pickering of Prentice Hall Europe, and Mary Harris, the tower of strength of VOLPROF. I also would like to record my gratitude to colleagues at City University Business School for their continuing support of this vital field of management and especially to our Dean, Leslie Hannah.

I.W.B.
October 1997

ABBREVIATIONS

AIDA	attention, interest, desire, action
AOP	Association of Optical Practitioners
BCO	British College of Optometrists
BCODP	British Council of Organisations of Disabled People
CAF	Charities Aid Foundation
CDI	Comprehensive Disability Income
DTI	Department of Trade and Industry
DBC	Disability Benefits Consortium
DIG	Disability Income Group
DLA	disability living allowance
FODO	Federation of Dispensing Opticians
FMCG	fast-moving consumer goods
LEA	local education authority
NACRO	National Association for the Care and Resettlement of Offenders
NOPWC	National Old People's Welfare Council
NSPCC	National Society for the Prevention of Cruelty to Children
ONS	Office of National Statistics
RADAR	Royal Association of Disability and Rehabilitation
RCSB	Royal Commonwealth Society for the Blind
RNIB	Royal National Institute for the Blind
RNID	Royal National Institute for Deaf People
RNLI	Royal National Lifeboat Institution
RSPB	Royal Society for the Protection of Birds
RSPCA	Royal Society for the Prevention of Cruelty to Animals
SWOT	strengths, weaknesses, opportunities and threats
USP	unique selling proposition
WWF	World Wildlife Fund (now Worldwide Fund for Nature)

1

WHAT IS CHARITY MARKETING?

What is charity marketing and why use it?

I am a passionate believer in marketing and in applying a marketing approach to the voluntary sector. In part this is because I was trained as a manager by Unilever where marketing was, and still is, the 'way we do it round here'. But the main reason for my continuing passion for marketing is that it is philosophically and practically well suited to the voluntary and public sectors. What a gift in finding a technique that has as its philosophy a dominant ethos of starting with the needs of the consumer, rather than the concerns of the provider. Doesn't it also just feel right to have a practical process which starts from where the consumer actually is, rather than where we would like them to be? Such a philosophy and practice rings all sorts of bells in my background and current life. For me, as a child of the 1960s, a marketing approach has similarities with community work and community development, i.e. giving to what were previously regarded as passive recipients of services, a major role in their creation and delivery. Being married to a Froebelian educator whose core philosophy and practice is the dictum 'begin where the learner is' (Friedrich Froebel 1782–1852) has produced an unexpected harmony between an educator and a manager.

Essentially marketing is a way of fitting our planning and implementation of goods, services or ideas together in a practical but sophisticated way; and in a way that emphasises the needs of the customer, client or person in need rather than simply trying to improve the efficiency of existing processes or ways of doing things. So much of voluntary sector activity development takes place in what the commercial world would call a product- or production-orientated way. Superficially this can increase efficiency but the risk in this rapidly changing world is that the product or process becomes increasingly less relevant or appropriate to what customers or clients need and want.

The majority of definitions of marketing describe it as an activity to help the organisation achieve its goals by providing consumer satisfaction. This description should reassure the charity reader because it describes the key role of the goals of the organisation. But it also establishes the key focus on the customer/user/client/patient, etc. In texts on commercial marketing the term 'customer' is almost always used. In this book I use the term 'customers' to cover all of a charity's target groups and, depending on the context, divide this term into prime subsets of 'beneficiaries' and 'suppor-ters' (see pages 26–30). However, at best the selection of the appropriate term is a matter of sensitivity and at worst it is a matter of fashion. Too much concentration on terms, in my experience, simply holds up a discussion of the more fundamental issues of charity marketing.

But for many people the term 'marketing' does have negative associations. It describes a process for selling people things they do not need. For those with a centre-to-left political orientation it is associated with an intensely capitalist and commercial environment which is antithetical to the public and not-for-profit sector. For those with a centre-to-right view, it is more acceptable generally, but its application in our sector can seem irrelevant or inappropriate. Even where marketing is accepted, it is often only readily associated with areas such as fund-raising and public rela-tions.

So if the term starts with such a bad press, why continue to use it in the public and voluntary sectors? Over the last fifty years the approach, practice and techniques of marketing have transformed the commercial world and its provision of goods. It is also now significantly affecting the world of services. Our world needs to take advantage of these advances. But should we use a new name? I think not. Attempts have been made to use the term 'public relations' as an alternative for marketing, regarding the public and voluntary sector (Bruce 1973), but PR also has negative overtones and is too narrow a concept. Professional practices (lawyers, architects, etc.) tried a similar approach (A. Wilson 1984, pp. xi–xiv) by substituting the term 'practice development', but it did not catch on.

Marketing as a term and a process is value-neutral. It can be used for good or ill. It can and has been applied not only in the commercial world, but also in the not-for-profit world, and even in the erstwhile planned economies of Eastern Europe.

Marketing is not unknown in public and not-for-profit organisations in the United Kingdom. As a rough benchmark, best practice is probably at the quality and penetration levels experienced in the commercial world in the 1960s. Over the last few years it has penetrated into strategic planning, service provision and campaigning. But in the main it is restricted to fund-raising and public relations. But best practice in these two areas is extremely impressive and can teach the commercial world a thing or two, e.g. direct mail.

Despite its bad press, the voluntary sector may want marketing more than it thinks. A survey of the 200 largest British charities (Bruce and Raymer 1992, Table 6.5) showed that understanding customer needs was rated as the third most important attribute that charity chief executives were seeking in their managers.

Definition of marketing in the public and voluntary sectors

A whole host of definitions of marketing exist. Most of the more sophisticated ones could be applied to the area under discussion. However, the one quoted here is by Philip Kotler. Kotler is Professor of International Marketing at Northwestern University, United States, and has the longest standing interest of any academic in the field of public and not-for-profit marketing. He developed an early version of the following definition in the 1970s which has essentially stood the test of time.

> *Marketing is the analysis, planning, implementation, and control of carefully formulated programmes designed to bring about voluntary exchanges of values with target markets to achieve institutional objectives. Marketing involves designing the institution's offerings to meet the target markets' needs and desires, and using effective pricing, communication, and distribution to inform, motivate, and service the markets. (Kotler and Fox 1985, p. 7)*

This comprehensive, albeit tightly packed, definition is helpful because it identifies the different elements of marketing which help to indicate how it can be applied in the charity sector. Kotler uses the term 'offering' in place of 'product' which is the generic term used universally to describe physical goods and services. In this book I use the generic term, product, to cover a charity's physical goods, services *and* ideas. Where it is important to draw particular attention to the type of product, the terms 'physical product', 'service product' and 'idea product' are used.

Four short case studies follow which exemplify what the different elements in the definition can mean in practice. While two of the four case studies have been taken from the social services and education, they could equally have been taken from health, transport, the arts, sports, etc. The social services study is of a voluntary visiting service for elderly people run by a local charity, but it may equally have been a study of a service for families under extreme stress or any other personal social service. The example from education is a school run by a national charity, but again any education service may have been selected. The example from fund-raising is a charity dinner but could have been big-gift fund-raising, a jumble sale or any other fund-raising method. A pressure group involved with the arts forms the final case study, but once again could just well have been drawn from social welfare, the environment, etc.

Case study 1: a voluntary visiting service for older people

In the text that follows, references to the terms in Kotler's definitions above are italicised.

The Social Services Department, whether as purchaser or provider, has an *institutional objective* of helping older people to stay independent in the community for as long as possible. *Analysis* of local and national research among old people shows that those living alone, or those with a dependent spouse, can become isolated and spiral rapidly down into high levels of dependency. The *target market* is therefore identified as over-75-year-olds living alone; over-75-year-olds with a dependent spouse; and over-65-year-olds with a health problem or a disability. The *needs and desires* of this target group are obviously many and varied. However, research shows that, to a lesser or greater extent, people want to be able to share their concerns and worries, and to be able to have the opportunity on a regular basis to signal the occasional need for help. They want to be able to do this with someone they know and with whom they are friendly, but they also want to feel that the person can get something done in the official structure. It might be argued that in an ideal world, this would be a question of a social worker calling in once a week, but the *analysis* and *planning* immediately indicate that this would be impossible within the given resources. Research and knowledge of other local authority provision suggests that visiting schemes (the product or, more specifically, service product) using volunteers might well meet the Social Services Department's objectives, provided that there is a *carefully formulated programme* which is well *planned* and subsequently *controlled* and evaluated. Research shows that the interaction between the volunteers and the clients is the key to success or failure. In other words, the programme has to enable a *voluntary exchange of values* between the volunteers and clients which is satisfying to both parties. If this does not happen, either the exchange will become sterile, or one of the two parties will drop out. In this service the volunteers therefore also become a *target market* with *needs and desires* which have to be met. Early retired people are identified as potential volunteers because the visiting scheme gives them an important role in the community but does not give them the feeling of an open-ended commitment which may drain them.

In this situation it is felt that charging (*pricing*) for the service is not appropriate to the quasi-friendship relationship and would hinder the *voluntary exchange of values* (although both volunteers and the visited are paying a 'price' of loss of free time, loss of privacy, etc., and so the benefits must outweigh this hidden price). However, the remaining elements of what is called the marketing mix, i.e. *communication, and distribution to inform, motivate and service the markets*, are particularly problematic in a voluntary visiting service. Starting with *distribution*, how large a geographic or population area should be served by the scheme? Should it be delivered directly by the Social Services Department or contracted out to a voluntary organisation on a fee basis? These and other issues concerned with the distribution of the service will need to be carefully formulated if the programme is to work. In this example the marketing mix needs to be applied to the volunteers as well as to the people being visited, but in this example we shall concentrate on the latter. *Informing*, let alone *motivating* elderly people to become involved, takes a lot of planning. Informing people can be achieved through publicising the programme via churches, day centres, old people's clubs and leisure interest groups that often involve elderly people, e.g. bingo halls and bowls clubs, but informing people is not enough. They have to be sufficiently *motivated* to want to take the service up. Word-of-mouth recommendations from people already involved become crucial in promoting this type of service. Similarly word-of-mouth recommendations from doctors, social workers and health visitors can be very important in motivating people to actually ask for the service. Perhaps most important of all is the *effective servicing* of the *market*. If the recipients do not get an effective service and see obvious benefits, then the exercise is clearly a complete waste of time. Structures and processes have to be developed so that voluntary visitors can trigger a process of wider service and delivery if the elderly person appears to want this. At the level of quasi-friendship, the voluntary visitor has to be at least prepared, and probably trained, in order to deliver the service in a way in which both sides gain satisfaction.

From the above example we can see that a marketing approach to service delivery involves an awful lot of common sense; importantly it involves a checklist of analysis, planning, implementation and control that needs to go on if the service is to be successful; and it achieves all of this with a very strong emphasis on the needs and desires of the end recipient of the service, i.e. the customer in a commercial environment, or the client or user in a social service environment.

There may still be some readers who are saying that a strong user orientation with careful planning and implementation procedures are so obvious and so much like common sense, that marketing, as defined above, is simply making the whole thing far too technical and sophisticated. The lie to that can be shown quite simply by the impressive research of voluntary visiting schemes by Shenfield and Allen (1972, pp. 163–9). In the period of the late 1960s and early 1970s, voluntary visiting schemes were springing up rapidly. Research showed that a majority were ill conceived and badly implemented. Some of the key problems were that the planners had not identified the main target groups that needed/wanted visiting (i.e. they did not identify the *target market*); second; they did not analyse or understand the *needs and desires* of the people being visited, nor of the volunteers, and so there was either a non-existent or unsatisfactory *exchange of values*; and finally, to put the tin lid on it, there was no *control of the programmes*, i.e. in the form of monitoring and evaluation. As a result of not adopting a marketing approach, many schemes were set up which visited the wrong people, delivering a 'service' that was unappreciated and, even worse, went on for many years involving the time and energy of volunteers who felt guilty about throwing in the towel.

Case study 2: a school for children with special educational needs

From the 1920s onwards the Royal National Institute for the Blind (RNIB) set up an increasing number of what were called Sunshine Homes for Blind Babies. In their heyday there were nine such residential homes (service products) taking children from the age of two years. Two key changes in the external environment resulted in the number of these schools being reduced to three by 1984. Both were social policy changes. The first was the growing view that it was undesirable for blind children, certainly as young as two years old, to be taken away from the family environment and placed in residential institutions. The second, in part a concomitant of the first, was the growing view that young blind children should and could be educated locally, and as a consequence necessarily integrated into educational settings with sighted children. Both these changing social policy views were encouraged by RNIB, which shows an essential difference between commercial and social marketing. In the world of commercial marketing it is highly unlikely to see the parent company encouraging policy shifts that would damage one of their leading products.

At first these changes in the external environment were seen as indicators that the role of these schools should diminish and eventually disappear. However, the marketing approach produced a radically different view, and as a result a radically different service product.

The educational objective of RNIB was and is to ensure that young blind people get the best possible education. Experience in parts of Scandinavia had shown that changes to a completely integrated system, while having many advantages, had one particular disadvantage – namely the dissolution and eventual degradation of any specialist knowledge in particular educational needs of visually handicapped children. In other words, as the separate schools for educating visually handicapped children disappeared, specialist staff either retired or were distributed around the country, so specialist knowledge of educating visually handicapped children became dissipated and eventually began to reduce.

RNIB's approach was different. First, while it was losing/encouraging the loss of its singly handicapped blind children, it identified a new need – namely the education of multi-handicapped blind children. These were youngsters who, in addition to having a visual handicap, might well have one or more other difficulties, i.e. severe learning difficulty (mental handicap) and/or severe behavioural problems. Severe learning difficulties or behavioural problems alone would have meant that they would not fit in well into the existing network of local special schools, but the overlay of severe handicap made the educational challenge that much more complex and appropriate for the special knowledge and skills of the Sunshine School. Second, the service developed an outreach arm, helping with the assessment of singly handicapped blind children and giving advice to mainstream education.

The name had become both a strength and a weakness. It was changed from Sunshine Home for Blind Babies into Sunshine House School.

The Sunshine House Schools also moved away from the exclusively residential form of service delivery. First, weekly boarding, i.e. going home at weekends, was introduced wherever possible. Second, the number of day pupils was increased via the use of taxi services. The location of two of the schools close to the M25 motorway ring around London was a distinct advantage which was exploited.

The change in the service and its method of delivery was significant, but the challenge of getting this new form across to intermediary customers, i.e. local education authorities, and to the parents of visually handicapped children was a major task. Sunshine House School heads invited local education special needs advisers to visit the schools; RNIB's own education advisers made the revised form of service more widely known; more active PR was employed, partly for fund-raising purposes but also in order to get the new form of service across; and the parents of newly visually handicapped children were welcome to visit the school on a regular basis, both in order to sample the school and in order to make contact with the parents of other visually handicapped children. (The numbers of blind children are small and therefore parents can easily feel isolated. They need to be able to make contact with the parents of other blind children.)

The price of the service was also radically revised over time. The declining numbers of children in the remaining schools had initially encouraged RNIB to keep the price artificially low. At a time when it was increasing school fees in other schools, it felt that it could not afford to raise prices in the Sunshine Homes. However, the recruitment of children with far greater educational challenges and the provision of an educational service appropriate to their needs gave the logical basis for fairly significant price rises. Local education authorities, which paid the fees, were prepared to accept quite significant fee charges for children they felt they could not educate locally; this was in contrast to being unprepared to pay the earlier, relatively lower, prices for singly handicapped children, when local education authorities felt that they did not need to pay such charges when they could educate the children in their own locality. Individual pricing was also introduced so that local education authorities funding less severely handicapped children were not subsidising those sending more severely handicapped children.

Pricing the outreach service has, however, proved problematic. Local education authorities have not been used to such outreach services, and while they were prepared to spend tens of thousands of pounds paying fees for children to attend a special residential school, they will have proved remarkably reluctant to pay the few hundred pounds per day required for specialist advice and assessment. This is in part because the budget heads in the local education authority are different, and partly because the increase in outreach service coincided with the relative pressure on local government income, both from central government and via local taxation.

It is important to point out that these changes took nearly ten years to identify and implement. In the early stages, the changes were not even identified as part of a marketing process, although in essence that is what they were. Nor were these changes planned or even implemented holistically. This is because, although RNIB is probably the leader among British charities trying to introduce a marketing approach to services, it was at that time still in the early stages of development. Nevertheless, these changes did take place in an evolutionary and complementary fashion. As we shall see later, they also took account of all of the elements of what is known as the 'marketing mix' (Borden 1964, pp. 2–7). In Chapter 2 we shall see the marketing mix as it functions in the commercial sector. In Chapter 4 we shall look at its contribution to the charity sector.

Case study 3: a fund-raising event

Charities put on a myriad fund-raising special events such as local or national theatre first nights, film premières, ticketed receptions, etc. One of the most basic and frequently used special event is a fund-raising dinner. What is not widely known is that, unless these events are organised from a professional marketing viewpoint, they may only just break even, and on occasions can lose money. These are many reasons why these events can be relatively unsuccessful, including insufficient analysis and planning; poor implementation; designing offerings that are not attractive to the people that the charity is hoping to entice to the event; poor promotion and/or incorrect pricing which results in too few people turning up to make a profit; and enticing too heterogeneous an audience (e.g. inebriated Hooray Henries insulting abstemious, rich, regular donors). The list is endless and the cost of failure is both short and long term. Not only does the event lose money, but it may make it virtually impossible for subsequent events to be put on successfully. The following example is a major and quite sophisticated one, but it is not unusual among the larger charities. While a simpler example could be given, its purpose is to show the marketing approach in action.

A major national charity is selected each year to receive the proceeds of an Ascot race day. The day usually offered is one that the race organisers know will not conventionally attract a large attendance; the understanding is that the charity will bring in additional punters, and benefit as a result. However, careful analysis of previous events shows that they are complicated to organise and raise relatively small sums of money. The charity decides to have an associated fund-raising dinner, a product that it is well used to organising.

The fund-raising dinner will be putting forward all three basic products, i.e. an idea product ('come to the dinner and you will be helping the charity's beneficiaries through your expenditure'); a service product ('pay a price for the ticket and come along and have a wonderful meal in good company'); and a physical product ('come along and bid for items in the auction which will go at very keen prices'). Delivering three such different products all at once is an unusual challenge for a commercial marketer. Clearly a credible idea product (i.e. the purpose of the charity itself) is an underlying essential. The service product is essential to attract people and make a modest amount of money. The physical product, i.e. the auction, is crucial, because this is where the majority of money will be raised. In the charity auction, the goods are very valuable, but donated, and the auction audience is prepared to bid figures only a little below, and sometimes considerably above, market value.

There are, broadly speaking, two target markets: the volunteer organisers of the dinner coming from the leadership of the racing fraternity; and the people attending the dinner, especially those who can be expected to bid for the expensive items.

The voluntary organising committee membership is attracted by a conventional method of persuading a leading aristocrat, well known in the racing fraternity, to chair the committee. Organising committee members are leading owners and/or their partners who enjoy each other's company, gain pleasure from contributing to an important charity and enjoy the more intimate social preserves of the chairperson. They offer the charity advice on a dinner venue that will be attractive to their peers and the prices that can be expected to be paid; most importantly they bring in the donated auction items, and equally importantly they sell the tickets. (It is not unusual for charities to organise first-class special events but be unable to attract sufficient numbers of people to come.)

The service product of the dinner is a fairly straightforward affair which is not detailed here other than to say that the three remaining elements of the marketing mix, i.e. pricing, communication (promotion) and distribution (place), have to be effectively worked out in relation to the anticipated needs and desires of the diners. However, as this is a service product, a fifth element of the marketing mix, namely *people*, is crucial. Services in general, and fund-raising services in particular, only work effectively when the participants have a natural affinity with each other. The participants effectively help to create the product through their approach, attitude and behaviour.

The physical products of the event, the auction items, are arguably the most crucial in fund-raising terms. The key items to be auctioned, it is decided, are nominations. (There may be some readers who do not know what nominations are. I sat through the whole of my first committee meeting not knowing what they were either, and was sorely tempted to ask. Luckily I did not do so until the privacy of a later conversation. Given that the nomination was being priced at £60,000 in 1985, what could be worth so much? In essence, it is where the owner of a thoroughbred stallion allows one relatively short opportunity for the purchaser's mare to be impregnated.) The organising committee, through its contacts, gained offers of four nominations, two to be auctioned at £60,000 and two at £40,000, related to the quality of stallions on offer.

The next vital ingredient for marketing success was to attract sufficient numbers of diners who would be motivated to bid for the nominations. So within the target market of diners in general there was an absolutely crucial submarket of people prepared to bid up to £60,000 for a nomination. Once again the organising committee with their contacts came up trumps. However, a 'carefully formulated programme' comes in again because a successful auction requires more than a rich, motivated audience and a good product: it requires a professional auctioneer, and a master of ceremonies to create the right kind of atmosphere. This the committee achieved through their contacts in the world of Sotheby's and Christie's, and they persuaded one of the leading television racing commentators to speak.

So what could have been a fairly mediocre dinner raising very little money, but requiring a lot of organisational effort, was transformed into a prestigious event which raised nearly £400,000! This was only achieved due to careful analysis of previous Ascot race days, and careful planning, implementation and control (right down to making sure that the auction purchasers wrote out a cheque on the very same evening), with three carefully formulated product offerings. The target markets were carefully subdivided and the 'needs and desires' of each group identified and met. In addition to the standard four 'P's of product, price, promotion and place, the fifth one of 'people' was added because of the service nature of the event.

Case study 4: an artists' pressure group campaign

The Arts Council of Great Britain was established primarily to subsidise the performing arts in order that art in all its various forms could be available to a wider cross-section of people. This meant that the bulk of the financial subsidies did, and still do, go to those responsible for the performing arts (e.g. theatres, galleries, orchestras, etc.) rather than to the artists who create the original work (e.g. painters, composers, playwrights, etc.). A group of artists had got together to try to persuade the Arts Council to amend its policy, and provide more financial help and encouragement to individual creative artists who, they argued, were creating the arts of the future. Informal discussions had largely failed on two counts. First, the Arts Council argued that it was the responsibility of the performing organis- ations to encourage and put on the work of new artists, and second, the Council did not really 'rate' new, largely unknown artists who were not part of their central remit. The campaign had relied on informal contacts between unequal partners (the Council and the unknown artists), the goodwill of the Council (which had run out, regarding the unknown artists as somewhat 'potty' and self-seeking), and a somewhat superficial analysis of the patterns of expenditure of the Arts Council on individual artists (which the Council had dismissed as spurious).

The leading artist involved, David Castillejo, decided that he needed more broadly based help with the campaign. He drew together an organising group consisting of an established and respected composer, the dean of the Royal College of Art, a young practising painter who also happened to be a member of the House of Lords, and a marketing expert. Together they set up a formal pressure group which they called Artists Now.

Given that negotiations with the Arts Council had effectively broken down, and the arguments, in the eyes of the Arts Council, had been disproved, it was necessary to go back to the drawing board. The Arts Council's key argument was that the performing organisations which it funded would be satisfactorily supporting living creative artists of today and that Castillejo's argument that less than a half per cent of the Council expenditure went directly to artists was misleading. It was therefore decided that the pressure group's offering or *idea product* should be two-fold: first, an analysis of how the major recipients of Arts Council's funds supported living artists; and second, the development of a number of proposals as to how money and support might be devoted to living creative artists. There followed a very careful programme of analysis using the national press whereby the performances and annual reports of all the major Council-subsidised companies (e.g. orchestras, theatres, galleries, etc.) were analysed to estab- lish what percentages of performances were of the work of living and dead artists respectively (i.e. painters, composers, writers, etc.). This gave the pressure group access to information which was not available to the Arts Council. It established that the figure of Council financial support going to living artists only rose from a half per cent to less than two per cent of total Arts Council expenditure. Further, the group developed a range of ideas as to how budding individual creative artists could be helped with their careers, for example through playwrights or composers being given access to performance possibilities.

So the pressure group now had a *carefully formulated programme*, but it still had no way of getting into serious negotiations with the Arts Council over the evidence and the proposals. Rather than go back into private discussions with the Arts Council, which gave them all the cards, it was decided to launch the report via the media, and so put the debate into the public domain. This, it was argued, would establish a more equal partnership, and would force the Arts Council to have to respond publicly. Artists Now felt they had an 'offering' which was effectively *priced* and was capable of *communicating* and *distributing* to the target market.

Their report, entitled *Patronage of the Creative Artist* (Bruce, Castillejo, Cornford, Gosford and Routh 1974), was launched with a suitable press release, embargoed for midnight on a Sunday, and distributed well in advance. The report got coverage in every serious national newspaper, in Radio Four's 'Today' programme and in five other national radio programmes, two of them about the arts. Even though in those days (the mid-1970s) the Arts Council seldom defended itself in public, it was forced into doing so.

In so far as the *target market* was other creative artists, the campaign was very successful and gained a lot of support through the national publicity. However, the key target market was the Arts Council and its administrators, and such a public method of negotiation, while it was effective at *informing* the Council, was not designed to *motivate*. So, as the establishment always does when under some public pressure, it made one or two relatively minor concessions, but the campaign of 'hearts and minds' was lost. It is also interesting to note that these concessions were largely achieved by what commercial marketers would call *'personal' selling*. In short, the concessions were achieved by subsequent private discussions, not between the public leadership of Artists Now and the Arts Council, but through the personal promotion of the more established members of Artists Now, i.e. the dean of the Royal College of Art and the established composer.

Conclusion

I hope that these examples have made Kotler's definition more concrete and have given some small taste as to how a marketing approach can be a helpful analytical and implementation tool for the full range of charity activity.

The next chapter goes to the wellspring of marketing, the commercial world, prior to Chapter 3 which proposes a philosophy and techniques, albeit in an adapted form, for the charity sector.

2

CLASSICAL MARKETING

Introduction

This chapter describes the classical marketing models as applied to:

☐ physical goods;
☐ (to a lesser extent) services;
☐ and (as we shall see later) ideas.

It is a basic description of the tools of marketing, and will be familiar to business students and others acquainted with commercial marketing.

It might seem that the most logical place to start would be with the definition, but here we hit a problem: there are so many of them! Crosier (1975, pp. 21–5) reviewed over fifty definitions which he classified into three major groups: those that regard marketing as a 'process'; those that see it as a 'concept or philosophy of business'; and those that regard it as an 'orientation'.

Kotler's definition given in the previous chapter (see page 3) is probably the most useful and comprehensive to apply in the charity world, and arguing for and against different commercial definitions is outside the purpose of this book. In essence, marketing is producing and delivering goods, services and ideas from a consumer standpoint rather than from a production one.

Graphical representations of marketing abound in the literature. Inevitably, they are somewhat crude and do not take account of all the intricacies of real life. However, they do give us a clear framework.

Figure 2.1 represents the main elements to the core of marketing. Around this core, which tends to concentrate on individual products in particular customer groups, there are several other concepts and realities which affect it, e.g. the impact of the changing social, political, technical and economic environment (test analysis).

Before looking at the different elements of the marketing core, an example of how they fit together and interact with each other might be useful. Let us take an example of an up-market credit card. In terms of marketing jargon, it is a *product* even though the credit card is probably 90 per cent a service and

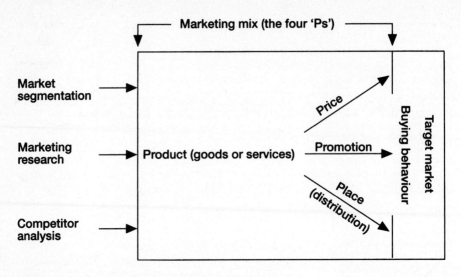

Figure 2.1 Classical core marketing model

only 10 per cent a physical good. It is physical in that you have a plastic card which performs rather practical miracles inside shops, hotels, etc., but essentially it is a financial service. The marketing manager of this up-market credit card has *segmented* her market (all adults) by socio-economic groups. Her *target market* is in the two upper socio-economic groups, i.e. those who have the highest incomes. *Marketing research* among a representative sample of the target markets has shown that there is a significant correlation between certain attitudes towards the credit card and the likelihood of people taking up the credit card. Put crudely, possession of the credit card is a sign of status. The marketing manager has done a *competitive analysis* of other cards on the market which has helped her to undertake a fairly sophisticated SWOT analysis (strengths, weaknesses, opportunities and threats) of her own product. This has been the basis of a review of the marketing mix (the term commonly used to describe the individual elements of product, price, promotion and place). She has identified that one of the USPs (unique selling propositions) of her card is its high status. Unfortunately, in terms of expanding sales of the card, it is only available to account-holders at a small, up-market banking chain. (The fourth 'P' of place is quite a difficult term to grasp immediately. Many writers on marketing turn 'place' into 'distribution', i.e. how the product is distributed.) She decides that there is a major opportunity to expand sales of the card if it is made available to people who do not have ordinary accounts at the bank. However, obviously she wants to maintain the distinctive *differentiation* of her product (i.e. its high status) and decides therefore to charge a much higher entry fee (*price*) for non-account-holders than for account-holders. In order to *promote* this product's enhancement she purchases a number of names from up-market mailing lists and carries out a discrete test market direct mail campaign.

I have chosen the above example partly because it will help us to lay out what the Americans call our emotional luggage. Marketing a high-cost status symbol to rich snobs is hardly likely to appeal to would-be voluntary sector marketers, but, as we saw in Chapter 1, marketing is value-neutral. It can be used for good or ill. It can be used for what most readers of this book would regard as high-priority activity, such as ensuring that appropriate and effective overseas aid is engendered and delivered; or it can be used for what some people might regard as low-priority activity, such as marketing top-of-the-range credit cards. As far as the voluntary sector is concerned, what matters is that it works and helps us to achieve our objective, which is to meet need.

Having taken the credit card as an example of the use of the key tools for marketing, the remainder of this chapter runs through the core marketing elements one by one. It is difficult to know where to start because the different elements interact with each other and change and modify as they integrate.

Market segmentation

While the basis of marketing is to produce products that your customers need and want, most companies or organisations are not starting from scratch – they already have a range of products and services. Therefore the technique of dividing, or segmenting, the potential market into groups of people to see whether they are more or less likely to buy the existing or proposed product was developed. Credit for the origination of this idea and technique of market segmentation is attributed to Pigou (1932, chs VIII, XI and XII) and Chamberlin (1938).

The key to successful market segmentation is to divide the market up according to attributes that are likely to make sense in terms of the product's attractiveness, but at the same time to divide it up in such a way that it is possible to reach the segment with your product. In other words, you may discover a segment of the market which is panting to buy your product, but if you have no physical way of reaching it, then it is all rather academic. For example, when fabric conditioners first came on the market, research showed that the most likely purchasers were flexible innovators. But, given that there was no mass circulation/mass audience medium reaching this group, the soap companies had to hit housewives with expensive TV advertisements in order to reach the target purchasers and as a consequence the brands had to be repositioned.

Ways of segmenting the market have become increasingly sophisticated over recent years. This is in part because of increased data collection, and in part because of the sophisticated cross-tabulations which can now be done quickly and easily by computer. The bases for segmentation can be categorised as follows (Thomas 1980, pp. 25–7):

☐ geographic (region, density, climate, etc.);
☐ demographic (age, sex, family size, income, occupation, social class, etc.);
☐ psychographic (lifestyle, personality);
☐ behaviouristic (behaviours exhibited towards the product, e.g. purchasing rate, usage rate, particular benefits sought, etc.)

Marketing research

Segmentation and marketing research are symbiotic. If we identify a market segment which is a likely, valuable purchasing source, then we need to do research among the actual and potential consumers to find out more. Similarly research on the product among consumers and how they use or do not use it, and how they like or do not like it, will help us greatly with effective market segmentation. Such research should at least be exploratory and, at best, identify correlations (such as the fact that credit cards tend to be purchased by upper socio-economic males aged 35–45 years); or even better, go further and reveal *why* they purchase.

Blyth (1989, p. 290) emphasises the distinction between 'passive' market research and 'dynamic' *marketing* research. He talks about *marketing* research being 'the collection and synthesis of primary or secondary data by their transformation into *information* that is relevant, timely and accurate for the task'.

Marketing managers new to the job quite often assume that very little consumer information is available and can easily rush into proposals for marketing research. However, this is the second stage. The first stage is to find out what is known already, and here the technique used is desk research, e.g. what sales records tell us about seasonality, average volume of sales, frequency and loyalty of purchaser; whether customer records reveal sex, age and geographic representation, etc. Once this information has been gathered, you are in a position to decide what else is needed.

In terms of a framework of questions, Blyth (1989, p. 291) gives a useful *aide-mémoire*:

1. Who are you?
2. What do you buy?
3. How much do you buy?
4. What do you pay?
5. Where do you buy it?
6. When did you buy it?

7. What else could you have bought?
8. Why?

He then argues that from this list you can infer the answers to the following:

9. What will you buy next?
10. What if (for example) price/advertising/distribution/packaging/product specifications are changed?

Dibb, Simkin, Pride and Ferrell (1991, p. 175) describe the five steps of the marketing research process as follows:

1. Defining and locating problems.
2. Developing hypotheses.
3. Collecting data.
4. Interpreting research findings.
5. Reporting research findings.

There are a variety of ways of gathering data. Although seldom acknowledged, reinterpretation of personal experience is frequently used. More objectively, *desk* marketing research, as mentioned above, is a crucial starting point. *Qualitative* marketing research, sensitively done, can be crucial. Here we gain insights into the user group in some depth, but we cannot be sure how widely applicable these conclusions and insights might be. Such research normally takes the form of in-depth interviews with individual or groups of potential or actual customers. *Quantitative* market research is by far the most expensive but can be incredibly effective, provided that a representative sample can be drawn or later constructed. As the name implies, one can begin to quantify some of the hypotheses about a product and the reasons for its success or failure, and, more importantly, hypotheses about how sales can be improved.

Competitor analysis

Even in the commercial world there is a tendency for marketing managers to concentrate too much on their own product and to fail to recognise the impact that competitors are having on sales. For example, when a now defunct soap powder, Omo, was in terminal decline, Lever made several attempts to relaunch and strengthen it. They failed primarily because the retailers and customers believed Daz to be a better product.

Competitor analysis tends to go wider than core marketing issues. Certainly competitors have to be evaluated according to marketing issues such as market share, distribution strengths, geographic coverage, price competitiveness, sales competitiveness, etc. However, in addition a good competitor analysis will look at the manufacturing capacity of competitors, their financial position and their organisation strengths or weaknesses.

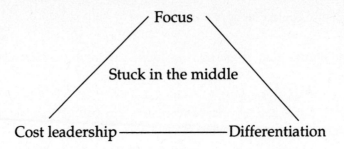

Figure 2.2

The most widely quoted expert on competitive strategy is Porter (1985). He created a model which is shown in Figure 2.2. Porter argued that the successful product needs to be close to an apex rather than 'stuck in the middle'. *Differentiation* means having a product that is clearly differentiated from others in the market and is seen to have real advantages. Bird's Eye fish fingers are set apart from the competition by the avuncular Captain Bird's Eye who reassures consumers that eating Bird's Eye fish fingers is wholesome and good fun. *Cost leadership* may mean low price, but not necessarily. It may mean that the product or product range is so dominant in the marketplace that it sets the guideline price and achieves economies of scale to allow the company to plough large profits back into new product development and launch. IBM was a classic example of this in the 1980. *Focus* is an approach to be adopted by smaller companies in the market which do not have the capacity to become market leaders. Essentially a focus strategy is to concentrate on providing a product to a well-defined group of customers with a well-defined need. For example, Cussons Imperial Leather soap has competed successfully against Lux and Camay, albeit on a smaller scale, for decades. It has a focus or niche for purchasers aspiring to an up-market toilet soap that reassures the purchaser and gives a coded message to visitors. This particular competitive strategy assumes some importance for voluntary sector organisations, as we will see later in this book.

Product

The term 'marketing mix' was introduced in Chapter 1 and its crucial contribution is pointed up in Figure 2.1. It is attributed to Borden (1964, pp. 2–7) and was popularised by McCarthy (1981, 7th edn, pp. 42–3) into the four 'Ps' of product, price, promotion and place.

Doyle (1991, p. 275) reframes McCarthy's key components of product as follows:

☐ features;
☐ quality;

☐ name;
☐ packaging;
☐ services;
☐ guarantees.

Within certain limits all these attributes are clearly variable. It is the marketing manager's job to adjust these features to take account of the needs and wants of the target market, bearing in mind marketing research findings and what the competitors are doing.

In marketing language, product is a generic term covering *physical goods* (e.g. soap powder, televisions, cars) and *services* (e.g. fast-food restaurants, hotels, air travel). Later we shall see that in the voluntary sector the third category of product, namely *ideas*, assumes a far greater importance than in the commercial sector.

Although the term 'product' is generic, it is no coincidence that in a lay person's mind it is equated with physical goods. Companies selling fast-moving consumer goods (FMCGs), such as frozen foods, toiletries and soap powders, were arguably first into the commercial marketing field and still have a dominant position in it. Although it is beginning to change, the vast majority of marketing books have either an explicit or implicit focus on the marketing of physical goods. However, because the service sector is growing fast and is becoming dominant, we can expect this situation to change.

Services such as products can be further split into two, namely non-professional services (such as fast-food restaurant chains, hotel groups, financial services) and professional services (such as architectural and law firms). Attention to this latter area is fairly new, and is in part prompted by deregulation (for example, law firms can now advertise). It is useful to note the lack of popularity of marketing terms in the professional services area, a relevant point to the voluntary sector. Indeed A. Wilson (1984) managed to write a book on marketing for professional practices where, in three pages of contents, the word 'marketing' is hardly mentioned.

Zeithaml, Parasuraman and Berry (1985, pp. 33–46), building on an earlier work, summarised a number of characteristics that have been suggested to help distinguish services from goods:

☐ *intangibility*, i.e. it is often not possible to experience services through taste, feel, sight, etc., before they are purchased;
☐ *inseparability*, i.e. services that cannot often be separated from the person or the seller;
☐ *heterogeneity*, i.e. it is often difficult to achieve standardisation of output in services;
☐ *perishability*, i.e. services cannot be stored – a spare room in a hotel for one week represents capacity loss forever.

All these service characteristics create marketing challenges needing solutions that differ, in the main, from those applied to physical goods. For example, there has to be a greater focus on benefits from the service; service reputation is absolutely critical; personnel need careful selection and training; standards need to be monitored regularly and frequently, etc.

Price

Doyle (1991, p. 275) reframes McCarthy's elements within price as follows:

☐ list price;
☐ discount;
☐ allowances;
☐ credit.

Baker (1991, pp. 309–10) quotes several studies which indicate that pricing is only a middle-order critical factor in the success of a product. However, its ranking may well vary in relation to macro-economic factors (e.g. in recession, price will be more critical) and a product's life cycle. For example, a highly innovative new product with major advantages over competitors is likely to command a premium price in the early stages of its life. As volume builds (and costs come down) and other copycat products come on the market, its price is likely to drop – although packaging and features may need to change in order to avoid antagonising earlier purchasers. Pricing of video cameras and personal computers over the last ten years has exhibited this life cycle phenomenon.

Of the elements in the marketing mix, price is usually a more flexible tool of intervention, with more immediate impact, than other elements of the mix. Price comparison between similar products is one of the most immediate and absolute comparisons that the potential customer can apply to a buying decision. A change in price is likely to have an immediate impact. However, a price change also has a very major impact on the profitability of the product. Simon (1989) gives six reasons for price being an important element in the marketing mix:

1. Price elasticity is twenty times greater than advertising elasticity, i.e. a 1 per cent price change has a sales effect twenty times as big as a 1 per cent change in advertising expenditure.
2. The sales effect of a price change is often immediate, and so measurable, while changes in other mix variables are usually lagged and difficult to quantify.
3. Price changes are easy to effect compared with other mix variables.
4. Competitors react more quickly to price changes.
5. Price does not require an initially negative cash flow unlike other marketing expenditures such as advertising, which also have a lagged impact.

6. Price and the product are the only two mix elements that feature significantly in strategic planning concepts.

Price is one of the most difficult conceptual and practical elements of the marketing mix when it comes to not-for-profit marketing. Blois (1987, p. 410) argues that Borden (1964, pp. 2–7) stressed that his concept of the marketing mix was a flexible one and therefore it is quite possible to think of a marketing mix with no 'P' for price. However, we shall discuss this later.

Promotion

The elements within promotion are sometimes called the promotional mix, namely:

☐ advertising;
☐ personal selling;
☐ sales promotion;
☐ public relations.

Advertising is probably the best-known element of the promotional mix, given that we all experience it daily. Dibb *et al.* (1991, pp. 400–401) describe advertising as a 'paid form of non-personal communication about an organisation and its products that is transmitted to a target audience through a mass medium such as television, radio, newspapers, magazines, direct mail, public transport, outdoor displays, or catalogues'. Advertising is highly flexible in its application, in that broadly based mass markets as well as tightly targeted audiences can be addressed. It is also attractive because the message can be delivered exactly as the promoter wishes, which is not the case with, for example, public relations.

Personal selling is, as its name implies, a direct contact with the potential purchaser and can be 'in person' or over the telephone. It is more expensive per customer contact than advertising, but is usually more effective.

Sales promotion, say Dibb *et al.* (1991, p. 404) is 'an activity or material that acts as a direct inducement, offering added value, or incentive for the product, to resellers, sales persons or consumers'. In FMCGs this is most commonly recognised as 'money off' for supposed 'good value' offers, provided that so many coupons or package tops are sent with the order for the offer. Promotion is a tactical weapon in the selling process to encourage either the consumer to increase consumption temporarily or indeed the retailer to stock more heavily. Over-promoting a product can often give the impression of desperation and may encourage people to think that the product has insufficient inner value.

Public relations uses many of the media employed by advertising, i.e. television, radio, newspapers or word of mouth, through editorial channels. Unlike advertising, it is 'free' in that space is not paid for. However, the promoter has far less control over an accurate interpretation of the message. Obviously news reporters want to put their own angle on the story, and in many cases the story is not covered at all. The kind of message that the product promoter wishes to put across is seldom of great interest to the editor.

Place

The term 'place' is used in order to maintain the consistency of the widely used four 'Ps'. However, I find it one of the least descriptive headings in the marketing mix, and on occasions just plain confusing. The term 'distribution' rather than 'place' is often used and is probably easier to understand.

Doyle (1991, p. 275) reframes McCarthy's list of elements of place as follows:

☐ distributor;
☐ retailer;
☐ location;
☐ inventory;
☐ transport.

In essence, place is meant to identify how we are going to get the product from wherever it is being manufactured or constructed (in the case of services) to the end consumer. Traditionally in the area of FMCG marketing it has been the Cinderella element of the mix – handled by the operations side of the business and associated with warehouses and diesel fumes rather than the glamour of advertising agencies.

However, if place (distribution) is ignored for too long, or if it is not thought through carefully at the beginning of a new product launch, the results are disastrous – the product does not reach the customer. Distribution is particularly challenging for small and medium-size companies with growing products. At one time, trying to find a retailer who sold Teasmades was like looking for a needle in a haystack.

When we look at the application of marketing in the voluntary sector, it will be seen that lack of attention to place (distribution) in the marketing mix is often the cause of products (goods/services/ideas) not reaching their target market.

Consumer buying behaviour

The majority of commercial marketing texts (e.g. Dibb *et al.* 1991, p. 112) describe the buying decision-making process as a flow diagram as shown in Figure 2.3.

It is widely acknowledged that the process is much more complicated than

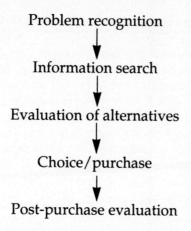

Figure 2.3

this simple model would suggest, with greater or lesser concentration on each of the stages, and complicated loop-backs to an earlier part of the process. However, Foxall (1987, p. 129) reports that while consumers *claim* to like more rather than less information, they do not use it extensively and do not necessarily make more rational decisions. In particular, he reports that even when relatively expensive, infrequently purchased consumer durables are bought, customers are often quite cavalier in their purchasing behaviour. For example, when purchasing an expensive video recorder they often only visit one retail outlet and consider only one brand, using price and their own and the shop staff's view of the reputation of suppliers in order to make a purchase. The description, translated into a social marketing context, is a familiar one. Donors often contribute on a less than rational basis. Clients, often under real pressure, take up the first service they come across.

One's own personal experience immediately suggests that there are a myriad factors that affect buying decisions. Some marketing authors have attempted to group these (e.g. Dibb *et al.* 1991, pp. 115–27) into personal, psychological and social factors. Baker (1991, pp. 115–30) groups them into psychological and social influences. Of all the areas of commercial marketing, I find the literature on consumer buying decisions the least satisfactory. At its most basic, it seems to be over-dominated by lists of factors that *might* influence behaviour, but it is difficult to predict which factors will be dominant and what the interaction between them will be. A typical list of factors affecting the buying decisions includes culture, social class, other demographic factors (such as age, sex, race, income, family life cycle and occupation), reference groups and lifestyle. There are also psychological influences such as perception, motivation, attitudes, personality, etc. (see Hibbert and Horne 1996).

Where does the manufacturer or service deliverer come into all this?

The majority of the basic marketing texts pay very little attention to the interaction between marketing and manufacturing, and not much more to the interaction of marketing and service construction/delivery. In my experience one of the hardest parts of marketing in the FMCG field is trying to stop the manufacturing/production side of the business adding 'knobs' to the product that one feels are not wanted by the customer; and, much more frequently, trying to persuade the manufacturer/producer to add those 'knobs' that the manufacturing arm feels are not necessary/too expensive/too difficult.

In the field of services marketing the relationship with the person running the service (e.g. the hotel manager) is even more critical because the service is both constructed and marketed simultaneously. Introducing or maintaining a marketing approach in this situation is often extremely difficult. Once again, we shall return to this subject in relation to the voluntary sector.

Conclusion

Marketing dominates the field of fast-moving consumer goods and there is a mass of literature to support the would-be marketer in this area. Marketing is beginning to establish itself in the field of services and is becoming dominant in certain sectors, such as mass delivery services (e.g. fast-food chains). However, in this area, there is much less literature available to support the would-be marketer.

For voluntary sector personnel, there are a number of basic commercial marketing texts which are very clear and elaborate the field (e.g. Dibb *et al.* 1994; Kotler *et al.* 1996; Thomas 1980; Baker 1991).

However, the rest of this book looks at marketing when applied to the charity world, to help us in our prime task of meeting broadly social needs. Although it seems at first sight unlikely, the philosophy and practice of commercial marketing, suitably adapted, can help us to become more effective in our work of identifying and meeting need.

Key points

Commercial marketing theory and practice involves the interaction and integration of a number of core elements:

☐ Segmentation – dividing up the market according to geographic, demographic, psychographic, behaviouristic or other criteria in order to understand and assess the likely demand for the product.

☐ Marketing research – best carried out in stages, first collecting data on what is already known, in order to establish what further information is required – looks especially at consumer buying behaviour.

☐ Competitor analysis – evaluating the impact of competitors, including assessing market share and strengths and weaknesses (for example in distribution, pricing, geographic coverage, and manufacturing capacity).

☐ Marketing mix – the four Ps: product (includes goods, services and ideas), price, promotion (covers advertising, personal selling, sales promotion and public relations) and place.

FUNDAMENTALS OF A CHARITY MARKETING APPROACH

Whom are we here for?

At its most straightforward, we are here to help the beneficiaries explicitly or implicitly identified in our charitable purposes. As a first level of analysis that is quite useful: the Royal National Institute for Deaf People (RNID) was established to provide services for deaf people; Shelter, for homeless people; Age Concern Southwark, for older people in Southwark, and so on.

However, is the primary purpose to focus on today's beneficiaries or on future generations? For example, the Imperial Cancer Research Fund operates largely to find a cure for cancer: this means helping future generations rather than present ones and, technically, not helping cancer patients at all because the discovered cure will prevent cancer. How does the Royal Society for the Protection of Birds (RSPB) achieve a balance between its activities to save birds that already exist (e.g. through oil clean-up operations) and activities to reduce pollution and guarantee future bird stocks? There are many charities where the end beneficiaries are not clearly spelt out. Is an arts charity, set up to promote modern music, primarily aiming at supporting contemporary composers producing modern music or is it aiming at audiences who like modern music?

Even where the end beneficiaries appear to be very clearly identified, such as with the RNID, there are additional layers of complexity. First, there is the balance, as described above, between the interests of today's deaf people (services) and preventing deafness in the future (prevention research). Second, how do you define deafness? Does the charity only help people who are totally deaf, or does it encompass people who 'only' have a hearing loss? If it does help people who are hard of hearing, where is the cut-off point, and is this cut-off point measured medically (e.g. 60 per cent hearing loss) or functionally (e.g. someone who is profoundly deaf may cope quite well through being very able at lip reading, whereas someone with a comparatively minor hearing loss may not be able to cope at all socially or economically)?

Then, there are the myriad charities that have gained charitable status under the legal category of education or religion. Charities in these categories (unlike the relief of poverty) allow an enormous flexibility in deciding a charity's customer group.

Thus it is clear that deciding who a charity's 'customers' are is absolutely crucial if the organisation is to have clarity of purpose, work effectively, stay within the legal limits of its 'purposes', decide how to apply its resources and, most important of all, provide effective help in the area of need.

Definitions of 'customers'

Charities have a wide variety of groups of people with whom they have to interact, and consequently whose needs and wants they must meet. Typically these include beneficiaries, funders, trustees, the Charity Commission, etc. What inclusive term can we use? Drucker (1990, p. 83) calls them constituencies. Gwin (1991, p. 43) calls them constituent groups. Kay (1993) calls them stakeholders. Despite being politically fashionable it does not seem realistic to claim that beneficiaries have a 'stake' to the extent that an individual beneficiary can exert any rights arising out of that stake; similarly with individual donors unless they are major donors. The term constituency (but not constituent group) conveys appropriate meaning but I prefer 'customer' because it brings home the importance of recognising that each of the disparate customer groups of beneficiaries, funders, trustees, staff, regulators have needs and wants which need to be met or at least accommodated.

Beneficiaries

While the individual charity's target groups might be clearly specified, e.g. older people with a hearing loss, charity marketing has to have some terms that allow general discussion. Commercial marketing often uses the term 'consumer', but this does not always sit easily in the charity world. Social welfare charities often talk of clients. Educational charities talk of students. In health care charities it is normally patients. Arts charities talk of audiences or patrons. An environmental charity might refer to them as members. A local charity might use the term 'residents', or 'Londoners', etc.

So what generic term can we use to cover those who benefit from a charity's fundamental aims? Rados (1981, p. 14) uses the term 'clients'. While this can work well with social welfare charities, it does not sit comfortably with educational, environmental and religious charities. 'Users' as a term is attractive but does not include a major segment of charity customers who benefit from a charity's product but do not 'use' them. This is particularly true of pressure group activity on behalf of large numbers of beneficiaries, e.g. Age Concern may, through its pressure group ideas, achieve a benefit for many more older people than actually use its services or even have any contact with it. The term I prefer to use is *beneficiaries*, i.e. deriving from the word 'benefit'. This term can be used generically to cover a wide range of people such as clients, patients, students, audiences, members, etc. It can also accommodate future generations of customers as well as those who do not 'use' or 'consume' but do benefit. Applying a marketing approach to products for not-for-profit beneficiaries is crucial but is much less used than in the fields of fund-raising and public relations to the general public (Bruce 1994; Ali 1996; Pyne and Robertson 1997).

Supporters

Support comes from individuals, groups or organisations in the form of money, gifts in kind or (unpaid) professional, skilled or unskilled time. While there can often be considerable overlap between beneficiaries and supporters (resource providers) to charities, there are also many occasions when they are separate with different needs and wants and in charity marketing terms need to be identified separately. The most obvious group of supporters are *donors* who might be individuals, companies, trusts, government departments, etc. But in addition there are *volunteer fund-raisers* (e.g. volunteers who place and collect charity collecting boxes, or who organise coffee mornings or jumble sales) and *voluntary service workers* (e.g. voluntary visitors to a charity residential home; volunteers who repair talking book machines in blind people's homes; volunteers in playgroups, etc.). Another supporter group, quite often ignored, is what I would call *advocates*: these are people relatively unconnected with the charity who voluntarily speak up on behalf of the charity and its cause. For example, an advocate may be an individual (who may or may not be a donor or voluntary service worker) who writes to the local MP on a particular issue directly or indirectly at the behest of the charity; or, less formally, this may be the woman in the sub post office putting money in a collecting box for NSPCC and saying to a friend 'I always support NSPCC because it does such good work with children'. Lastly there are the *purchasers* who will typically be statutory authorities. The term *supporters* covers those who back the charity, e.g. through donations, voluntary fund-raising, voluntary service, advocacy or purchasing on behalf of a third party.

Regulators

External *regulators* can usefully be regarded as a separate target group, albeit only addressed infrequently. Charity services may be inspected by local authorities (e.g. education or social services), the Charity Commission or the Home Office. Less formal regulation comes through groups such as the

National Council for Voluntary Organisations. Even local communities can be informal regulators, e.g. opposing the building of a home for disabled people in 'their' street.

Stakeholders

The last target group of people who are crucial to a charity marketing approach, especially where the charity is providing services, is *stakeholders* including trustees, representatives of beneficiaries and staff, etc. Commercial service marketers always emphasise the importance of staff in the marketing mix. Indeed two of the leading service marketing writers, Berry and Parasuraman (1991, pp. 157–72) devote a whole chapter in their book on service marketing entitled 'Marketing to employees'. In essence stakeholders are those who have rights and responsibilities over the running of the charity. So beneficiaries are not stakeholders in any legal or realistic sense, but *representatives* of beneficiaries, recognised by the charity, are.

Conclusion

So, for a discussion of marketing in charities, it is useful to divide customers into *beneficiaries*, *supporters*, *regulators* and *stakeholders*. Within each of these four groups there will be subgroups that will regularly need to be specified, and examples are laid out in Table 3.1. Intermediaries are absolutely crucial to charity marketing. These are people not directly connected to the charity who can improve the benefits going to beneficiaries, and can improve the resources gained from supporters. In the beneficiary field of activity, intermediaries have been the subject of increasing attention from charities. Pressure group work is a prime example where many charities spend a considerable amount of energy in trying to persuade *intermediaries* such as policy-makers to make decisions that will help their beneficiaries (e.g. improving social security for single parents). In addition to pressure group work, increasing numbers of charities (e.g. Age Concern, Barnardo's, RSPB, RNIB, etc.) have set up (indirect) services aimed at influencing other providers (i.e. intermediaries) to the charities' beneficiary groups. These providers might be statutory services such as local authorities, or commercial companies such as retailers and public utilities. For example, RNIB runs advisory, training and consultancy services aimed at NHS ophthalmology services, social services departments, local education authorities, public utilities (e.g. BT, electricity companies, etc.) and commercial companies (e.g. banks, supermarkets, etc.) in order to advise these services on how they can better serve the needs of blind and partially sighted people. An example of intermediaries in the supporter field would be chief executives of commercial companies where a charity was trying to gain access to significant payroll giving opportunities from a company's workforce. Here the chief executive would be persuaded to encourage the staff publicly to make monthly donations out of their pay packet.

Table 3.1 Voluntary organisation customer groups with examples

Beneficiaries	Supporters	Stakeholders	Regulators
Clients	Donors	Staff	Charity Commission
Students	Volunteer fund-raisers	Representatives of beneficiaries	Local authorities (eg. inspection of homes, schools)
Patients	Voluntary service workers	Committee members	Local community
Users	Advocates		
Purchasers	Purchasers		
Local public			
Members			
Audience			
Patrons			
Beneficiary intermediaries	Supporter intermediaries	Stakeholder intermediaries	Regulator intermediaries
Statutory providers	Church leaders	Staff managers	MPs
Statutory purchasers	Company chief executives	Union representatives	Home Office
Commercial providers	School head teachers	Committee leaders	Local councils
Family purchasers			
Other voluntary organisation providers			
Policy-makers			
Decision-makers			

So it can be seen that the target markets of charities are various. Multiple constituencies, says Drucker (1990, p. 83) make managing a charity very difficult; this is a distinguishing feature between charities and businesses, which have fewer constituencies. Similarities between businesses and charities are reviewed by Leat (1993).

Customer take-up behaviour

Commercial marketing tends to use the term 'customer buying behaviour', but for the charity sector I use the term 'customer take-up behaviour'. Many of the transactions in the not-for-profit sector cannot easily be described as buying ones, e.g. recruiting volunteers or free services to clients. Even where money changes hands, buying does not seem an apt description. For example, even where charity beneficiaries buy goods or services, they are often at non-market, or heavily subsidised rates. Also, while I argue that a supporter is 'buying' an idea, it still seems a far cry from a comparable commercial purchase.

Because charities have such a bewildering variety of customers, take-up behaviour in the marketing process is extremely complicated. This complexity is all the more difficult to handle because there are disagreements among theorists in this area in commercial marketing. So how do we approach this complexity?

Social and psychological influences

All the social and psychological factors that influence commercial buying decisions (mentioned in Chapter 2) are relevant in the charity marketing setting, but unfortunately are probably even less understood in terms of their practical impact on take-up behaviour. In charity marketing we need to spend a lot more time understanding customers' psychological interaction with our goods, services and ideas, their motivations for taking them up or not, the impact of their personality, and their attitudes, etc. Also, while the social factors affecting take-up are quite crude – culture, social class, reference groups and the whole gamut of socio-demography – they are very important too. If the voluntary sector does not get better at taking account of these factors, charities in particular will retain too much of their Victorian heritage of forcing themselves onto relatively small minorities, while having very little contact with the majority of their target groups, i.e. potential beneficiaries and supporters.

However, charities quite often have one or more factors of the beneficiary transaction process defined for them because of their legal purposes. For example, the key attributes of beneficiaries of Marie Curie Cancer Care, Age Concern and a charity housing advice centre are fairly easily defined. Subfactors associated with the key attributes are often very pertinent, e.g. length of time since onset of cancer and its location and spread; numbers and needs of the very old; and homeless versus poorly housed people.

However, broad categories only take us so far. In the next section we look at what it is that turns a potential charity customer into an actual customer.

Voluntary exchanges between the not-for-profit organisation and its consumers

Kotler and Andreasen (1991, pp. 121–34) and Lovelock and Weinberg (1984, pp. 43–64; 1989, pp. 37–43) use traditional exchange theory used in commercial marketing and apply it to our field. They use the idea of voluntary exchanges between the not-for-profit organisation and its customers to explain take-up behaviour. Marketing is concerned with increasing the number and quality of the voluntary exchanges.

At a simplistic level, an exchange results in costs and benefits to each party. Classical theory suggests that when the benefits to each party outweigh the costs, then a voluntary exchange will take place.

What are the costs and benefits associated with not-for-profit exchanges? Lovelock and Weinberg (1984, p. 47; 1989, p. 39) list five categories drawn from commercial marketing and apply them to the not-for-profit world. They are as follows:

☐ sensory benefits (how does the product feel, sound, smell or taste?);
☐ psychic benefits (how does the product stimulate a positive psychological state of mind?);
☐ place benefits (how does the product become more attractive because of where and how it is sold or passed on?);
☐ time benefits (how long does it take to find and get hold of the product?);
☐ monetary benefits (does the product save money in the medium term, is it likely to have a higher resale value over time, does it enhance a person's earning power? etc.).

These categories of benefit can be translated by mirror image into costs and can provide a useful checklist for helping a not-for-profit organisation make sure that it has covered all the pros and cons of any product it is delivering.

However, for charities which, in extreme cases, can literally be dealing with the life or death of beneficiaries, and on a very regular basis with products that dramatically change a beneficiary's quality of life, these categories, and the order in which they appear, come across as superficial. They appear to have been constructed at the behest of the cosmetics marketing manager focusing heavily on sensory, psychological and convenience factors. Taking account of the much more dramatic impact of many charity products and of Maslow's Hierarchy of Needs (Maslow 1943), I would construct the following list of costs and benefits that need to be evaluated for a charity product. Such products could be physical goods, services or ideas, and could be aimed at any intermediary or end customer group, i.e. beneficiaries, supporters, stakeholders or regulators. While virtually all the following benefits will apply to each kind of product and customer group, the mix will vary, i.e. benefits/disbenefits will assume greater or lesser importance in encouraging a transaction between customer and charity.

☐ *Physical benefits/disbenefits*. Will it keep the beneficiary alive and relatively well, e.g. feeding programme; will it keep them longer in their own home rather than in an institution; will it enable them to get out of the house when previously they could not; will the supporter get a well-constructed item through its purchaser catalogue (e.g. T-shirt, coffee mug, etc.); do staff have satisfactory equipment? etc. Disbenefits can literally be the opposite of these, e.g. will it put a person's life at risk (e.g. hanggliding); will it require them to be institutionalised for lengthy periods in order to aid recovery (e.g. hospital drug recovery programmes, residential rehabilitation for disabled people)? etc.

☐ *Quality-of-life benefits/disbenefits*. Will the product increase or decrease the beneficiary's range of life opportunities (e.g. vocational training course for a disabled person would increase the range of employment opportunities; the provision of talking books to blind people would increase a person's daily enjoyment); is the work programme organised in a way not only to help beneficiaries but also to give staff a better quality of work life? etc.

☐ *Psychological benefits (equivalent of psychic benefits above)*. These are different from quality-of-life benefits in that psychological benefits have less basis in physical reality than quality-of-life gains, e.g. membership of an organisation entitling members to put letters after their name or wear badges publicly on their lapels (e.g. professional associations or Rotary); supporter or staff association with a group that has a high status, perhaps with royal involvement and patronage; beneficiaries being offered more involvement in a service, thus improving self-esteem; acceptance of a pressure group demand, thus enhancing the status of the decision-maker within their organisation.

☐ *Access benefits and disbenefits*. How physically accessible is the product to beneficiaries (e.g. posting talking books directly to blind people's homes as opposed to placing them in their local library); how psychologically accessible is the product to beneficiaries (e.g. Alcoholics Anonymous where it is a requirement that one admits to being an alcoholic before joining, as opposed to other organisations where it is not); how physically or psychologically accessible is the supporter programme (e.g. are events wheelchair accessible; do the procedures inhibit minority groups)?

☐ *Time benefits/disbenefits*. How much time must the supporter devote (e.g. how many committee meetings); how long is the beneficiary's rehabilitation course; how much overtime do staff have to work? Arguably this is part of access but it is an important subhead of that category in that so many charity products are time-consuming to take up.

☐ *Monetary benefits/disbenefits*. How much does it cost; is it worth it; can beneficiaries afford it; can supporters afford the price (e.g. of a fundraising dinner, or the frequency of direct mail solicitations); is an intermediary prepared to spend their budget in this way (e.g. one residential school placement will cost as much as three placements in local mainstream schools)?

☐ *Sensory benefits/disbenefits.* The disbenefits of old people's homes that smell of urine and overly antiseptic hospitals, and the benefits of good food at charity dinners, etc., are not inconsiderable.

The above is a list of benefits and disbenefits which are important in any theoretical consideration as to whether a voluntary transaction between a customer and a charity is to take place; it is also useful as a checklist in designing and assessing new goods, services and ideas, and assessing continuing ones: for example, in assessing a residential rehabilitation service which is resulting in psychological over-dependency of beneficiaries; in assessing a centrally located facility which is being under-utilised because of transportation difficulties and physical access problems for disabled people; where a pressure group proposal is rejected because it was too expensive in year one, but could have been phased in over five years. All the charities concerned would have done well to consider the above checklist in some detail. To fail to do so is to risk being an enthusiastic amateur who ends up with what they feel is a good product but which is under-utilised or even rejected. But how can we get the information to allow the use of the above benefit categories? Here we have to turn to marketing information and marketing research.

Marketing information and research

Why marketing research?

Marketing research is at the heart of charity marketing. It is the prime tool of understanding customer, and in particular beneficiary, need. Espy (1993, p. 90) argues that marketing research helps organisations to reach out to actual and potential consumers, to understand their wants and needs, and to assess the extent to which they are satisfied by existing products. If we want charities to be needs-led, not process or resources-driven, then we must undertake significant amounts of marketing research. For example, RNIB spends approximately £200,000 per year in this field. As a passionate marketer, two of the projects that have given me most satisfaction in the voluntary sector have been initiating and directing two major needs surveys, one on the older people with Age Concern England (1974), the other on blind and partially sighted people with RNIB (Bruce, McKennell and Walker 1991, and Walker, Tobin and McKennell 1992).

Marketing research is essentially gathering information about our actual and potential end customers and actual and potential intermediary customers, and reflecting these findings and conclusions onto the design and delivery of our physical, service and idea products. This research needs to be undertaken among all the customer groups, i.e. beneficiaries, supporters, stakeholders and their intermediaries. The only group that cannot easily be formally researched are some regulators, but even there informal sounding out is important.

Of the customer groups, research among actual and potential beneficiaries is the bedrock which supports work directed at them *and* informs work with other customer groups. The RNIB needs survey referred to above has not only helped us to modify our services to blind and partially sighted people, but it has also been fundamentally important to pressure group work, public relations and fund-raising. For example, it was crucial evidence for convincing civil servants that a new social security allowance should be designed in such a way as to fit the particular needs of blind people (estimated full value: £40 million per year); it provides the basis of our most successful cold mail appeals letter; it achieved five national TV news slots when it was launched. What is also fascinating is that research among our stakeholders (representatives of organisations of blind and partially sighted people, major backers, government contacts, associated charities, etc.) as part of our strategic review showed that the RNIB needs survey was felt to be one of the three most important pieces of work that the organisation had undertaken in the last ten years. So marketing research can have wide range of benefits.

There are a variety of ways of *gathering* data and of *structuring* it, and these are laid out below.

Structuring the required information

By adapting Blyth (1989, p. 291), referred to in Chapter 2, in order to be more relevant to the charity sector, we have the following questions:

☐ What do I know?
☐ What do I need to know in addition?

The first question is dealt with in the section on desk research, below. The second question is one of the hardest to answer. Unless it is answered, the subsequent research will be much more expensive because more data will be collected than is necessary and may not answer the questions (*later* identified as needing answers) because the right data may not have been collected.

For example, RNIB wanted to know if age of onset of visual impairment was a critical factor in take-up of services and so asked the question 'At what age did you become visually impaired?' This allowed cross-tabulation of age of onset with a whole variety of products, e.g. Braille services. We should also have asked how long after onset did the respondent take up our various services. We did not do this, and only managed to calculate the time by undertaking complicated extra work.

So basic questions that need answering are as follows:

Existing customers

- [ ] Who are you?
- [ ] What products have you taken up? (If none, see below.)
- [ ] How much product are you taking up?
- [ ] What is being paid and who is paying it?
- [ ] Where and how did you take up this product?
- [ ] When did you take it up?
- [ ] What else could you have taken up?
- [ ] Why?

Potential customers

- [ ] Who are you?
- [ ] Which products of ours do you know about?
- [ ] Which ones might you consider taking up and why?
- [ ] Which ones do you definitely not want and why?
- [ ] Of these products which you did not know about, which are the most attractive to you and why?

Personal marketing research/experience

The method which is used too often in charities is data collection and drawing conclusions from personal experience, either on the basis of 'I have been through it and therefore know these things' or 'I have seen other people go through it'. This kind of data collection can be extraordinarily effective because it is based on first-hand experience and is totally absorbed into the mind of the committee members and managers concerned. It therefore avoids one of the problems of more rigorous market research, i.e. that of the findings being left to gather dust on the shelves. The findings of personal experience are very often rapidly absorbed into practice. However, the disadvantage is very clear, namely it is only *personal* experience and may not be typical. Even where it is typical of a large customer subgroup, it will most likely result in an over-dominance of services to this particular subgroup.

Information via representation and experience

Some charities are able to achieve formal representation of their customer groups, especially beneficiary ones, on their committees. This can have a number of advantages (e.g. giving an implicit seal of approval to the charity's products) but is particularly helpful in marketing research terms. Such representation gives a useful blend of the views of leaders and opinion formers, as well as those of the rank and file of the customer groups. In my experience charities outperform commercial companies in this respect.

Desk marketing research

Another very useful and readily achievable form of marketing research is desk research of information which is available *externally* and *internally*.

There is almost always more market information available on an organisation's target groups than conventional wisdom suggests. If there is no appropriately qualified member of staff to undertake the desk marketing research, modest outlays of money to a postgraduate student will gain the organisation an invaluable annotated bibliography of virtually everything published that is relevant. Many charities are luckier than commercial companies in that universities will have undertaken extensive research into at least their beneficiary target groups, the results of which are in the public domain. A review of this literature indicating which documents are most valuable and drawing some of the most basic conclusions can be vital.

This desk research can be particularly crucial in taking the organisation a stage further in identifying the customers. In my experience of desk research in charities, there is frequently a reaction on the lines of 'I didn't realise there were so many people in our potential as opposed to our actual customer groups' or 'we didn't realise how much our services were skewed towards a particular subgroup within our overall target market'. Assessing the size of the potential user group is not only crucial to giving a marketing perspective on existing services; it is also crucial because it will help with subsequent sampling for the organisation's own marketing research.

As for internal customer information, an undergraduate or MBA marketing student will leap at the chance to do an audit of any already gathered customer information. There is often a wealth of customer data 'hidden away' in sales order processing, in the accounts department, at various distribution points or even in the post room. With luck the data will go back several years and trends will therefore become available.

Qualitative marketing research

Qualitative marketing research at its simplest allows us to gain insights into our user group in some depth, but does not enable us to be sure how widely applicable these conclusions and insights might be. It can take the form of depth interviews with individual potential or actual customers who, you have predicted beforehand, have some of the attributes in which you are interested. For example, if a service charity is aware that the majority of its target group are elderly women, but it is not successfully reaching this group, then a dozen depth interviews with individual elderly women, both users and non-users, is likely to be very instructive. It is important to be aware that to be done well, qualitative research is difficult and expensive. Good depth interviewers are hard to come by (for example, they have to be sympathetic and encouraging but not over-prescriptive) and the design of the interviews is just as complicated, if not more so, than larger surveys. However, such a process has the immediate advantage that it can be tried out by service managers (assuming that they are not dominating by predisposition, or can at least control this in the interview) and thus draw the research directly in to the line manager.

Group interviews are a variation on individual interviews. Here between six and twelve individuals are brought together into a group discussion about a particular service or problem area. Obviously group dynamics are important here; the group leader needs to have many of the attributes of the depth interviewer but must also be able to facilitate a group. With careful selection of group participants it is possible to introduce a semblance of a quantitative or pro rata set of conclusions. Such groups can be useful to help assessment of products at the pre-test stage such as a new technical aid or charity logo.

Quantitative marketing research

Provided that there is sufficient budget for a robust random sample, or that a representative sample can be drawn or later constructed, quantitative research is excellent for sizing the market for your product or service and for measuring the extent of individual strengths or weaknesses. It is particularly good at measuring the physical, social and demographic characteristics of the target group, e.g. how many are over 65 years old, how many are men/women, how much money they have or do not have, their economic/class background, etc.

In essence, in quantitative research one asks similar questions of hundreds of actual and potential customers through either a printed questionnaire or trained personal interviewers. The questions to be asked must always be tested out on a small subsample, and indeed the questions are often constructed on the basis of initial qualitative work.

The results and conclusions can come close to measuring hypotheses, attributes, attitudes and behaviour that have been identified in preceding qualitative research.

The process of marketing research

Experience of research in general can be widespread in charities, and so there will be some expertise to transpose into marketing research. As with any form of research it is vital that the stages of planning, execution, analysis and presentation of findings are gone through meticulously. As with any good marketing approach, close involvement of the staff and committee members who are going to have to act on the research findings is vital from the earliest stages. It is so easy for conclusions to stay on the shelf. Where the market researcher involves managers and committee members before and especially after the research, the chances of the findings being acted upon increase enormously.

Impact of marketing research

Marketing research can make discoveries of dramatic importance to a charity and its physical, service and idea products, but in the main they come up with evolutionary conclusions. For example, market research by Cancer Relief Macmillan discovered that professional support and advice was directed at sufferers, with little support going to carers (Scott 1993, p. 2) and as a result charity services were modified. An example of evolutionary impact is where charities have worked with the Department of Employment on research into programmes to help unemployed disabled people acquire work. This research discovered which programmes were most successful, and in turn this information was related back to programme cost so that the Department was able to focus its activities on the most cost-effective ways of bringing disabled people into the employment market.

Market segmentation and targeting

The process of dividing the organisation's total market of customers into subgroups or market segments is one of the most useful conceptual and practical tools in marketing. This then enables decisions about which segments to target with which products.

For example, the RNID does not think of its target market as simply 'deaf people'. People with a hearing impairment have as many needs and wants as hearing people – arguably more. There are as many kinds of deaf people as there are hearing. It thinks in terms of hearing-impaired people under 16, of working age, and over retirement age. Among hearing-impaired people under 16 it has to think of the needs of the singly handicapped as being different from the multi-handicapped hearing-impaired. It has to think of the different needs of those who can communicate through speech and those who can only communicate through sign language; of the different needs of people who have been hearing-impaired from birth from those who become so later in life.

Such segmentation allows a charity to construct products that take account of the particular needs of a more homogeneous group than 'deaf people'.

Why segment?

There are two fundamental pressures which should persuade a not-for-profit organisation to segment its market. The first is an apparently negative one, namely that the organisation cannot serve every need of its whole market simply because there is almost certainly not enough resource in the form of money or expertise. If the organisation does try to do this, it will fail and at the very best will provide a low-quality service which is not appreciated by very many people in its market. The positive pressure for segmentation is that it allows, and indeed encourages, the development of products that are much more likely to be appreciated by the customers. The associated downside is that this means that some consumer segments may be ignored by the organisation simply because, on the basis of institutional aims, they have been selected as lower priority or are judged to be relatively inaccessible.

Lovelock and Weinberg (1984, pp. 106–7; 1989, pp. 157–9) list seven reasons for segmentation, namely that it helps the spotlighting of relevant segments, the development of responsive strategies, efficient allocation of resources, effectiveness in attracting funding, efficiency in media selection, reducing competitive impact (i.e. choosing an area where few others operate), and focusing organisation efforts. In addition, in charities it is important because segmentation helps us to identify under-served groups.

Process of market segmentation leading to target marketing

Kotler and Fox (1985, p. 176) identify three progressive stages of market segmentation leading to three more progressive stages of target marketing, as follows:

1. Identify bases for segmenting the market.
2. Develop profiles of resulting segments. } Market segmentation
3. Develop measure of segment attractiveness.
4. Select the target market(s).
5. Develop positioning for each target market. } Target marketing
6. Develop marketing mix for each target market.

Lovelock and Weinberg (1984, p. 109; 1989, p. 160) identify two previous stages which are particularly important to the not-for-profit organisation. These stages are as follows:

1. Define institutional objectives and set priorities.
2. Identify which market(s) within overall population is/are key to successful achievement of objectives.

Criteria for segmenting the market

Traditional criteria for segmenting the markets are the following:

☐ geographic (e.g. region, density, climate, etc.);
☐ socio-demographic (e.g. age, sex, family size, income, occupation, social class, etc.);
☐ psychographic (e.g. lifestyle, personality, attitudes, etc.);

☐ behaviouristic (e.g. benefits being sought, purchasing rate, usage rate, etc.)

In a charity setting, the behaviour basis of segmentation is likely to be of highest priority for beneficiary customers. The only danger to avoid is doing the selection and then discovering that there is no way of implementing the segmentation in terms of reaching the target market.

A talking-book service is available to all blind and partially sighted people. However, within this market it is much more likely that the service will be taken up by people who used to read a lot before they lost their sight, and not by those who did not read much. Since it takes twelve hours to listen to a whole book (approximately three times longer than for a sighted person to read an equivalent size printed book), the service is more likely to appeal to visually impaired people with a lot of leisure time, e.g. older and unem- ployed people. There is no reason for believing that the tastes in reading are any different than for sighted people. The market segments are divided primarily by age. Taste in reading is solved by recording the most popular books on the sighted market. Target markets are older, newly visually impaired people and the unemployed. A separate library is developed for the target market of students and working people on the basis that their needs and time availability are different.

Another example of target marketing which indicates the extreme complex- ity (greater than in the commercial sector in general) is that of a special school run by a charity. In this situation there are four quite distinct target markets whose needs and wants have to be satisfied. First, there are the children attending the school who are the ultimate beneficiaries, i.e. educa- tion has to be designed to serve them best. However, as with any school, parent(s) may be involved and they have views as to the design of the education their child might best receive. In addition, as parent(s) they have an important educational role with the child, i.e. they are, in part, a provider. Third, there is the local education authority (LEA) which will decide whether or not to pay for the (expensive) education and will have its own needs and wants. Fourth, there is the regulator in the form of what used to be called Her Majesty's Inspectorate (which inspects the school and has the power and authority to require the school to provide education in an appropriate manner).

Donor market segmentation and targeting often uses all the traditional criteria for segmenting. For example, many charities when aiming fund- raising at the general public try to target couples and single women over 50 years old from upper socio-economic groups (socio-demographic) who have a religious orientation (psychographic) and who have an established track record of giving to charity (behaviouristic). While all parts of the United

Kingdom are targeted, the South East and South West are often most lucrative (geographic).

Conclusion

Market segmentation and target markets are some of the most useful tools available to the charity manager. They allow the prioritisation of different target markets according to the aims and objectives of the organisation. However, they explicitly recognise that not everyone in the overall needs group (market) of the agency can be served, and so many charity managers initially feel uncomfortable with the concept. However, even if they ignore explicit target markets and market segmentation, they will be undertaking it implicitly and will have little idea about which groups they are prioritising and which groups they are in fact ignoring.

Other-player analysis and positioning

As described in Chapter 2, competitor analysis is essential in the commercial world if a product, product line or even company is to survive and prosper.

In the charity sector the term 'competitor' seems inappropriate in a number of settings, and unhelpful in others. The term 'other player' is not only more acceptable, but it is also more appropriate. Other players in the charity world consist not only of other charities in the subsector (e.g. other cancer charities), but also all other charities, in some instances statutory services (e.g. charity and statutory services to beneficiaries interact and intertwine in a complicated and interdependent manner) and other commercial organisations. For example, in the world of residential care there are four different kinds of providers: charities, statutory organisations, housing associations (which are not technically charities) and commercial organisations. So other-player analysis, especially when it comes to beneficiary markets, has to be very broad if it is to be meaningful. For example, an other-player analysis of charity services to beneficiaries in 1945 would have come to some very strange conclusions if it had omitted the role of statutory provision, bearing in mind the rapid and widespread extension of the welfare state between 1945 and 1950. Indeed, as it is argued in Chapter 10, one of the most important aspects of other-player analysis in charities over the last fifty years has been the interactive but changing roles of the statutory, voluntary and commercial sectors as far as beneficiary provision is concerned. This interaction has also spilled over into supporter markets, with changing attitudes towards voluntary work (varying degrees of encouragement or discouragement) and donations (changing tax advantages/disadvantages), as well as changing attitudes towards the acceptability and legitimacy of pressure group work (changing views as to legitimacy).

Components of other-player analysis

Other-player analysis is the closest that this book comes to strategic planning. As is mentioned in Chapter 10, the world of strategic planning in commerce has been increasingly colonised by strategic marketing. However, in the charity and statutory sector, strategic planning has had, for a long time, a powerful and legitimate role. It seems more helpful that a marketing approach should be subsumed within more general models and applications of strategic planning, provided that the latter accept the dominant customer ethos. That is an important qualification because in the past this has not always been the case. Strategic planning has in many instances appeared to be a tool for ensuring organisational survival rather than for developing the backcloth to the creation of products relevant to customers. For example, strategic planning abounded in public utilities, such as the old gas board, which were hardly renowned for their customer sensitivities!

This introduction indicates that other-player analysis, as alluded to in the previous section, requires components of broad environmental analysis – economic, political, social and technological. Unless charities analyse and understand what is happening in those important areas of the environment, particularly where they may impact on the charity, the fortunes of the charity and its beneficiaries are likely to wane.

Leaving this broader environmental scan aside, there are, from the commercial world, some generally recognised factors that need to be analysed in other players and that we can apply to any organisations, whether they be other charities, or statutory or commercial players.

- ☐ What is their product? (Physical, service or idea). How modern and up to date is it? What is the quality like? Does the organisation have a track record of product innovation?
- ☐ What are the organisation's marketing skills and capacity like? What share of the market do they have? How strong are they on the marketing mix? In particular how are the services spread geographically, and how good is the market penetration, etc.?
- ☐ What is their manufacturing strength? This is less relevant to most charities given their service base, but still needs considering.
- ☐ What are their resources like? How does the other player compare in terms of financial reserves, income, staff and volunteer capacity, land and buildings, etc.?
- ☐ What is their overall organisational effectiveness like? How good are the managers, the directors and lay committees? What is their organisational structure like? Can it deliver products effectively, directly and flexibly, or is it a sluggish organisation, etc.?

Strategies to follow in relation to other players

In the commercial world, as was mentioned in Chapter 2, Porter (1980) recommends adoption of one of three strategies to maintain success against competitors, namely *cost leadership* (where the dominant market leader establishes the price rules), *differentiation* (where the company establishes a product which is so positively distinctive from its competitors that it becomes difficult to challenge), or *focus* (where the company focuses its product on a market niche of customers and becomes the market leader in that narrow area).

Many charities occupy market *niche* positions, e.g. Guide Dogs for the Blind in the field of blind welfare generally, the Donkey Sanctuary within the field of animal welfare, etc. As was mentioned above, charities are quite often rather poor at achieving differentiation between themselves, but they have a very strong *differentiation* from other players such as statutory organisations and commercial ones. However, even here resource shortages and the organisational mutations of NHS hospitals into hospital trusts and LEA schools into opted-out schools are reducing this differentiation between some charities and other types of providers.

Cost leadership is difficult to translate into the charity sector. For this strategy to be effective the organisation has to be a dominant player in the consumer field, and very few charities achieve this (perhaps the one exception is the Royal National Lifeboat Institution).

Kotler and Andreasen (1991, p. 206) describe four choices of position, two of which are close to those of Porter. The position of 'market leader' is very close to that of cost leadership, because only the market leader can establish cost leadership. The position of 'market nicher' is close to that of focus. However, they introduce two strategic positions which are different and have some particular relevance to the charity sector. The first is 'market challenger' – a strategy that can be adopted more easily against other players such as statutory and commercial organisations through the use of greater flexibility and volunteer involvement, etc. (e.g. charity hospices expanding at the 'expense' of nursing homes). The fourth strategic position is that of 'market follower' where a charity can let some other organisation (often a commercial one) develop the expertise and/or practical capability and then follow. RNIB is currently holding back on changing its talking-book format away from tape to an electronic form, until the market dominance is decided between the competition of compact disc, digital audio tape and video disc. Saxton (1996a) proposes four strategies for competitive advantages in charities: externally driven, niche (which has two sub-categories – issue/emotional and geographic), differentiation (which has three sub-categories – by customer group, by product, and by belief) and awareness. These strategies have been developed with charities in mind and deserve empirical testing.

Positioning

Positioning the charity's physical, service and idea products is a concept that follows on logically from segmentation, targeting and other-player analysis. Harrison (1987, p. 7) defines the position of a product as:

> *the sum of those attributes normally ascribed to it by the consumers – its standing, its quality, the type of people who use it, its strengths, its weaknesses, and any other unusual or memorable characteristics it may possess, its price and the value it represents.*

This definition makes it clear that while the charity can have a major impact on how customers view the position of its products, e.g. through the product quality and through the associated advertising and promotion, at the end of the day it is the customers who position the offering, not the charity.

In the commercial world the positioning of service products and the associated service companies is more challenging than for commercial companies marketing FMCGs. Whereas Unilever need to position only their brands, a service company like Forte need to position their individual services in a way that adds up to a coherent and supportive positioning for the company as a whole. In effect the company brand is dominant. With charities the situation is even more complex than with commercial service companies. This is because the charity is the brand, but it also has a larger number of customer groups who may be expecting to receive different messages. The positioning challenge for charities is that they have to have an openly recognisable and consistent position to beneficiaries and supporters, as well as stakeholders and regulators – with such a consistent position being acceptable to all four groups. Some charities, e.g. SCOPE, when it was called the Spastics Society, or War on Want, have on occasions failed to achieve this. War on Want attracts supporters because of its radical stance on social and political change required to improve the position of the developing world, but because of this stance it has attracted criticism from a regulator, namely the Charity Commission. Key stakeholders in the then Spastics Society were parents of beneficiaries; significant tension over policy arose between them and adult beneficiaries, which has made it difficult for the society to have a consistent approach.

Positioning a charity with is variety of physical, service and idea products to its various customer groups is undoubtedly an art rather than a science. In the vast majority of cases it is also done unconsciously, rather than consciously. However, lack of attention to positioning in the charity sector generally, and within specific subsectors such as the various cancer charities, provides us with a developing, long-term problem. For example, the comparative positioning of the Imperial Cancer Research Fund, the Cancer Research Campaign, Marie Curie Cancer Care and Cancer Relief Macmillan is very indistinct. As competition in the supporter market intensifies, charities with clearly identified positions, such as Save the Children and NSPCC, are bound to be at a competitive advantage.

Positioning is equally important in the constituency of beneficiaries and their intermediaries. Service-giving products in the field of child care are relatively indistinct and undifferentiated. For example, over fifty different charities provide some form of support to children. NSPCC and Barnardo's occupy the dominant positions in the market, but differentiation confusion abounds. More distinctive positions would not only benefit the charities, but also the beneficiaries and their intermediaries. It is generally thought that whatever the customer group, the market leader (at least in the customer's mind) benefits from indistinct positioning. So, for example, unbranded or weakly branded work by one of the smaller children's charities will often be attributed to Barnardo's or NSPCC.

Conclusion

In summary, a charity marketing approach requires analysis of other players in the market – both immediate and obvious competitors (as in the fund-raising field) or other charities, statutory services and commercial organisations in the fields of offerings aimed at beneficiaries. However, this is the natural interface with strategic planning which has long been strong in the statutory sector, and is growing fast in the voluntary sector. Provided that strategic planning has a strong customer focus, it is probably the best specialism to deal with the complexities of a charity operating in the rough seas of changing economic, political, social and technological environments.

Key points

☐ Identify the separate target groups or 'customers': beneficiaries, supporters (donors, volunteers and 'advocates'), stakeholders (including staff) and regulators.

☐ Understand the social and psychological factors that influence customer take-up behaviour in the context of charities and social marketing.

☐ Marketing research – collect data to understand customer and beneficiary need via personal experience, desk research, individual/group interviews (for qualitative assessment) and large samples (quantitative research).

☐ Segmentation – segment the separate market groups to target specific products and services to particular need.

☐ Other-player analysis – analyse the activities, products and services of other players (other charities, statutory services or even commercial organisations) operating in the same sector. Consider their skills, resources and organisational effectiveness in comparison to yours (SWOT).

☐ Positioning – how do customers view your products and how should you change the marketing mix in the light of these views and the position of other players?

4

THE CHARITY MARKETING MIX

This chapter, like the previous one, introduces the concepts and terms of the commercial marketing world and puts them into a charity context. Chapters 6–10 then put them into a functional setting.

Construction of the marketing mix

The marketing mix is what is required to bake a successful marketing cake. The marketing mix has a more or less constant list of ingredients which interact with each other. Unlike making a cake, however, the marketer has to construct each of the ingredients as well as simply mix them together in known proportions. In short, the marketer has to ensure that the individual ingredients are valid in their own right as well as that the interaction between the ingredients is successful. The term 'marketing mix' is attributed to Borden (1964, pp. 2–7). The marketing mix has also been encapsulated into the well-known dictum of the four 'Ps' (McCarthy 1981, 7th edn, pp. 42–3):

☐ product;
☐ price;
☐ promotion;
☐ place.

Doyle (1991, p. 275) reframes McCarthy's elaboration of the four 'Ps' as follows:

☐ product (consisting of quality, features, name, packaging, services, guarantees);
☐ price (consisting of list price, discounts, allowances, credit);
☐ promotion (consisting of advertising, personal selling, sales promotion and public relations);
☐ place (consisting of distributors, retailers, locations, inventory, transport).

It is clear that this commercial definition of the marketing mix is heavily orientated towards physical goods rather than services and was constructed with no reference to the pressure group work or fund-raising activity of voluntary organisations.

As we shall see later in this chapter, and in Chapters 6, 7, 8 and 9, despite the initial unattractiveness of the language to the charity manager, the terms and the concepts behind them are useful and applicable in the voluntary sector. However, given the strong orientation of the list to physical products, other writers, Booms and Bitner (1981) in particular, have argued that it needs adaption to be useful to service managers. Since there is a preponderance of services in the charity sector, this is useful.

Booms and Bitner (1981, pp. 47–51) argue that three extra 'Ps' should be added to the list where services are concerned, namely people, physical evidence and process of service assembly:

☐ People: consisting of *personnel* and their training, discretion, commitment, incentives, appearance, interpersonal behaviour and attitudes; but also includes *other customers* and their behaviour, degree of involvement, customer-to-customer interaction.
☐ Physical evidence: consisting of environmental factors such as furnishings, colour, layout and noise level; facilitating goods; tangible clues.
☐ Process: consisting of policies, procedures, mechanisation, employee discretion, customer involvement, customer direction and flow of activities.

The reason for including the two groups under people is straightforward. Unlike physical goods, the *staff* of services are absolutely crucial in customer assessment and will have a major impact on whether they use the service again and what word-of-mouth recommendation they will give. This is particularly true for charity products. The attitudes, behaviour, commitment, etc., of charity staff are crucial in retaining and developing donors and, in particular, fund-raising volunteers. These factors are similarly crucial in service provision to beneficiaries who can be active promoters or detractors of charity services depending on the quality of staff providers. *Other customers* in the fund-arising context make this difference to the success or failure of an event and whether the volunteer organisers will remain involved and do another one. Other customers are also important in services delivered to beneficiaries. For example, charity beneficiaries are not naturally homogeneous groups of people and the peer group interaction of beneficiaries can make or break some charity service offerings. If empathy develops between contemporary clients, say, on a rehabilitation course, then peer group support after, as well as during, the service experience can provide very positive benefits. If the service clients are poorly or unimaginatively grouped, then peer group antagonisms can easily develop which will be destructive in themselves and will undermine the value of the service provided.

The next 'P' of physical evidence covers things such as environment (furnishings, colour, layout, noise level), facilitating goods and other tangible clues. The argument for the inclusion of physical evidence is that so much of a service is intangible, at least before experiencing it. Physical evidence, such as the cleanliness and modernity of school buildings, can have a triggering effect on a decision whether or not to take part in the service.

The last area, *process*, includes policies, procedures, mechanisation, employee discretion, customer involvement, customer direction and flow of activities. This rather abstruse list includes activities absolutely fundamental to successful service products. Chapter 7 looks at these and builds in particular on the important contributions of Berry, Parasuraman and Zeithaml.

Marketing mix for the charitable sector: add philosophy

Do the seven 'Ps' – product, price, promotion, place, people, physical evidence and process – provide a satisfactory marketing mix for charities? I would say yes but for one important omission – *philosophy*. The philosophy of a charity in delivering goods, services or ideas is absolutely fundamental to a good marketing approach in our sector. Is the philosophy of the charity one of empowering beneficiaries to become as independent as possible? Or is the philosophy one of trying to change the beneficiaries' environment with less emphasis on personal empowerment? Or is the philosophy one of caring for and segregation of the beneficiary with little emphasis on empowerment and environmental change? The philosophy that a charity (and, I would argue, a statutory or public organisation) adopts will have a fundamental effect on the organisation's offerings. Similarly, lack of clarity about the organisation's overall guiding philosophy may also result in an inconsistency among the services, ideas and even physical goods offered by the charity, in accordance with the differing individual philosophies of the various managers involved.

Is the marketing mix relevant to charities?

Some people have questioned whether the marketing mix as it is currently interpreted is relevant to not-for-profit organisations. Blois (1987, pp. 386–97) argues that Borden (1964, pp. 2–7) did not have a rigid list of what must be part of the marketing mix but provided illustrative lists, stressing that other people and other situations will require different ingredients. This is helpful and will be taken up later. Blois argues that over-concentration on the four 'Ps' are distracting from the essential task of not-for-profit managers which is to identify the following:

1. The organisation's product features and controllable variables and, separately, those features that they can alter.
2. Those market forces that influence demand and, separately, those forces that they can modify.

Clearly both these factors are crucial but do not detract from the usefulness of a charity marketing mix.

The charity marketing mix

The (now) eight 'Ps' of philosophy, product, price, promotion, place, people, physical evidence, and process provide a useful checklist of all the factors that a charity manager needs to consider in constructing and delivering an effective physical, service or idea product. Three additional sub-elements have been added and are shown in italics.

☐ Philosophy: consisting of philosophy of the charity as a whole, and philosophy to be applied to the specific product.
☐ Product (goods, services or ideas): consisting of quality, feature, name, packaging, services, guarantees.
☐ Price: comprising price, discounts, allowances, credit.
☐ Promotion: consisting of advertising, personal selling, *intermediary referral, customer referral*, sales promotion, public relations, *coalition building*.
☐ Place: consisting of distributors, retailers, locations, inventory, transport.
☐ People: consisting of personnel (training, discretion, commitment, incentives, appearance, interpersonal behaviour and attitudes) and other customers (including behaviour, degree of involvement and customer-to-customer interaction).
☐ Physical evidence: consisting of environmental factors such as furnishings, colour, layout and noise level; facilitating goods; tangible clues.
☐ Process: consisting of policies, procedures mechanisation, employee discretion, customer involvement, customer direction and flow of activities.

The next sections look in more detail at the different elements of the marketing mix as applied to charities.

Philosophy – the bedrock of our work

A major new element of the marketing mix which I would add for the charity (and indeed public sector) market is that of philosophy. By philosophy is meant an explicit recognition of the value-laden approach to be taken or encouraged in the product, be it a physical good, a service or an idea aimed at the beneficiary, supporter, stakeholder or regulator markets. For example, part of RNIB's organisational philosophy is that we aim to empower blind and partially sighted people to be more independent, not inadvertently to make them more dependent on us or anyone else. Therefore each RNIB product has to be judged in this light and there needs to be an explicit part of the marketing mix that looks at this issue. Is the educational content and curriculum of one of our schools such that it helps the child become more autonomous? Does the promotional activity, including the prospectus, give a dignified image of the multi-handicapped child? Do the people (staff) involved in the school treat the children with respect and encourage maximum independence? In other words, the philosophy to be used in the marketing mix has to be explicit, and understood and applied to all the other seven elements.

The purpose of this section is not to say what the philosophy of any charity, or its individual offerings, should be. That has to be a decision of the individual charity. What is being proposed is that voluntary organisations should be explicit about their values and philosophy, and ensure that these are integrated firmly into the marketing mix in an explicit and understood fashion. If the philosophy is not explicit, it will still surely exist. However, it will probably be more apparent to the customers than to the organisation; it may well vary from one unit of the organisation to another; the variance may well be contradictory; and the philosophy applied to any individual product or product line may change as staff change. If the philosophy is explicit and is made a clear part of the marketing mix, everyone will know where they are and what is expected of them. Its very explicitness will allow this element of the marketing mix to be reviewed from time to time.

So how does a charity go about creating a philosophical position for incorporation into the marketing mix, and on what should it be based? The most obvious answer is that the philosophy should be based on the needs and wants of the beneficiary customers. It is beneficiary customers' interests that should be paramount in a charity (subject to the legal expression of its charitable purposes, although even these can be changed). However, immediately this prompts a distinction between needs and wants. The term 'needs' implies some objective assessment of the end beneficiaries' situation. The term 'wants' implies pre-eminence to the views of the end beneficiary. These views and objective assessments may be identical, but there again they may not. Another problem is how to balance the needs and wants of the present generation of beneficiaries with those of future generations (or even non-generations in the case of a charity undertaking research to prevent a medical condition such as cancer). Third, is it possible to adopt the same philosophical or value position for all beneficiaries? In other words, the development of a philosophical position for the organisation and its offerings is extremely challenging.

To a large extent the responsibility for developing this position is outside the prime responsibility of charity marketing and is within the purview of charity strategic planning. Indeed it is within a charity's vision and/or mission and/or value statement that we can look for evidence as to the required content of the philosophy element of the marketing mix. Increasing numbers of charities are creating mission statements and a fair proportion of these have vision and value statements. For example, Shelter's vision and value statement (McKechnie 1993, p. 47) says:

> A home is somewhere affordable, of adequate size and design, in good repair, safe, secure and with support when required. To be without a home is unacceptable. It is degrading and damaging to individuals and the community and has enormous social and economic costs for us all ...

It goes on to say:

> As an organisation we recognise that we can only achieve our aims through effective management and promoting equality of opportunity in the widest sense. Shelter's integrity and independence will be safe-guarded by its Trustees.

It will quickly be seen that, while significant parts of the above statement are to do with aims and objectives, there is a strong value-laden philosophy. This is shown in words like 'unacceptable', 'degrading' and 'damaging'. By implication it follows that any provision or proposals that Shelter makes must give dignity to the individuals and must not inadvertently give support to certain forms of homelessness, etc.

Save the Children Fund also has a mission statement which contains the sentence 'In all its work Save the Children endeavours to make a reality of children's rights' (Hinton 1993, p. 11). The rights referred to are those adopted by the United Nations in 1989 and include the following:

> The child must be protected beyond and above all considerations of race, nationality or creed. The child must be cared for with due respect for the family as an entity. The child must be brought up in the consciousness that its talents must be devoted to the services of its fellow men ...

Once again the philosophical position that needs to be adopted in the marketing mix of any Save the Children offering is to ensure that the marketing mix at least does not inadvertently damage the implementation of the rights of children, and at best enhances them.

Does this eighth 'P' make charities different from commercial organisations? It is certainly true that the commercial marketing texts seldom, if ever, make reference to the philosophical or value-laden position of a product as a separate section of the marketing mix. It is interesting to question why this has not occurred. However, things may be changing. Embley (1993) has titled his book *Doing Well While Doing Good: The marketing link between business and non-profit causes*. He lists over fifty examples of mainly American commercial companies that have developed their business platform on the basis of 'doing good'. One of the companies he quotes is The Body Shop which will be familiar to UK readers. Embley (1993, p. 100) describes seven principles under which the company operates, which include the following:

'all the products do is cleanse, polish, and protect the skin and hair. The Body Shop makes no promises about rejuvenation; it promotes health rather than beauty. Ingredients and products are obtained in an unpatronising, non-exploitative manner ...'. These statements, along with The Body Shop's position on product testing on animals, give a very clear philosophic position for the organisation's various marketing mixes. So The Body Shop certainly has an eighth 'P' for philosophy. Embley (1993, p. 2) argues that companies with a social mission as well as a business mission will become the models of the future.

Product – what is it we are offering?

It is vital in charity marketing to emphasise that the term 'product' covers not only physical goods, but also services and ideas. At one level it would seem unnecessary to emphasise this because, in theory, all are covered by the term. It is simply that, in lay person's language, the word 'product' is associated almost entirely with physical goods. Further, marketing arose out of the fast-moving consumer goods (FMCG) world and all the academic and practical literature is dominated by physical goods. While the American Marketing Association includes equal emphasis on physical goods, services and *ideas*, this latter area hardly ever gets a mention except in the more thoughtful academic texts where such consideration is consciously excluded as requiring more attention than a general book can give (Cowell 1984, p. 36). In the charity, and indeed statutory, sector, ideas as products are very important and come in three main guises: in pressure group work, public education activity and fund-raising.

Kotler and Fox (1985, p. 221) suggest 'offer, value packages or benefit bundles' as alternative names for product in the not-for-profit organisations. Kotler and Andreasen (1991, e.g. p. 389) use the term 'offering' as an alternative to product and this is used from now on as synonymous with 'product'.

Physical goods

Little elaboration of this heading is given here, first because overwhelming attention is given to this area in the literature and, second, such differences as there are between charity goods marketing and commercial goods marketing are covered in Chapter 6.

Lovelock and Weinberg (1984, p. 285; 189, p. 202) argue that physical goods represent a relatively small area of output for not-for-profit organisations. This is true but it is still valid and significant output for quite a few voluntary organisations (e.g. disability organisations selling/giving technical aids to their beneficiaries). Physical goods sold by charities to realise income for their primary mission (such as direct mail catalogue activities) also appear to be on the increase. Charities are putting growing emphasis on trading, particularly in the area of physical goods. Hiscock (1991, pp. 5 and 9) reports that 79 per cent of the top 200 British charities trade and that 110 have set up trading companies; of these, approximately 20 per cent have been set up in the last five years.

Services

What is overwhelmingly clear is the dominance of services in the public and charitable sectors. This means that the relative lack of writing and research in commercial services marketing is a real problem. For every one book on services marketing, there are between ten and twenty on marketing in which the dominant concern is physical goods, and a chapter or two at most will be devoted to services marketing. This is ironic given the fundamental tenet of a marketing approach, i.e. being customer focused. Manufacturing industry as a proportion of GDP has been in decline for some while. The EC reports (Eurostat 1988) that in Europe as a whole, approaching 60 per cent of the workforce is in services, around 30 per cent in industry and a little less than 10 per cent in agriculture. In the United Kingdom the figures are approximately 67 per cent, 30 per cent and 3 per cent. So it is not only the charity sector that needs more marketing writing and research on services!

What is so different about services in comparison to physical goods, and what does the literature on commercial marketing say about them? Building on the earlier work of Eiglier and Langeard (1977), Gronroos (1980) and Shostack (1977), and on their own original research, Zeithaml, Parasuraman and Berry (1985, pp. 33–46) conclude that the unique features of services are as follows:

☐ *intangibility*: it cannot be stored, protected through patents, readily displayed or communicated; prices are difficult to set;
☐ *inseparability*: the consumer is involved in production; other consumers are involved in production; centralised mass production is difficult;
☐ *perishability*: services cannot be inventoried (i.e. stored);
☐ *heterogeneity*: standardisation and quality are difficult to control.

These unique service features and their resulting marketing problems help us to understand the nature of a service and the marketing approach required. These ideas fit well into a charity service context. Take the service examples from Chapter 1. The special school is intangible (prior to experiencing it); customers (children) are inseparably involved in the education; an empty place for a term cannot be recovered (perishability) and standardisation of the service is difficult and not necessarily desirable.

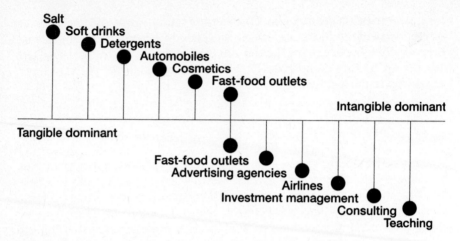

Figure 4.1 A goods–service continuum (source: Shostack 1997, p. 77)

Shostack (1977, p. 77) proposed a continuum ranging from a pure tangible good, through a tangible good with accompanying services and a service with accompanying goods and service through to a pure service (see Figure 4.1).

A. Wilson (1984, p. 10) adjusted his model from its concentration on consumer/commercial subjects to include professional services and extended her continuum further right to include medicine, architecture and the law.

Berry and Parasuraman (1991, pp. 15–21) argue that in services marketing, quality is of paramount importance – indeed they go as far as arguing that in the traditional product marketing mix of the four 'Ps', there should be a fifth 'P', only this time it would be a 'Q' for quality! They have conducted extensive research among customers of service companies which suggests five dimensions that influence customers' assessment of service quality, namely:

☐ Reliability: consisting of the ability to perform the promised service dependably and accurately.
☐ Responsiveness: consisting of the willingness to help customers and to provide prompt service.
☐ Assurance: consisting of the knowledge and courtesy of employees and their ability to convey trust and confidence.
☐ Empathy: consisting of the provision of caring, individualised attention to customers.
☐ Tangibles: consisting of the appearance of the physical facilities, equipment, personnel and communications material.

They argue that all these factors are crucial in the quality assessment that a customer inevitably undertakes when receiving a service, rated in that order of priority (i.e. reliability is the most important factor that customers are looking for).

This quality, they argue, can be delivered first through providing service leadership from top managers who believe that high quality, reliable services are essential all the time; second, through thoroughly testing and retesting services in relation to customer expectations; and, third, through building and nurturing an organisational infrastructure that delivers error-free services.

My experience of service delivery to both beneficiaries and supporters suggests that this list and its application makes a lot of sense for charity services managers.

Shostack (1982, pp. 54–63) argues that one method of ensuring quality is through 'blueprinting'. Physical goods can be specified minutely so that substandard variations are reduced to a minimum. She argues that 'services are very often defined in terms of poorly articulated oral and written abstractions' (Shostack 1982, p. 55). She argues, rightly in my view, that service marketers should make much more effort in directly and indirectly specifying the service blueprint, concentrating particularly on those parts of the service process that seem to cause problems.

Ideas

The third product area of ideas needs greater explanation. Products composed exclusively of ideas are seldom found in the commercial world except perhaps in trade associations (which in themselves are voluntary organisations), promulgating positive ideas about their membership and business concerns. However, ideas as products gained full legitimacy when the American Marketing Association (1985, p. 1) announced its revised definition of marketing as 'the process of planning and executing the conception, pricing, promotion, and distribution of ideas, goods and services to create exchanges that satisfy individual and organisational objectives'. Voluntary organisations spend a significant amount of their time on ideas activity outside the context of a physical good or service. Such ideas are products in themselves, certainly within the context of the marketing mix. Lovelock and Weinberg (1984, p. 285; 1989, pp. 202–5) have argued that this third category under 'product' should be 'social behaviours'. If this logic is accepted, then the first category under the first product, i.e. 'physical goods', might well be 'commercial behaviours'. The overall aim might be to change customer's social behaviours, but the product is 'ideas'.

Ideas as products in charities are normally exemplified in three ways, namely pressure group work, public education and fund-raising.

Pressure group ideas

Pressure group work tends to be aimed primarily at organisations/institutions such as legislatures, the civil service, established/establishment organisations, etc. Examples of pressure group work are myriad, for example: trying to change Sunday trading laws; campaigning for better treatment of prisoners; pressuring for an increase in foreign aid; demanding a higher value social security benefit, etc. Pressure group campaigns may be focused on the broader public, but only as a means to an end, i.e. to build broad-based sympathy in the public in order to influence decision-makers in, say, legislatures.

Public education

Public education tends to be the aiming of ideas at larger swathes of people to try to change their behaviour as an end in itself, for example energy conservation, smoking reduction, keeping the countryside tidy, health education, etc. While there are important exceptions (e.g. ASH on anti-smoking) very few charities engage in significant public education campaigns to change mass behaviour. This needs extensive resources which are usually only available to governments and their agents, e.g. the Health Education Council. Where charities do claim to be implementing public education campaigns, they are often superficial 'nine-day wonders' that do more for charity awareness than they achieve in changed general public behaviour. Even heavily resourced government campaigns on smoking make little impression on behaviour. For more detailed consideration of public education initiatives, see Fine (1990) and Kotler and Roberts (1989).

Fund-raising

There is a third group of charities' idea products, namely fund-raising. At first sight, fund-raising seems too practical and down to earth to be thought of as an idea product. However, it is seldom a physical good (except when charities market goods for profit), and it cannot easily be described as a service; it fits primarily as an idea. Charities raise money for a product which for the donor is essentially an intangible idea. Funds are raised by response to a direct mail letter, or a shaken collection tin, or a written proposal or brochure. Even where the prospective donor visits a charity building to which they will contribute, or visits a service to which they will contribute, there is no absolutely concrete connection between the donor and the service or the building. The donation goes into the charity coffers and the donor trusts the organisation to make sure that the money gets converted into the chosen building or service. In other words, the donor is contributing to a distant idea, which they cannot experience in the way they could a physical good or a service.

It is useful to note that the fund-raising idea product aimed at a donor is only an interpretation or partial representation of a charity's physical or service product aimed at beneficiaries. Unique selling propositions (USPs) for products aimed at beneficiaries may not be the ones that readily appeal to potential donors. In my view it is legitimate to propose different USPs to donors than to beneficiaries. However, two things are essential. First, the beneficiary product must not be modified in order to attract supporters. Second, the tone and content of messages being relayed to potential supporters must be acceptable to beneficiaries. For example, it is not unusual for a talking-book direct mail appeal letter from RNIB to land on the doormat of a visually impaired talking-book member. A key criterion in the final clearance of RNIB direct mail letters is that that talking-book member should find the tone and content of the letter acceptable if by chance they should receive one. Nevertheless the points in the letter, promoting the idea product, may not be the ones that are top of the beneficiary's list of product features. For example, two key features to a visually impaired member is that the book arrives by post and listening to the book is a stimulating experience which relieves boredom and loneliness. The appeal letter will feature the latter attribute because it is more likely to prompt a potential donor into action, but the postal feature will not, because experience shows that it does not have 'pulling power' with donors.

Action arising from idea products

There is an important difference, at least in degree, between action arising out of a pressure group/public education idea product and a fund-raising idea product. In the former the 'seller' (i.e. the charity) has virtually no control over how the idea is actioned. Indeed the idea could be actioned in a way that the charity regards as totally unsatisfactory (see below). With a fund-raising idea product the charity can institute much more control over the immediate action of the target customer, and responsibility for actioning this idea is with the seller or charity.

For example, we shall see in Chapter 8 how the Disability Benefits Consortium was proposing (a) a fundamental review of the UK benefits system for disabled people and (b) its modification to adopt a disability income and costs allowance scheme. The pressure group was successful in getting the first idea adopted, but only partially successful in persuading the government (the target customer) to adopt the second, at least in the form that the pressure group wanted. In short, the Conservative government, of the early 90s, adopted the second idea, but implemented it on its own terms, with far less money than the pressure group was seeking.

Customer behaviour arising out of fund-raising products are easier to control, in part because the behaviour response required is more modest, and in part because promotion and distribution mechanisms can be put in place more firmly. Raising money via a direct mail letter to an individual potential donor allows the fund-raising idea to be set out clearly, e.g. £25 to purify an existing water well in a developing country. The response mechanism is there in the letter, i.e. a reply slip and envelope addressed to the charity. So in this way the customer take-up behaviour arising out of the idea product is simple and reasonably well controlled. However, even here things are not straightforward. The letter recipient may be quite convinced about the proposal but before they have time to act in the way requested, they may have passed a competitor overseas aid charity collecting box in the street and, prompted by the direct mail letter, decided to contribute to that instead because it is easier and more direct. But the marketing twist in the tail of the fund-raising idea product is that although the customer (donor) pays for the idea product, it is the seller (charity) who implements it, normally without any involvement of this purchaser (donor). In a sense the donor is paying 'something for nothing'.

Implementation of idea products
A successful approach to ideas marketing requires the voluntary organisation to develop ways in which it can be involved in implementation, rather than to feel that its job has been done once the idea has been 'sold'; for example, by being invited to join the civil service implementation group for the new benefit, or by gaining a ministerial commitment that the charity will be consulted at each stage of implementation. In the case of action by a mass of individuals, this can be through down-to-earth practical advice on the detailed steps that need to be taken via public relations and promotional material. Table 4.1 shows who does and does not control implementation in the case of three common categories of charity idea products.

Features of idea products
Ideas have to be developed (manufactured), and put across (sold) and then implemented (acted upon). Ideas are all of the following (Bruce 1994):

Table 4.1 Implementation of idea products

Idea product	Who controls implementation	Who does *not* control implementation
Pressure group idea product (e.g. new social security benefit)	Decision-makers	Pressure group/charity
Public education idea product (e.g. anti-smoking)	Individual members of the public	Promoting agency/charity
Fund-raising idea product (e.g. to build a new rehabilitation centre)	Charity	Donor

☐ Intangible: idea products are the ultimate in intangibility.
☐ Separable: voluntary organisation idea products are almost always developed separately by people who are different to those to whom the idea product is 'sold' and to those who implement it.
☐ Durable: idea products are highly durable – some have been around for thousands of years.
☐ Precise: in description they can be precise, i.e. carefully and accurately designed and promoted.
☐ Heterogeneous: in application and implementation there will be almost as many versions as there are individuals or units implementing them.

Comparison of goods, service and idea products

Using the features of ideas above and the service features presented by Zeithaml *et al.* (1985, pp. 33–46), an interesting grid emerges in which the service features have been modified and the ideas column added (Bruce 1994) (see Table 4.2).

Table 4.2 Comparative features of goods, services and ideas

Goods	Services	Ideas
Tangible	Part tangible	Intangible
Separable	Inseparable	Separable
Relatively durable	Perishable	Highly durable
Homogeneous	Heterogeneous	Homogeneous in presentation, heterogeneous in implementation

As described above, Shostack (1977, p. 77) proposed a continuum, see Figure 4.1 (page 56), ranging from a pure tangible good (salt comes near to this), through a tangible good with accompanying services (e.g. cosmetics) and a service with accompanying goods (e.g. investment management) to a pure service (teaching could approach this). In other words, most products have a goods element and a service element.

But Shostack does not place the idea element in the frame. The place of idea products would seem to be further along the continuum to the right, past 'intangible dominant'. This leads to the additional idea that the continuum is not from goods to services only but from goods to services to ideas. Just as services enter into the continuum shortly after goods, so do ideas.

GOODS   SERVICES   IDEAS

However, let us take this much-favoured example of Shostack (1977, p. 77) and subsequent writers – salt (close to a pure physical good). The customer has more opportunities to engage with the product in addition to its use as an additive to make food salty. For example, the customer may be buying it to pour into hot water to soothe tired feet. There again the potential customer may be refusing to buy salt at all because of the *idea* that salt is bad for blood pressure. In short, there are traces of ideas and services lurking around what one might think of as pure physical goods. At the other end of the continuum, approaching pure ideas, we shall find traces of goods as well as services.

Pursuing these ideas with a variety of products, the following models can be constructed.

Salt (Figure 4.2): unbranded, bulk-purchase cooking salt is virtually 100 per cent pure physical good (no service elements, and virtually no idea element).

Fast-food (Figure 4.3): from a highly regarded chain, fast-food has strong

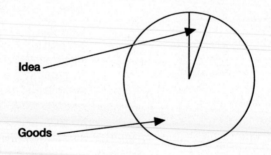

Figure 4.2 Salt

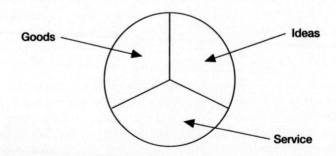

Figure 4.3 Fast-food

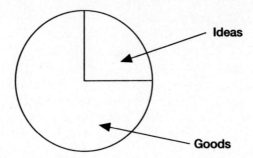

Figure 4.4 Liquid level indicator

physical goods, service and ideas components (i.e. by buying here I know I shall get good food cooked how I like it; served by people who are quick and friendly; and eating fast food confirms to me and my friends that I am so busy, I don't have time to cook and can afford to pay someone else to do it).

Liquid level indicator (Figure 4.4): sold at subsidised prices to (mainly) newly blind people, it hooks over the rim of the cup and makes a buzzing noise when the beverage reaches 1 cm below the rim. This is mainly a physical good; and there is no service element, but there is a significant ideas element in that use of the device encourages/empowers the newly blind person to entertain sighted friends once again.

Talking books (Figure 4.5): complete books are recorded onto tape and posted to a blind person's home on request, backed up by volunteer service engineers who visit to explain how to use the recording machine and to give useful information on other services available. The books relieve boredom and loneliness (especially among newly blind people) and are a source of pride and accomplishment to friends and family in that the majority of older users have never used a tape recorder before. Without the sense of pride in using the machine and, more importantly, without the service back-up, many newly blind older members would not have taken up or sustained the

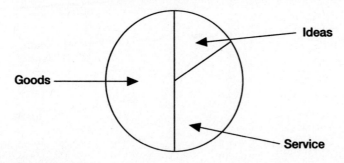

Figure 4.5 Talking books

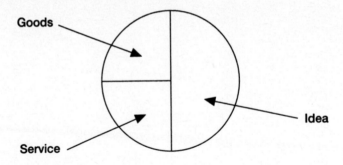

Figure 4.6 Empowerment

activity. The books have a high physical goods component, with significant service and ideas elements.

Empowerment (Figure 4.6): the idea of empowerment of disadvantaged groups is fundamental to many charities. However, without supplying some resources (goods such as wheelchairs for disabled people, and food and shelter for homeless people) and services (such as self-help/mutual aid organisations), the idea of empowerment will not be taken up by disadvantaged groups. (As an aside, devising structures to deliver the goods and services in a way that empowers, rather than encourages dependency, is problematic.)

Religion (Figure 4.7): in organised religion, ideas and service components dominate and physical goods feature less (depending on the religion and the particular subdivision), i.e. the essence of religion is belief in certain ideas which are supported and developed through services such as regular communal worship, where physical items such as an altar may play a role but only as part of the service.

Politics (Figure 4.8): the (ideal) essence of politics is in its ideas. The individual 'buys into' a set of beliefs which others will put into practice (if elected). Because of their extreme intangibility, these ideas need to be

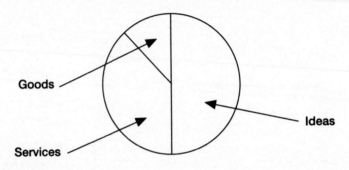

Figure 4.7 Religion

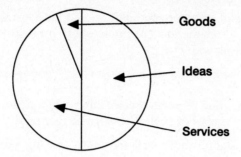

Figure 4.8 Politics

supported by service organisations (political parties) which run a whole range of activities to recruit and sustain supporters (ranging from recruitment events and leafleting to social occasions, etc.). Physical goods are seldom involved except at the periphery, e.g. sale of T-shirts indicating support for a candidate.

Comprehensive model
All the above products, indeed all products in theory, can be placed in a three-dimensional model, in relationship to each other (see Figure 4.9). There are three axes at right angles: degree of idea element, service element and goods element.

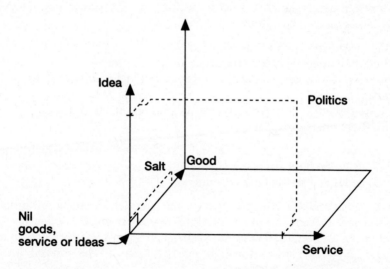

Figure 4.9 Comprehensive product model, positioning products according to the relative weighting of their constituent elements of goods, services and ideas (plotting two examples – salt and politics)

Conclusion: rules of product composition and marketing

The simple, but fundamental conclusions on product composition and marketing are as follows:

1. All products have actual or latent physical goods, service and ideas components.
2. Successful marketing requires that all three components are attended to if the maximum number of customers is to be recruited and retained.

So, for example, organisations will sell more cooking salt if they brand it, offer guarantees, give advice on usage, etc. At the other extreme, political parties will gain and retain more supporters if they not only put forward ideas, but also increase the penetration and effectiveness of services such as regular party meetings, social and community events, advice to and representation of individuals with problems; and, albeit less importantly, and within the limits of the law, if they sell and distribute branded physical goods such as badges, pendants, pens, T-shirts, etc. Empowerment of disadvantaged individuals and groups will not just happen. It also requires significant goods and services to be delivered, albeit within the enabling structure of rights, not largesse.

New product development and the phasing out of existing products

Development of the new products (physical goods, services or ideas) or modification of the existing ones depends fundamentally on relating the charity's aims to the target markets selected.

The kinds of issues which need considering in new product (good, services, ideas) decisions are as follows:

☐ What is the intensity of unmet need?
☐ How many people in the target market are so affected?
☐ Do we have or can we develop a product which can wholly meet those needs?
☐ Do we have the resource of money, expertise, etc., to deliver?
☐ Are there other providers?

The answers to these questions do not give the final answer which requires an overall judgement from management (and sometimes committees). But they do provide a framework of evidence.

Ansoff (1965, pp. 109–10) proposed a useful model for considering market development (which he called 'product–market posture') which has been widely used and adapted over the years (see Figure 4.10). Increased market penetration gives growth through market share of the present product markets.

An example from quadrant A would be to increase the number of existing Braille readers purchasing RNIB's Braille magazines and/or to increase the

Growth through

A	B
Existing products in existing target markets (market penetration)	Existing products in new target markets (market development)
C	D
New products in existing target markets (product development)	New products in new target markets (diversification)

Figure 4.10

number of magazines taken. In B, it might be to increase the numbers of Braille readers through education programmes (i.e. a new market) and to sell existing magazines into this market. In quadrant C it might be to introduce new Braille magazines into the range to promote to existing purchasers. In quadrant D it might be to introduce new magazines on subjects designed to appeal to newly Braille-literate people.

The above examples are ones of evolutionary growth. However, more revolutionary ones can also be adopted. For example, in quadrant D the logic could be as follows. Only 20,000 out of one million blind and partially sighted people read Braille. This is because most of the one million are relatively newly visually impaired in older age and so reduced finger sensitivity makes learning Braille very difficult. One of the products they miss is being able to read national newspapers in full on the day they are published, rather than 20 per cent on an audio tape version arriving three days later. Electronic technology has advanced to such an extent that a computerised newspaper in voice output form can be beamed direct from the editorial offices of a national newspaper over the night via the home television aerial into a home computer, ready for listening to in audio or Braille form by 6 a.m., i.e. the same time as an ordinary newspaper falls on the mat. This might be attractive to newly blind people of 40–60 years of age who previously could type or were familiar with personal computers. RNIB has already launched such a scheme.

Ansoff's growth framework is equally useful for other markets such as the environment and the arts. Rodger (1987, pp. 40–52) provides interesting examples from the visual arts.

While the above model provides a framework for a strategic analysis of development, how does new product development happen in practice? This is discussed in more detail in Chapter 7 on charity services. However, in short, the process consists of developing proposals, giving them preliminary analysis in relation to target markets and the resources of the charity and relating the proposal to the objective of the charity. If the product gets through this stage, one then undertakes more sophisticated business analysis and development of the product in some detail (this needs to occur more or less simultaneously because one feeds on the other), takes the product in the form of physical goods, services or even ideas out to an actual or simulated test market situation, and if the pilot is successful, launches the new physical good, service or idea.

Deleting a product in whatever form is very difficult in any organisation, but especially in a charity where commitment to beneficiary groups, however small in number, is very high; and the straightforward pressures of profitability do not often apply. To avoid snap deletion decisions being made because of a funding crisis or customer complaints, all charity offerings should be reviewed on a regular basis. The review ideally should not be simply on the basis of whether to remove a product or not. It would obviously be much more broadly based and would be part of regular effectiveness reviews. However, the basic question 'do we need this product any more?' should always be asked in such reviews. Some of the questions to ask in reaching a decision are as follows:

☐ Is it central to our mission?
☐ How do our customers regard its quality?
☐ How many customers does it reach?
☐ What is the subsidy in total and the subsidy per customer?
☐ Are there other providers of better or comparable quality?

If there are other providers and the other answers are negative, this offering is a candidate for closure.

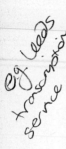

The handling of deletions or closures needs to be very carefully thought through. It is fairly easy for Unilever to cope with complaints about the deletion of the soap powder Omo. It is much harder for a charity to deal with (especially organised) complaints by beneficiaries about the removal of a product, for example closure of an old people's home, particularly when the closure has the effect of dramatically disrupting the lives of existing residents by placing them in other homes away from the staff and fellow residents whom they have come to know and love.

Conclusion

The field of charity products or offerings is extraordinarily complex, involving not only physical goods and services, but also ideas. Successful product design requires attention to the eight 'Ps' of philosophy, product, price, promotion, place, people, physical evidence and process. Next we turn to one of the most challenging elements of the charity marketing mix, namely price.

Price – important but very underrated

As has been noted above, this has traditionally been one of the most difficult of the 'Ps' to use in not-for-profit marketing. There are areas where it is readily, and normally, well applied, e.g. the pricing of fund-raising catalogue items, or giving donors target response levels in direct mail letters, etc. However, outside the field of fund-raising, and within the product areas of services and ideas, the charity track record is generally very poor. Even the most fundamental information for considering price, namely cost, is missing more often than not. Even accepting that setting a price greater than cost is normally inappropriate for activities associated with core charity aims, failing to understand the true relativity of price and cost is amateurish. For example, it is only in the last ten years that the RNIB has properly costed all the items within its sixty or so product lines (comprising physical goods, services and ideas); and the last 20 per cent are proving particularly intransigent. Hardest to cost are those products that are part of a multiple product line and are handled by several different parts of the organisation. The field of costing the services of the charity sector has much to learn from other professional service providers such as lawyers, management consultants, etc., who charge out every working moment in time chunks of fifteen minutes (or even five minutes). Going this far will seldom be necessary when profit is not the bottom line, but charities should have a better idea of the subsidy going into products as well as product lines.

Having costed our charity offerings, is it worthwhile or even appropriate to price them? It is worthwhile in many more cases than at present. Every product has to be resourced – something which properly idealistic service managers often forget! If the customer (whether they be end beneficiary, intermediary or supporter) is contributing nothing to this, a number of dangers emerge, such as the intermediary or beneficiary customer not valuing the product, the beneficiary feeling patronised as a recipient of charity rather than a customer with consumer rights, relative over-usage by some customers which blocks off access to non-users, etc.

If this seems like an esoteric argument we only have to look at the contribution of income from priced products to get a shock of realism. Sales of goods and services are the largest single source of income for general charities with turnovers of more than £1 million. Even for smaller general charities with turnovers between £100,000 per year and £1 million it is the second largest source of income after donations and grants (Hems and Passey 1996).

When it is realised that sales of general charity goods and services provide around one-third of charity income, the importance of appropriate pricing is very clear (see Table 4.3). However, the importance of pricing is even further underlined by the dramatic growth of income provided by priced products (goods and services) over the last few years. Between 1991 and 1994/5,

Table 4.3 Gross income of general charities by income bands – percentages

	Less than £100K	£0.1m to £1m	£1m to £10m	£10m +	All
Sales of goods/services	12	33	42	34	33
Grants and donations	54	49	34	31	40
Legacies	2	3	5	13	7
Investment and disposal income	32	15	20	22	20
Total	100	100	100	100	100

Source:
Table 3.1 ONS Survey, Hems and Passey 1996.

while total grants and donations only grew by 2 per cent, sales of goods and services grew by massive 30 per cent (Table 4.4). In fact for medium-sized charities (£1m–£10m) grants and donations dropped by 31 per cent, while sales income rose by 16 per cent.

It is likely that sales growth is being fuelled by contracting, especially for medium-sized charities which saw government grants (as opposed to purchasing or contracting) drop by 7 per cent (Hems and Passey 1996); even in the £10 million plus charities increasing purchases by government (+ 46 per cent) outstripped government grant rises (+ 25 per cent).

So a key conclusion is that sales income and pricing are crucial to general charities and are growing in importance. Charities ignore this at their peril.

So much for goods, services and ideas which can be priced, but what about others which superficially cannot be priced? A good example here might be pressure group proposals, trying to persuade the government to increase social security benefit or introduce a new one. The charity can hardly charge the civil servants for battering them with ideas they do not really want to hear! However, here and in relation to many services and some physical goods as well as ideas, I suggest using the term 'impact price'. The price is obscured to the seller but not the buyer. This concept is widely applicable to idea products, partially applicable to service products and marginally applicable to physical goods products. These impact prices are often ignored by the seller, but readily appreciated by the consumer. Returning to the example of the pressure group proposal, many charity pressure groups come up with calls for immediate changes which are very difficult for politicians and civil servants to implement. This is for a variety of reasons, including the fact that the resources are simply not available and/or the procedural changes involved are very significant and would create opposition from other government departments, let alone the fact that other pressure groups might lose out as a consequence. In short, the impact price that the politicians and civil servants would have to pay is too high, even if

Table 4.4 Percentage change in income of general charities 1991–1994/5, using general charities surveyed in both 1991 and 1994/95

	Income strata (ONS based)		
	£1m–£10m	Over £10m	All over £1m
1 Total income	–8.2	30.9	25.8
2 Total sales of goods/services	15.9	32.7	30.4
2.1 Total sales of goods/services to persons	38.9	19.7	22.3
2.2 Total sales of goods/services to companies	–81.1	9.7	–16.6
2.3 Total sales of goods/services to non-profits	–50.7	165.5	108.9
2.4 Total sales of goods/services to government	31.3	46.2	44.3
3 Total grants/donations	–30.6	7.7	2.2
4 Legacies	34.4	8.0	9.1
5 Total investment income	–32.9	82.3	61.4

Source:
Table 3.7 ONS Survey, Hems and Passey 1996.

they think that the pressure group idea is a good one. When challenged on this impact price, campaigners will offer a variety of justifications for not having thought the issue through. One is that they are trying to establish a bargaining position which can later be reduced; another is that it is not up to them to become involved in resource and procedural deliberations, as that is the role of government; and another is that it would be letting down the interest they represent to demand anything other than the full proposal. In their way, all of these points have some validity, but on many occasions they are simply excuses for the pressure group not having thought carefully enough about the full price their customers are going to have to pay. A marketing approach would be to think about the impact price from the point of view of the potential implementers of the proposal. It may be that while the full demand is retained, suggestions can be put forward as to how the change could be introduced incrementally. The first increment would take account of resources likely to become available and would be in a form that is less likely to encourage opposition from other interest groups both within and without government, etc. Such a pricing process is not dissimilar to a commercial company offering significant discounts to customers in the early stages in order to get them 'hooked'.

Chapter 3 described the application of exchange theory to understand customer take-up behaviour, listing costs and benefits to the target groups of taking up the offering. Such an approach helps us to assess the impact price.

In short, the 'P' of price is undervalued by the public and not-for-profit sectors in two main ways. Overt pricing is often not considered in relation to true costs and under-pricing too readily accepted. Second, impact prices, especially of ideas and to a lesser extent services, and also occasionally of goods, are seldom considered by charities, which accounts for many important 'sales' not being made. Charities need to use the concepts behind such commercial terms as price discounts, allowances and credit. These ideas are explored further in Chapters 6–10.

Promotion – what we are good at

If pricing is an element of the marketing mix where many not-for-profit organisations are weak, promotion of offerings is an area where they are strong and frequently outperform their commercial counterparts. The traditional list of the promotion mix is advertising, personal selling, sales promotion and public relations. Three additional important areas, relevant to services in general and to charity service and idea products in particular, need to be considered, namely coalition building, intermediary referral and customer referral.

Advertising

Within the limits of relatively low spending levels, charity advertising can be among the best, giving high impact, high memorability and significant awareness. Among the classics are the Salvation Army's 'For God's sake care', Christian Aid's 'Give a man a fish and you feed him for a day. Teach him to fish and you feed him for life'; and Great Ormond Street's Wishing Well Appeal with the childlike face and falling teardrop.

Personal selling

Personal selling, where it happens, can also be highly effective and professional. The volunteer fund-raising forces of charities such as Save the Children, Oxfam and NSPCC make commercial sales directors green with envy. Personal selling of ideas (particularly in pressure group work and fund-raising) by middle and senior management is also widespread and effective. This assessment is based on informal feedback from civil servants, politicians and senior business leaders who have been on the receiving end of such initiatives. However, personal selling of services – especially beneficiary services – by middle managers to intermediaries such as local authorities can be a problematic area. There is a widespread feeling among charity service middle managers that selling, self-publicity and even publicising the organisation is 'not why we are here'. Rather they feel that constructing and delivering the service is the key task. This fails to recognise the fact that without very active promotion, including personal selling, no one is going to want the services. A good example of the benefit of effective personal selling can be seen among special schools run by charities. Here it is usually the responsibility of the head or a senior staff member to travel to interested local authorities and prospective parents. When prospective parents visit the school, this is not seen as an unwelcome intrusion but is valued by all staff as an opportunity to meet prospective parents and to form a view as to whether the child will benefit from the school's education. Schools like this are full.

Sales promotion

Sales promotion is probably one of the less useful methods and is certainly not widely utilised in the charity sector. An important exception would be in fund-raising where gifts to donors associated with donations are becoming more widespread; also special opportunities for major valued donors are becoming increasingly the norm, e.g. meeting aristocratic and royal patrons, attendance at prestigious first nights, etc.

Stripping back the purpose of sales promotion to its very core, i.e. promoting sales of a particular offering, one can see far wider applicability in the charity sector. All voluntary organisations have services and ideas that are reasonably well known and well regarded but are not expanding as fast as the agency would wish. A greater concentration on trying to create events either in isolation, or as part of other third-party activity with a specific objective of clinching a sale, could reap rewards: for example, a disability charity providing 50 per cent of the costs of the extra equipment that a mainstream school needs to integrate a disabled child, provided that the LEA will provide the extra professional staff support.

Public relations

Public relations is once again an area where charities are among the market leaders. They have products that are intrinsically interesting and news-worthy, and they achieve massive TV, radio and newspaper coverage of their interests through the editorial rather than the paid advertising chan-nels. Charities have made a fine art of marketing their interests to journalists and researchers in all three media. They treat these groups as the inter-mediary customers they really are. Indeed, so good are charities at commu-nications that some have argued that this emphasis is disproportionate and that charities need to adopt a more strategic or long-term marketing perspective (Conway 1997).

Pharoah and Welchman (1997) surveyed public communication methods and development in one thousand charities showing a very wide range of techniques and strategy contributing to effectiveness. Deacon, Fenton and Walker (1995) interviewed media professionals and concluded that they were most receptive to stories which are topical (i.e. pertinent to broader issues current at the time) or stories which are demonstrably of general interest. This bears out two important media relations rules: (a) try and ride on the back of bigger stories, and (b) establish your story's relevance to as wide a group of people as possible. *e.g. eclipse*

Coalition building

A further addition to the list of promotion activities, particularly relevant to the charities sector, is 'coalition building'. The promotion of services and, in particular, ideas can be greatly enhanced by building coalitions between statutory, voluntary and in some cases even commercial organisations with a common interest (see Chapter 8). Because of the superficially altruistic basis of the work, quite surprising coalitions can be achieved which greatly enhance their power. It is not unusual for a variety of charities to join together with representatives from local government to promote a particular cause area, e.g. child protection. Employers supported by disability charities have built a coalition to promote the recruitment of disabled people into employers' workforces, and as a side-effect this coalition has had a strong influence on disability policy. In 1987 a consortium of 250 charities in Britain concerned with disability (Disability Benefits Consortium) gathered together to present one voice during a period when it was known that the government was prepared to amend existing benefits and introduce new benefits for disabled people. These coalitions significantly increase the impact of charity proposals.

Intermediary and customer referral

Another area absent from traditional elaborations of the marketing mix relates to services and ideas. A. Wilson (1984, p. 161) points out the importance of professional referral for professional services and, along with Berry and Parasuraman (1991, p. 7), emphasises the importance of the word-of-mouth recommendation – especially from customers – as being that much more critical for a service which can only be experienced, as opposed to a physical good which can be inspected.

These forms of promotion are of critical importance to charity services and idea products and also to physical goods aimed at beneficiaries. Anything up to 100 per cent of new beneficiary customers to education and social service charities will come from professional referrals from social workers, doctors, teachers, lawyers, etc. The relative take-up of physical goods aimed at beneficiaries may also be highly related to the degree and nature of referrals from professionals. In Chapter 8, which covers pressure group work, the importance of professional referral, commendation and advocacy will be discussed. So the obvious conclusion is that professional worker intermediaries are an important customer group which needs to be identified for each charity offering, be it goods, services or ideas. They not only need to be identified but also developed, even nurtured, if the charity products are to penetrate their end customer market significantly.

Satisfied (or dissatisfied) existing customers of charity offerings are also potent promotional forces. This area is covered in Chapters 6–10. It is sufficient to say here that satisfied and loyal beneficiary and supporter customers will spread the word and bring in many more beneficiaries and supporters. Strongly dissatisfied ones will do the opposite. Again, existing customers need to be well served and nurtured in their own right, particularly if customer word-of-mouth recommendations are to increase target market penetration.

Conclusion

Promotion in the charity field is rather like the curate's egg, good and bad in different parts. Even where it is good, however, there is room for drawing promotion in as part of the marketing mix and involving line managers in the promotional work. Promotion is often undertaken by staff separate from the product line and the promotion is not integrated into the marketing mix, but stands alone, losing effectiveness.

Place – how we distribute our products

Place, or distribution, is the activity that ensures that products get to customers when and where they want to buy them. Doyle (1991, p. 275) reframes McCarthy's list of elements of place as distributors, retailers, locations, inventory and transport.

Distributors and retailers

Public and charitable organisations often assume that they have a much harder task in reaching their end customer than the commercial world. In fact the list above shows that the commercial marketing organisation has many intermediary target groups to work through before it reaches its end customer, in the same way as a not-for-profit organisation does. Distribution intermediaries, Doyle (1991, p. 282) argues, have 'goals that are at least partially conflicting with those of the manufacturer'. This produces many of the difficulties experienced by charities in the area of 'place'. The key difference is that commercial organisations are much more prepared to bolster the common interest between the marketing organisation and its distribution channels through the provision of financial incentives. Charities seldom provide financial incentives to intermediaries and have to rely much more heavily on common goals in relation to the end consumer. For example, charities running home visiting services rely heavily on referrals from social workers. Social workers and social services departments receive no financial incentive or 'percentage' of the subsequent fee (if any). They introduce the service because they feel it will help the wellbeing of their client, i.e. they have common cause with the supply organisation.

Dibb *et al.* (1991, p. 698), in their brief discussion of voluntary organisation marketing, point out that an important element of the distribution mix (place) – that of independent wholesalers – does not exist in the charity sector. In the sense of wholesaler services which can be purchased, they are right. However, charities have a plethora of distributors which they can and do use to reach their end clients. (For example, national charities may use local charities for stock-holding, with even more localised old people's clubs or local churches drawing down stock for onward distribution to end beneficiaries.) The difference is that these distributor channels cannot normally be bought in the way that commercial wholesalers and other onward distributors can. Thus these intermediary distribution channels assume the characteristics of an intermediary target group or intermediary customer group whose needs and wants must be addressed in a funda- mental way if the charity is to be successful in reaching its end clients. Provided that this broader understanding of the terms 'distributors' and 'retailers' is understood, then Doyle's (1991) list is adequate.

As a generalisation, charities pay insufficient attention to this fourth 'P' of place. They tend to assume that because (in their view) their product, be it a physical good, service or idea, is intrinsically good, somehow everyone else will take up common cause and help to make it accessible and available to the potential end customer. This is not necessarily the case; greater study of the aims of intermediaries, and adjusting the product or the way it is designed, can increase its attractiveness to intermediaries and thus increase its chances of reaching the end customer.

Locations

'Locations' is a crucial checkpoint for the development of new offerings and assessing existing ones. Locations where charity offerings are delivered to customers can change quite dramatically over a number of years; or if they do not change, can result in the demise of the product. As shown in an example in Chapter 1, changes in social policy dictated that the delivery of education and rehabilitation to young visually handicapped children should change from sending them to a distant residential home towards concentrating on delivery at the local level. If the Sunshine organisation had not changed its point of delivery, it would have gone out of existence. Similar changes are now taking place in relation to rehabilitating newly disabled adults into employment. Previously this was provided regionally, but now the purchasing authority in the form of the government is insisting that this should be provided locally.

The headings 'inventory' (stocks) and 'transport' are all relevant to charities when dealing with physical goods but make less sense when considering services and ideas.

People – staff and volunteers who make or break

Booms and Bitner (1981, pp. 47–51) include personnel and other customers as the two-part breakdown of this area of the marketing mix with specific application to *services*.

Personnel

The checklist includes training, discretion, commitment, incentives, appearance, interpersonal behaviour and attitudes. By this time, charity marketing managers must be feeling that they are being asked to take on responsibility for managing the whole organisation; and general charity managers must be either feeling threatened or becoming exasperated at the cheek of these marketing people who think that such aspects as staff behaviour and attitudes have anything to do with marketing staff. Chapter 5 will deal with this in more detail. However, in essence, the marketing function's responsibility is to persuade line management of the importance of these elements if the service or idea product is to be attractive to customers and recommended by them.

Some line managers would argue that they already have all the above elements well under control. This may be true, but in my experience they are primarily under control in relation to other staff, their managers and the organisation in general. They are not always appropriately directed towards customers. Chapter 3 discussed all the various reasons that charities, in particular, do not always think along the philosophical lines of 'the customer is always right'. Too often charities appear to think and behave along the lines of 'the customers are lucky to have our help'.

For me, one of the most exciting bridges from marketing into service and idea delivery is a book by Berry and Parasuraman (1991). The reason for calling this book a 'bridge' is that they focus very heavily on quality as the way through to successful service (and, by implication, idea) products. However, their application of quality is intensely directed towards the customer. They argue that there is nothing better than quality to retain customers; nothing better to gain new customers through word-of-mouth recommendation; and nothing better to establish product differentiation.

At this point it is worth introducing the idea of high staff/customer contact and low staff/customer contact service systems. This distinction was developed by Chase (1978, pp. 137–42). In short, the greater the amount of contact between customers and (charity) service staff, the more important it is to get the staff personnel aspects up to a very high standard. At its most superficial, a charity can get away with grumpy but efficient staff provided that they are not in contact with the customer! For charity service products such as schools, colleges, hotels, training centres, day centres, etc., contact with staff is lengthy and intensive. The value that beneficiaries put on these services will be almost entirely the result of their interaction with staff.

Looking at the list of elements, it is immediately clear that charities should have a significant advantage over commercial companies under the headings of commitment, attitude and interpersonal behaviour. It is my experience of working in both the commercial and voluntary sectors that charities have the edge in these areas, but only just. A commercial organisation that involves its staff, praises them for good work and has good staff development programmes will almost certainly have better staff attitudes and commitment than the charity that does none of these things.

Discretion is a particularly interesting element. Berry and Parasuraman (1991, p. 49) make a very strong case for giving those service staff in direct touch with the customer significant discretion to satisfy the customer, especially if they are dissatisfied. They quote Federal Express where, even though the average transaction costs only $16, front-line company service representatives are empowered to spend up to $100 to resolve a customer problem. That principle translates well into the charity sector.

Other Contemporaneous Customers

The impact that other customers have on customer take-up is a fascinating one, and is clearly also crucial to charity services to beneficiaries and supporters. If the offering requires quite a number of beneficiaries or supporters all to be in one place for some length of time, then it is vital that they get on with each other. If they do not, then the offering will be much less well appreciated, they might not come back, and they will almost certainly not recommend it to their peers.

To some extent, good marketing analysis beforehand should overcome many of the potential dangers, because the customer group should be relatively homogeneous. However, problems or dislikes between con- temporaneous customers will inevitably happen, and it is therefore vital that staff are trained and skilled in resolving these. For example, quite a few disability charities run holiday schemes. There are normally fairly well targeted, either to involve younger people or older people. In theory there is no reason that the scheme could not involve both, but the chances of negative customer interaction increase, e.g. younger people staying up later and wanting loud music, and older guests not appreciating this! Similarly we saw in Chapter 1, in the fund-raising case study, that one of the reasons for the success of the fund-raising dinner was that it involved people interested in horseracing, i.e. all the attenders had a common interest and the event was planned around this. Figure 4.11 shows young people enjoying dancing together as part of a dance outreach service of the Birmingham Royal Ballet.

Physical evidence – necessary when so much of our work is hidden

Physical evidence of the product, and surrounding the product, can be very influential in establishing customer expectations before take-up, and can continue to be influential during take-up. While it is relevant to physical goods, it is particularly vital in the field of charity services and ideas because these are, in themselves, so much less tangible. In other words, the customer may well be placing particular reliance, especially before take-up, on the physical evidence simply because the experience is not yet there. Even while the experience is taking place, the tangible aspects may set a very strong backcloth for judgement of the intangibles. For example, the quality of tea, coffee and other food on a rehabilitation course may be a strong influencer as to the clients' judgement of the effectiveness of the course. It is hard to be positive about any kind of course where the food is delivered late, cold and of poor quality!

Charity services

Whether these services are aimed at beneficiaries or supporters, the design of the service environment needs to be well considered. Factors such as

Figure 4.11 Customers of services need to get on with each other if the service experience is to be highly valued – young people from a Birmingham school enjoying each other and the Jiving Lindy Hoppers dance group as part of the outreach services of the Birmingham Royal Ballet and the Royal Opera House (photographer Charles Baynon).

too small
room—hot etc.

physical layout, quality of furnishings, noise levels, etc., can quickly set an atmosphere, either good or bad. A charity nature reserve, hotel, college or rehabilitation centre, etc., needs to be laid out as well as possible in relation to its function and the expectations of its beneficiaries. For example, even if the hotel is old the lighting levels can be improved along with furnishings.

As far as services aimed at donors are concerned, similar considerations are important. The atmosphere of the fund-raising dinner would be quite different if held in the (aristocratic) president's own home as opposed to the Hilton. The sponsored swim is likely to be much more effective first in attracting swimmers, and second in encouraging them to support again, if it is held in a modern swimming bath with clean changing facilities.

Once stated, these points are obvious. But it is surprising how many charities either ignore them, or take the view that there is nothing they can do to improve matters substantially. There are always relatively low-cost initiatives that can be undertaken to improve the physical environment which will improve take-up.

Encouraging take-up of services relies heavily on adroit use of tangible clues both in advertising and promotion, and in responding to enquiries. Once again, if charity hotels, schools, rehabilitation centres, etc., respond to enquiries promptly with an attractive brochure and good covering letter, the intermediary or potential beneficiary is going to be much more reassured about the quality of the actual service. Two colleges may be providing comparable education, but if one has a poor brochure and responds late to enquiries, the enquirer is far more likely to go to the college with the prompt response and the good brochure.

Ideas

It is even more important to manage the physical evidence of ideas in a proactive way, simply because they are intangible. Take-up of fund-raising ideas can be much higher when tangible clues are offered. Direct mail letters get much better responses if a small sample of dehydration salts are included in an overseas aid appeal, or if a piece of Braille is included in a letter asking for support for services to blind people, or, at a most basic level, if a photograph of the school for which the appeal is being made is included.

At first sight one might think that tangible clues about pressure group ideas are either impossible or inconsequential. Surely it is the quality of ideas that counts, rather than any kind of physical evidence. In my experience physical evidence can be absolutely crucial in an idea gaining ground. Even something as simple as using a flip chart with computer-generated large print headings will nudge ministers out of their post-prandial doze! Drawing other knowledgeable or experienced people into the presentation, either in person or through video, adds to the credibility of the idea. Leaving well-printed and designed (but not expensive) proposal papers makes everything much more concrete.

This is not to dismiss the role of the informal discussion at a government reception, or over a private lunch, where not even papers change hands. However, when one has got through the door to the stage of formal presentation, physical evidence of pressure group ideas needs to be implemented very thoughtfully.

In summary, in order to encourage take-up, especially of services and ideas, a charity needs to look at the best possible physical evidence that it can present to potential customers before take-up. In addition it needs to look carefully at the physical evidence of services during their consumption.

Processes – are they customer-friendly?

The subheads under this element of the marketing mix as proposed by Booms and Bitner (1981, pp. 47–51) are policies, procedures, mechanisation, employee discretion, customer involvement, customer direction and flow of activities. Once again this list must prompt the charity manager reading this text to wonder if the marketing manager is trying to take over the whole world! What is being proposed is that operations managers have to 'think' marketing or, to put it another way, marketing has to go into the line. Policies, procedures, mechanisation, customer direction and flow of activities initially all look like straight operations responsibilities, i.e. the purpose is to undertake all of those activities as efficiently, effectively and cheaply as possible. But all these processes must be customer-friendly. If they are not, customers will either walk away or stay and harbour dissatisfaction.

When stated it is obvious that beneficiaries and supporters are crucial. Their satisfaction must dictate the changes, and the rate of change of operational activities. For example, too many charities have seized the advantage of computer systems to introduce much more 'efficient' invoicing and fee collection systems to customers. Invoices are issued much more promptly and accurately, and non-paying customers are identified automatically and regularly – something we could not have dreamed of since the days when skilled labour was cheap. However, more often than not, these new efficient billing systems have been introduced with little thought of the paying customer. The invoices are full of number codes which cannot easily be related to purchases, the first-generation financial systems do not allow many words to be included, and they are difficult for the customer to understand. RNIB's first generation of invoices were so unfriendly towards customers that some people actually stopped buying because they got so confused and upset by what they saw as the gobbledegook being thrown at them. Now RNIB issues invoices not only in large print but also in Braille to take account of our beneficiary customers' needs.

Another example of the need for operational managers to 'think' marketing and customers is in the field of employee discretion for those staff who work at the front line with customers. Superficial operational efficiency would suggest that the most junior employees need have little discretion. However, customer contact personnel are the first people (however junior) to learn that a customer has received a substandard physical good, or an unsatisfactory service. Berry and Parasuraman (1991, pp. 47–50) describe four crucial requirements for resolving customer problems effectively. They argue that, first, employees must be prepared/trained in recovering the situation; second they have to be empowered to undertake corrective action (the example was given above of Federal Express frontline employees being empowered to spend up to six times the average order cost to correct a problem); third, employees must be facilitated to correct problems (e.g. by giving them the right to access information urgently from other, often more senior, staff and/or giving them the most expensive high-tech equipment to help access other parts of the organisation); and fourth, employees must be rewarded for early and satisfactory customer complaints resolution and reporting them up the line so that problems can be grouped and solved as part of the system. This description seems to me to be an excellent example of how the common interests of operational trains of thought and marketing trains of thought can be brought together to the benefit of the organisation and customers.

As far as customer involvement and customer direction are concerned, this is an area of particular interest to charity goods, services and ideas as applied to beneficiaries, and it also makes good sense in services aimed at supporters. We can learn a lot from the educational philosophy that says that people develop far more effectively if they are 'active in their own learning'. Charity customers, whether they be beneficiaries, supporters, intermediaries or staff, are not there to be 'done unto'. As a general rule they need to be involved, and certainly in the area of services they have to be involved whether the charity likes it or not (and obviously the charity should 'like it').

In conclusion, this element of the marketing mix, process, is not an attempt by marketing managers to take over operational management. It is simply a proposal that marketing has a lot to offer to operations at the customer interface, especially in the area of service products and idea products where the processes of the charity are inextricably interwoven with the offering.

Conclusion

Charities and public organisations' products (goods, services and ideas) have a marketing mix whether or not it is recognised as such by the organisation. Adapting the commercial listings of the marketing mix can help charities and not-for-profit organisations make sure that their offerings or products are more in line with customers' needs and wants. However, defining a marketing mix for a product or product line is one thing; implementing it in the services-dominant environment of charities is another! The next chapter suggests how we can do this by looking at a charity's culture, resources, activities and processes, and structure.

Key points

The charity marketing mix – the eight 'Ps':

Philosophy
☐ Voluntary organisations should be explicit about their values and philosophy and ensure that these are integrated into the marketing mix. Failure to do so will lead to tensions and contradictions between different physical products, services and ideas.

Product (or offering)
☐ Charity products can be physical goods, services or ideas.
☐ Successful product design requires attention to all eight 'Ps'.
☐ Develop new products or adapt existing ones to the target markets selected.
☐ In marketing services, quality is key – achieved by reliability, ensuring that the service continues to meet customer expectation and constructing an organisation that delivers the service without errors.

Price
☐ Price is an element of the marketing mix where charities are often weak.
☐ Know the cost of each offering or product and beware of the dangers of under-pricing and over-subsidy.
☐ Understand the impact price of the ideas or services you are proposing.

Promotion
☐ Charity promotion is often very effective, but for best results make sure that it is integrated into the marketing mix.
☐ Be aware of the importance of word-of-mouth recommendation and referral.

Place
☐ Charities have a variety of distributors and potential distributors. Because they are often not paid in the conventional commercial sense, they need to be treated as intermediary customers with their needs

addressed in much the same way as any other intermediary target group.

☐ Check the locations (i.e. the points of delivery) of new and existing products.

People

☐ Charities do not always have the advantage over commercial companies in terms of staff commitment and attitude and there are useful lessons from the commercial sector which can be applied in the voluntary sector.

☐ Service customers often interact with each other. Segmentation will help ensure this is positive.

Physical evidence

☐ Remember that the service customer may be relying on the tangible evidence of an experience as a way of interpreting it, whether the service is aimed at beneficiaries or supporters.

☐ Give potential donors or supporters tangible evidence to help them understand and remember your appeal or proposal.

Process

☐ Think how your usual administrative procedures could become more customer oriented.

5

HOW TO INTRODUCE A MARKETING APPROACH AND A MARKETING REALITY

Virtually all marketing books, whether aimed at not-for-profit organisations or the commercial world, devote relatively little attention to introducing marketing into an organisation. My experience of this in three charities and one public body is that this is a very major challenge which is not at all easy to accomplish.

Charity acceptance of marketing as a managerial discipline – endemic reasons for its resistance

In the charity world of the early 1970s, marketing was not a word to be loved or hated, it was simply unknown. However, as advertising agencies became more influential with larger numbers of charities, the term began to be acknowledged. Yet the heavy involvement of the former only tended to encourage the view that marketing was simply advertising and selling. The growth, first of fund-raising advertisements (as opposed to awareness-raising ones) and then of direct mail, steadily introduced the term and its techniques into charity fund-raising. By the early 1980s the more successful charities were using marketing methods in fund-raising in considerable and sophisticated ways. However, the term 'marketing manager' was seldom, if ever, seen. If a post did have this title it was attached to the post of the manager in charge of some combination of charity shops, Christmas cards and catalogues. In 1986 RNIB introduced four posts with the title 'marketing manager', three of them wholly orientated towards physical goods and services aimed at beneficiaries (in education, employment and social services, and Braille and technical aids products). Fairly extensive enquiries at that time did not turn up any other charity marketing posts aimed exclusively at physical goods or services directed at beneficiaries. In the 1990s, it is still very unusual to find marketing managers in charge of offerings to beneficiaries. However, it is commonplace to find them in the fields of fund-raising and public relations.

The basic tenets of marketing crystallised in the commercial world in the 1950s. Why has it taken around 50 years for charities to begin to adapt the discipline in provision for beneficiaries? Even in direct marketing to supporters it took charities some 20 years and in fund-raising generally some 30 years. This remarkably slow penetration of marketing should warn us that resistance is of a fundamental, not superficial nature; also that its introduction needs to be planned and undertaken carefully. Such an introduction requires us to understand in some detail why meeting customer needs is, surprisingly, quite an alien concept in charities (Bruce 1995). The next sections explore why we often do not meet the needs of beneficiaries, supporters and stakeholders sufficiently; and indeed why we often do not value them sufficiently.

Why we can undervalue beneficiary needs and wants

1. Many not-for-profit organisations are in a *monopolistic situation* in relation to beneficiaries. This gives beneficiaries little or no choice and can allow, if not encourage, a 'take it or leave it' attitude in the not-for-profit provider. If unchecked this situation can lead to neglect and even, on occasions, arrogance towards, and contempt for, beneficiaries. Critical views expressed by beneficiaries, especially if they are organised or semi-organised, are dismissed as the work of trouble-makers.

2. A related reason for beneficiary neglect is that in many situations, even if there is competition between not-for-profits, *demand far exceeds supply*. In theory, two organisations serving old people, or two others providing low-cost housing may appear to be competing for beneficiary customers and offering choice. However, the reality is that the combined provision is still totally inadequate in terms of the number of potential beneficiaries and their needs. Indeed, some commercial marketers (e.g. Baker 1987, p. 7) have argued that commercial marketing only flourished when basic needs had been met and supply had outstripped demand. In the not-for-profit world this seldom happens except in the arts field (Hill, O'Sullivan and O'Sullivan 1995). This view, coming from such an eminent commercial marketer, needs careful consideration and I return to it later in this chapter. Ali (1996), Paton (1996) and Lindsay and Murphy (1996) also explore when and under what conditions marketing can be applied in the not-for-profit sector and O'Sullivan and O'Sullivan (1996) argue that marketing in our sector can best be described as 'naive' bringing a fresh and more individualistic approach than 'orthodox' commercial marketing. Where demand outstrips supply, not-for-profits can adopt a range of coping strategies nearly all of which result in an undervaluing of the beneficiary customer. One is to try and improve productivity through mass production of goods and services that help

everyone to a basic level, i.e. you can have your individual needs met provided it is through our standard product (goods or services). Another is to build in restraints on demand. The most customer-friendly restraint is not to make the product very widely known and this is a widespread technique in our sector. Less customer-friendly restraints are those that reduce demand by deterring beneficiary customers, such as means tests, complicated forms, lengthy queuing systems, or poor or patronising customer care.

3. Paradoxically, some not-for-profit workers' predilection for *concentrated attention on too few beneficiaries* (which looks like a pure marketing or meeting needs approach) can militate against an effective customer attentive approach. One regularly comes across situations where an organisation has spent an inordinate amount of time on a product (be it a good or a service) for one beneficiary. This can occur for several reasons such as compassion for a beneficiary in a desperate situation, or because an influential stakeholder (often a trustee) insists on an individual's needs being met. At the same time the organisation often runs standardised, undifferentiated products to its whole beneficiary group, which means that no one is particularly well satisfied. A marketing approach, which groups beneficiaries with similar needs, can avoid both the one-off help which ignores the silent majority of need, and the undifferentiated mass-production which is sub-standard for everyone.

4. Many not-for-profits are trying to meet fundamental and basic needs often in the bottom half of Maslow's (1943) Hierarchy of Needs such as food, shelter and security. Thus many not-for-profit beneficiaries are economically, politically, socially and sometimes even physically weak. As a consequence they are *too weak to make their voice heard* effectively. Organising themselves into representative groups is problematic.

5. Furthermore it is difficult to prevent *'haves' who run the not-for-profit from developing a patronising attitude towards 'have nots'* on the basis that the organisation is always right, rather than the customer. For example, if a charity has been providing a service in a given way for years, it is hard for it to accept the views of what it may see as a small, unrepresentative group of beneficiaries asking for change. 'Haves' serving 'have nots' are used to overwhelming gratitude, not criticism.

6. In many not-for-profits there are significant numbers of professionals (e.g. social workers, teachers, architects, accountants, lawyers, planners, etc.) on the staff and/or on the volunteer boards. Professional training, by its very nature in passing on an exclusive body of knowledge, can encourage professionals into *'I know what is best for you'* attitude.

7. Related to this last point is the practice of *professional distance* which can protect the professional from pressure but is not always conducive to meeting the needs of beneficiary customers.

8. Voluntary organisations that have been set up on the basis of *belief* can be particularly antipathetic to customer needs (Blois 1987, p. 408). The

most obvious ones concerned with belief are religious, but many others exist such as those promoting vegetarianism, opposing blood sports, etc. Blois argues that the effect of belief, in 'knowing you are right' can be two-fold. First, an organisation whose primary goal is based upon certainty (e.g. absolute belief in a deity with highly specific attributes) is much less likely to listen to the concerns and view of actual and potential customers. Second, even when these views are noted they are less likely to result in a change of the product, service or message because such changes are likely to be interpreted as a challenge to the fundamental precepts of the organisation.

9. Not-for-profits have an action orientated approach – 'let's roll up our sleeves and get on with it'. This approach linked with a desire to direct as much resource as possible toward the direct services means that *consumer research (especially independent consumer research) is not widespread*. Consequently not-for-profits are less knowledgeable about the real needs and desires of their beneficiary customers than might be expected.

10. Consumer sovereignty or *consumer rights may be seen as alien* to the fulfilment of the institutional mission. Lovelock and Weinberg (1989) give examples from social cause activity such as trying to stop people drinking too much, eating too much, etc.

11. Lastly, organisations involved in amelioration of disadvantage rather than removing its causes can easily slip into an underlying assumption that it is the *'beneficiary customers' fault'* simply through accepting the status quo of the socio-economic environment.

It is not argued here that all the above conditions occur in all not-for-profit organisations. However, even when only two or three exist, it is clear that the needs and desires of beneficiary customers may be undervalued and the, often unexpressed, perceptions of the beneficiary customers will be at variance with those of the not-for-profit supplier.

Reasons for not valuing supporter customers

One might expect that charities would value supporters and respect their needs to a greater extent than beneficiary customers. First, the supply of supporter opportunities far outstrips demand from potential supporters. Second, the competition in the market place for donors and volunteer service workers is intense and therefore potential supporters have a wide variety of choice. Lastly, a marketing approach, which values customer needs and desires, has penetrated much further into the fund-raising, if not the volunteer service, side of not-for-profit activity. So, ironically, given that supporters are not normally regarded as the prime customer group for charities, supporters are probably more highly valued and respected than beneficiaries.

Nevertheless, there is still cause for concern at the way donor supporters and volunteer worker supporters are valued. The over-riding reason for this is that many charities still operate in what marketers would call a production mode. The concentration is on processes and making these apparently more efficient, with far less concentration on the needs of supporters. In the most extreme cases supporters are seen as a necessary evil, simply required to get the job done.

1. Donor supporters often claim to being *bled dry* by strident, too frequent demands, which treat them as impersonal groups to be 'milked' of their money.
2. Donors frequently complain about *not being sufficiently appreciated and thanked*, or at least thanked in a way which recognises them as individuals as opposed to a class (i.e. of donors). Of the fund-raising methods, probably direct mail is the worst offender despite the supposed ability of sophisticated computer programmes to help build up a 'relationship' between the not-for-profit organisation and the supporter. The mail donor complains about the frequency of approaches; the lack of recognition of previous donating actions; and the not infrequent double and triple mailings caused by transcribing errors in the address or even worse the donor's name.
3. Volunteer service workers can also feel undervalued and undersupported. Mass volunteer recruitment campaigns can leave *volunteers lost or stranded* through the recruiting process being inefficient, for example, through recruiting too many volunteers in communities with fewer needs to be met.
4. Charities can treat volunteer service workers like so much *cannon fodder*: being marched forward to be overwhelmed by the massive need of many of the beneficiaries, which they simply cannot meet.
5. In many situations the volunteer service workers can feel *sustained more by the relationship they have with beneficiaries* than through any relationship with or appreciation from the charity. In the worst of situations volunteer service workers can be inexorably tied to one or more beneficiaries knowing deep down that they are not really able to help substantially. However, they feel it would be letting people down by withdrawing (Shenfield and Allen 1972).

Reasons for not valuing stakeholder customers

Structural conditions can also lead to an undervaluing, or at least a perception of being undervalued, of two of the main stakeholder groups, namely staff and committee members.

1. Staff on a job-by-job comparison with the commercial and sometimes the government sector can often be *underpaid*. When things are going well this is not normally a problem. However, when other hidden additions to

the pay packet (e.g. job satisfaction) are undermined, then this structural weakness is, in effect, an undervaluing of the staff stakeholder customers.

2. With the rapidly changing boundaries between the not-for-profit, government and commercial sectors so typical of the 1990s, security of job role has reduced. Pressure on voluntary income as well as demands from statutory purchasers for more value for money have led to *growing uncertainty* among the paid staff of charities. One hears more frequently the cry 'if they cannot look after us, how can we look after the beneficiaries?'

3. Often all is not well with committee member stakeholders. As charities have become increasingly professional and sophisticated then unpaid committee members with too little time to devote to the increasing complexity and with insufficient relevant knowledge and skills, feel *unwanted and powerless* in relation to the professional management team.

Interactive reasons for undervaluing customers

The very fact that not-for-profits have multiple constituencies or customer groups militates against valuing each constituent to the full. For example, when one customer is paying (and has needs) and another is receiving (and has different needs) then chances of meeting both sets of needs and desires fully is problematic. Add in stakeholder and regulator needs and the situation is even more problematic.

An example of this *inter-customer group tension* might be an avant-garde theatre where there is a tension between the need to keep audiences (beneficiaries) coming, bringing on new avant-garde writers (additional beneficiaries), satisfying the grant makers (supporters), the board (stakeholders) and the regulators (health and safety, obscenity, etc.). If the product is too avant-garde it will drive away audiences and upset the board. If the product is watered down to please the audience the avant-garde writer will be upset and perhaps walk out. The grant maker may want avant-garde performances but dislike low audiences. The regulators may try and close the performance because it offends the public (e.g. obscenity) or close the theatre because cost cutting is threatening safety. Such inter-customer group tensions pose major challenges to the not-for-profit marketers.

It can be seen that valuing customers and meeting their needs (i.e. a marketing approach) is very challenging in a charity context.

Support for adopting a marketing approach

Having identified so many oppositional forces to charity marketing, this heading may appear optimistic! But, paradoxically, all the opposition outlined above only confirms the need for charity marketing if one believes charities exist to help people, primarily beneficiaries. So marketing – meeting customer need within the objectives of the organisation – provides a philosophy, management approach and a set of operational tools which can address the anti-customer tendencies of charities.

However, there is the important technical challenge introduced by Baker (1987, p. 7) which says that marketing can only flourish and is only useful when supply outstrips demand. He argues that marketing as a discipline only received a huge push into prominence as the world's commercial ability to over-supply its market-places became the norm. It is therefore natural that marketing should find a secure and growing base in the charity fund-raising field where supply of fund-raising products vastly outstrips the amount of money that supporter customers are prepared or able to pay.

Applying Baker's commercial logic to offerings to beneficiary customers would suggest that, as the demand from actual and potential beneficiaries far outstrips the supply capability of charities, the ground would not be fertile for a marketing approach – a straightforward production approach should be sufficient. However, it is not possible to apply this commercial logic to the charity sector. Charities are committed to, and locked into, their beneficiary customers in a way that commercial organisations are not. At its crudest, if a commercial organisation found out that a particular customer group could no longer afford their products, an option would be for the company to walk away. That option is not open to charities who may well be legally as well as morally committed to certain beneficiary groups. Again, a commercial company that suddenly found that a business activity it was undertaking was no longer profitable, and was unlikely to become so again, would almost certainly close that part of the business down. Those charities that are not committed by their legal purposes to beneficiary groups will be committed to an area of charitable activity (e.g. education or religion). They cannot simply transfer their charitable activity into a totally different area. It is this legal requirement, which is essentially based on a moral imperative (e.g. the relief of poverty), that makes marketing so useful to charity work among beneficiaries. Charities are committed to their beneficiary customers in such a way and with an intensity that commercial marketing companies are not. Therefore a management approach, which has at its heart a commitment to meeting customer needs and wants, should have a welcome home in the charity sector.

Other reasons have been given as to why a marketing approach suits charities (Bruce 1993, p. 94). In particular it helps charities to act more responsibly and effectively in meeting the needs of beneficiaries in a market situation where the brutal reality is that beneficiary customers often cannot easily choose between a variety of alternatives, either because these alter- natives simply do not exist or because low incomes among beneficiaries means that they cannot be afforded. Therefore a marketing approach helps charities to improve the quality of their offerings to beneficiaries in situations where, because demand massively outstrips supply and there are few competitors, it will be easy to get away with delivering substandard offerings. Charities normally operate with a good deal of resource constraint, and so operational efficiency and cost saving is given a high priority. But operational efficiency can also easily lead to products being not very 'customer-friendly'. Conversely, changes that may make the products more customer-friendly will often add costs and are not therefore readily acceptable. Marketing can help us find a way through these two challenges. Last, given the dominance of professionals in charities, it helps the organisation to guard against the syndrome of 'professionals knowing best'.

However, this last point gives an indication of some staff attitudes which have to be addressed, especially among professional charity workers on the beneficiary side. A. Wilson (1984, p. 19) argues that groups of professionals such as lawyers, accountants and architects have a 'trained-in' antipathy to commerce in general and marketing in particular because of the way their very professionalism has been established over the centuries and their training delivered. This point is relevant to professionals in charities. But there is an additional attitude cluster which has to be addressed and which is particularly relevant to professionals such as social workers, teachers, doctors and nurses, all of whom are readily found in the charities sector. These professional groups, while having complete sympathy with the concept of 'meeting need', also associate marketing with commerce. For them marketing has the overtones of a 'hard sell' which they rightly feel is inappropriate for their vulnerable clients. Second, marketing can have the implication of payment with which they have not traditionally been involved (and are therefore not confident about it) and they know that many of their clients cannot afford to pay. So introducing a marketing approach into a charity needs to take account of, and meet, these objections.

Spillard (1987, p. 54) gives an additional reason for the introduction of a marketing approach being so difficult:

> because marketing so often acts at the boundaries of other groups' activities and achieves what success it does through pursuing its objectives effectively by a process of negotiation, most of what it claims to influence is subject to dispute by other groups. These groups are put on the defensive by the very act of marketing trying to influence the outcome of decisions which they traditionally have regarded as their own.

So, in summary, the reasons for introducing marketing are that as a philosophy, management approach and set of operational tools it will help ensure that charities, in meeting the needs and wants of beneficiaries:

☐ do not act as (arrogant) monopolies;
☐ operate services sensitive to real needs;

☐ do not concentrate on too few beneficiaries;
☐ do recognise the needs and desires of beneficiaries even if they are weak;
☐ do not develop patronising attitudes of 'haves' towards 'have nots';
☐ do not adopt 'professional' attitudes of 'knowing best';
☐ do not keep professional distance in the overall delivery of service;
☐ are sensitive to the tension between belief and customer need;
☐ use customer research and customer representation to understand and meet needs and desires;
☐ recognise that beneficiaries have rights;
☐ do not become institutionalised into the status quo, thinking it is their (beneficiaries) fault.

There are encouraging signs that charities are now becoming more cognisant of the need for a marketing approach.

A survey of chief executives of the 200 largest charities (Bruce and Raymer 1992, Table 6.5) showed that understanding customer needs was at that time the third most important attribute they were looking for in their managers, and that they anticipated this becoming even more important after the recession. However, marketing skills were only rated eighth, below financial control, strategic planning, understanding customer needs, concern for quality, raising income levels and flexibility/creativity. This apparent discrepancy can be explained by the chief executives' assumed understanding of the term 'marketing'. They would almost certainly have been using this term in relation to fund-raising/advertising/public relations activity. So my conclusion is that, while the term is not widely used or understood, the concept behind marketing, i.e. customer needs, is a very major preoccupation of charity management. This suggests a fertile environment for the significant extension of marketing into the area of beneficiary customers, and a further consolidation of marketing in the field of supporter customers.

How can a marketing approach be introduced into a charity?

Here the obvious needs to be stated, namely that the introduction of marketing requires a marketing approach! People in the organisation need to be treated as customers. For example, firm decision-making by top managers to introduce a marketing structure, without cultural acceptance by staff, is bound to fail. But sensitive development of the cultural acceptance of a marketing-orientated approach, without introducing new structures and processes, will also fail. Although it sounds challenging, what is required is concerted and coordinated action in the following areas:

☐ organisation culture;
☐ resources (both money and the expertise of people);

☐ activities, processes and marketing plans;
☐ structure.

It is difficult to work in all areas at once, and the areas of activities and structure can come after the injection of work in the areas of culture and resources. The next four sections deal with these areas in turn.

A needs-led (marketing) culture

If a marketing approach is to be introduced successfully it has to permeate the whole organisation. People's attitudes towards it have to be ideally welcoming, preferably accepting and at least acquiescent. So here is a major challenge to a marketing approach because of the widespread antipathy to the term 'marketing' and what many people believe it stands for.

The key axiom, as in all marketing, is 'start from where your customer is, not from where you would like them to be'.

So how does one encourage a cultural change towards being receptive to a marketing approach? An important starting point is to recognise how cynical charity staff are about commercial marketing, not least because of the behaviour of some marketers, e.g. apparently marketing alcohol and cigarettes to young teenagers. Nevertheless the strongest weapon is one of logic. Whatever the implicit assumptions and attitudes, it is probably more true for charities than for any other kind of organisation that the reason for its existence is to serve its beneficiary customers. Charities must be needs led. This gives marketing the moral and logical high ground. If this high ground is further promoted and defended by the chief executive and senior management and committees, this begins to set explicit standards for public opinions and actions inside the organisation, whatever some people's private opinion may still be. In short, the chief executive and the senior staff can give a strong lead on 'how we do it round here'.

Other actions will have important impacts, such as awareness-raising activities, role play both within and outside training activities and marketing training itself. Also the appointment and promotion of staff with a strong customer orientation will send out strong messages to staff. Concentrating initially on particular sub-activities of marketing which one has assessed are of interest to line managers can change views, e.g. service promotion, market research or customer care. Holwegger (1996) describes how introducing a customer care orientation and programme into RNID led to the adoption of a broader marketing approach.

Apart from gaining knowledge of marketing it is crucial to encourage all staff whose work impacts on customers to feel that marketing is part of their job, not something the marketing experts do.

Marketing resources

Resources in this situation come in two ways: first, as expertise bound up in people, and second, in the form of money and what it can buy.

Expertise

Increasing the quality and quantity of marketing expertise inside the charity is crucial to its success. In the early stages it may well be the most important factor. Organisation culture, activities and structures all require the time of knowledgeable and experienced marketing people to talk through, promote, design and implement. If this is left to hard-pressed existing staff, the introduction of marketing will at best be delayed and at worst will fail. A useful way of injecting expertise rapidly is to combine the early appointment of a very limited marketing staff resource with the use of external marketing advisers through a consultancy. The consultancy will bring in a breadth of knowledge and experience that will be impossible, and unwise, to install at such an early stage. But the weakness of the consultancy, i.e. not being regarded as one of the staff, can be overcome in part by the internal appointment(s). Any medium-sized charity will need one person. A small charity is unlikely to need or be able to afford a separate marketing person. However, just one champion of marketing in a small charity, especially at senior level, is likely to achieve more, and more quickly, than in a large charity. RNIB, as large charity, appointed four to cover the main operating divisions (then totalling 2,000 staff). In a medium-size charity the appointee will need to be accountable to the chief executive. In a large charity this may not be possible, but they should report to the second tier. Even though these posts will be staff, rather than line, their importance will be signalled by their accountability and access to the chief executive and senior manager. They will need to be given authority to call people together in meetings and make firm proposals for action. If these proposals are likely to be challenged they will do well to get their manager's backing first!

However, after a fairly short phase, e.g. six months to one year, sufficient initial work on cultural change, discussion of possible structural change, etc., will have been achieved to enable a more significant build-up of expertise. This next phase can be achieved through the training and subsequent promotion of internal staff as well as the recruitment of external staff.

The role of marketing training is absolutely crucial here and can easily be underestimated. Marketing training for charity personnel is not widespread. The marketing consultancy which has become familiar with the charity can be extremely useful in either modifying external training packages or developing in-house training packages which can make the training more user-friendly towards the specific charity. Simply sending charity personnel onto commercial marketing training courses can be a disaster if the trainee is unenthusiastic about the concept to start with. Even if they are enthusiastic about the external, commercially orientated training, it is quite difficult for them to translate what has been learned back into the charity.

Money/budget

It is clear that the initial staff recruitment and consultancy involvement will require money. Also, money will be needed in order to get additional short-term work under way, e.g. market research, training, etc. If at all possible, money for this phase should be 'new' rather than budget substitution from operational activity because the expenditure will bring no immediate and tangible gain to operational managers, and the budget transfer will antagonise them.

However, the budget for subsequent marketing activity should ideally be a mix of new money and budget transfers from existing spending heads. Such financial resource is likely to be spent on activities such as, once again, market research, but also promotional activity which ought to show short-term benefits to operational managers. The transfer of budget responsibility begins to show the iron fist in the velvet glove. Nevertheless whatever the source, money for the marketing function will be required. Marketing personnel without spending power simply become friendly, advisory appendages.

Activities, processes and marketing plans

Activities here refer to the things that the appointed marketing staff are likely to do, especially in the early stages. Processes refer to the things that need to be done as a matter of course, primarily by the existing operational staff in order to lock them and their work into a marketing framework. Marketing plans are particularly important to this last area.

Marketing activities

In the short and medium term the marketing person(s) will be wise to concentrate on activities such as market research, targeting and elements of marketing mix, rather than strategic marketing planning – this latter produces no short-term gains and can, quite reasonably, follow on later. Which of these activities the marketing person(s) works on should depend on the wants/needs of the operational managers, i.e. the internal customers. Interviews with these internal customers will reveal which operational managers are most open to additional help and what kind of help they need. The two activities most likely to be welcome early on are those of *promotion* and *marketing research*. Operational managers (such as heads of schools, theatre directors, social work managers, field fund-raising managers, etc.)

often feel that 'people' do not really appreciate or even know what their service does. But they also have little expertise in and are personally less comfortable with the active promotion of their work in order to gain additional customers. Therefore a marketing person turning up with suggestions as to how their goods, services or ideas can be more actively promoted is likely to gain a warm welcome. Further, the production of even fairly basic tools in a professional manner, such as leaflets, articles placed in external magazines and newspapers, advertisements, specially convened promotional meetings and professional conferences, etc., can be achieved fairly quickly and at relatively low cost. They are also very tangible to the internal customer.

Marketing research is also a potentially sympathetic intervention tool for the short/medium term which will give the marketer more locus in the medium term. It obviously must be designed in conjunction with the operational manager in order to ensure that the results are sufficiently service-specific and usable. The very process of deciding what to ask of whom for what purpose helps to educate the operational manager about marketing. The research data will also be a major resource not only to the manager but also to the marketer who can introduce the results into their work on the marketing mix. If it can be achieved with the goodwill of the operational manager, marketing research among the intermediary customer groups can be particularly important in providing the marketing person with new ideas and suggestions for operational improvement.

Both promotion and marketing research will cost money because the marketer will need outside help from an agency, hence the need for a marketing budget mentioned above. In the medium term the marketing person will need to intervene in all areas of marketing mix as well as be active in the area of marketing research and promotion.

Marketing processes and marketing plans

Marketing processes mean those activities of a bureaucratic (using the word neutrally) nature that need to be additionally built in to what is likely to be an operationally dominated organisation. Every organisation will need to develop its own tailor-made marketing processes which need to be followed. However, a good starting point is the annual plan for each of the major goods/service/idea areas. More often than charities would care to admit, service areas have only very patchy plans which are normally dominated by budgets and have little narrative. Nevertheless they are a starting point for a *marketing plan* which might be called a *service plan* if this will help acceptability. The plan needs to be timed to fit in particularly with the budget/financial planning cycle as this tends to be the major fixed point in any charity's planning cycle. If from the marketing point of view this is subsequently felt to be bad in terms of timing they can be changed, but it is an optimistic marketer who tries to cross the finance function in the early stages!

Marketing plans can be very sophisticated or very basic. One way of introducing service/marketing plans is to produce sophisticated marketing plans for a minority of products (services or goods), using the success of these to roll the idea out to the full range of the organisation's offerings. However, this method can easily get elongated and bogged down, and may never get rolled out across the charity. This is because a sophisticated marketing plan requires much fundamental thinking about the market-place of the whole organisation, and its strategic plan – which may not have been developed at all, let alone from a marketing orientation. The alter-native, which I have found to be more successful, is to produce basic marketing plans for a wider range of the organisation's goods/services/ ideas. These need to be produced with the close involvement of the operational manger and the finance representative. They should concentrate on the absolute core of the generic marketing plan, i.e. they should include the basic *marketing mix* (product, price, promotion and place); *target market*; *target take-up* in terms of quantity and quality; *unique selling points*; *marketing resources* to be applied; and all the financial *budget information* that has traditionally been required; and an *action plan* of who is going to do what by when and what results are expected. If quantified targets for the product area have been set and measured in previous years, then it would be sensible and reasonable to include these in the marketing plan. However, if they have not, it would be unwise to insert these in year one, but a good marketing discipline would require them in year two. If this approach to applying basic marketing plans is to be followed quite widely, it is unwise to include too many, or any, strategic marketing elements, e.g. proposals for *marketing research*, a broad situation analysis including *other players* and a *SWOT* (strengths, weaknesses, opportunities and threats) because of the 'slowing-down factor'. The remaining elements of the marketing mix, i.e. *people, physical evidence, process* and *philosophy*, could be included first time, but might be problematic for two reasons. First, they do intervene quite heavily in operations which the line managers will rightly regard as their territory. Second, they make the process that much more difficult, and risk the plan not being completed in time. The one exception might be *philosophy*, if this is attractive to the operational manager for inclusion (e.g. to buttress their activity from what they feel may become too commercial an approach). If the resulting marketing plan is more than five pages long, there should be a one-page summary capable of standing alone. Service managers will hate doing this, preferring other readers to have no choice but to read the whole plan; but senior managers and committees may have dozens of plans to read, and will skip-read if there is no summary.

The structure of a marketing (or service) plan might be as follows.

Basic voluntary organisation marketing/service plan

Where relevant the measures which follow should describe the last two years' *actual*, this year's *forecast*, and next year's *target*.

☐ Name and *very* short description of the product (goods/service/idea).
☐ Key volume data, numbers of units (of activity) incoming, expenditures and subsidy.
☐ Existing customers: who are they, how many of them, what characteristics, how segmented, etc.?
☐ Total market size: who are they, how many, etc.?
☐ Key customer needs and how the product meets them.
☐ Philosophy underpinning the product.
☐ Price.
☐ Promotion (plans including expenditure plans).
☐ Distribution (how is the product delivered?).
☐ People involved.
☐ Key physical evidence.
☐ Key aspect of processes to ensure take-up.
☐ Marketing and market research (include evidence of unmet need).
☐ Other players.
☐ Appendix of other/additional relevant data.

A one page summary of key facts and figures is essential.

Structure

Marketing organisation structure is simple to draw on a chart, but complicated to implement! Whatever structure is implemented in the early stages, it is likely to require revision after a few years, as the organisation comes to understand, accept and implement a marketing approach. It is to be hoped that the processes and activities described above, and the first structure, will have encouraged marketing to permeate the organisation, i.e. to be built 'into the line'. Indeed Baker (1987, p. 9) says: 'in a truly marketing orientated organisation the need for a specialised marketing function is probably far less than it is in a sales or production dominated company'. Even where the conscious attempt needs to be made to insert a formal marketing unit, Spillard (1987, p. 54) argues that it should be a 'soft form of organisation' which recognises that the

> boundaries are loose, constantly shifting and frequently ill defined and open to debate ... the responsibility and area of influence of marketing tend to be both diffuse and lacking in structural integrity, at least in the sense of possessing a well bounded and undisputed sphere of influence.

Many writers on marketing emphasise that there are a variety of marketing organisation structures that can be implemented, depending on such things as the size of the organisation, the variety of products (goods/service/ideas) that they offer, and the degree to which they are in the same or different market areas. However, what appears to be much more problematic is relating the particular situation in any one organisation to the particular form of marketing organisation that would suit it best.

For medium-sized and large charities the choices of organisation structure, crudely described, put the marketing function in one and/or more of the following locations:

☐ at the corporate centre;
☐ at each main operating area (containing several products);
☐ at the product level.

Where the function is at the corporate centre it may have effective line authority for strategic marketing, but it can only be advisory in relation to product lines and product groups. Kotler and Fox (1985, p. 33) give a sample job description for a university director of marketing, located at the centre of a university. Among other things the marketing director contributes a marketing perspective to the deliberations of the top administration in their planning of the university's future; prepare data that might be needed by any officer of the university on a particular market size, segment, trends, and behaviour dynamics; conduct studies of the needs, perceptions, preferences and satisfaction of particular markets; assist in the planning, promotion and launching of new programmes; assist in the development of communications and promotion campaigns and materials; analyse and advise on pricing questions, etc. So it can be seen that this is very much an advisory function.

The marketing function located halfway down the organisation at the level of a major operating division can either be at the advisory end of the continuum or more towards the line management end. If the operating division has a large number of service products going across several markets or if it runs services managed by technical professions such as teachers, social workers or doctors, it is more likely to be at the advisory end. If the products are in a fairly homogeneous market, and especially if they are physical goods, then it is possible for the marketing function to have strong authority over the marketing mix.

Where the marketing function is located at the individual product (goods/services/ideas) level, then the marketing manager is appointed as operational manger, or *in charge of* the operational manager, or the operational manager *is trained* in marketing. Which of these alternatives is chosen at the product level normally depends on staff turnover, availability of staff with the right qualifications, how complex the operational side is, and whether it is physical goods or services. For example, a marketing manager can call the shots if the product is a straightforward physical good. But if it is complex or the product is a service, especially a professional service such as a school or rehabilitation centre, then the marketing manager can only be advisory, and it will normally be better to train the operational manager in marketing.

RNIB: a case study of introducing a marketing approach

RNIB activities

In the middle 1980s RNIB drew up a corporate strategy, involving commit-tees, staff and beneficiaries. This strategy identified, among many other things, a need for the charity to undertake more market research among beneficiary customers, more promotion and more target segmentation. Clearly these three items are not a perfect description of marketing, but they were activities identified by staff and committees as things that needed to be done. Hence these became the starting point for introducing a marketing approach, which was formally stated in the strategy.

At that time RNIB involved over 25,000 volunteers, 2,000 paid staff and ran over 60 different direct services to end beneficiaries and indirect ones to intermediary customer groups. These *direct* services included schools and colleges, some for able youngsters who went to college and university, but most for multi-handicapped blind and partially sighted people; a wide range of educational support services for visually impaired young people in mainstream education; a Scottish and English national residential rehabilita-tion centre for newly blinded adults; two vocational training colleges, which ran a wide variety of courses such as telephony, office skills, computer programming, physiotherapy and many more; an employment service to support people getting into work; three hotels catering for about 7,000 blind people each year; the RNIB Talking Books service which lent over three-and-a-half million books a year to 65,000 members; a weekly large-print national newspaper; an electronically delivered daily newspaper; the largest Braille publishing house in Europe; a large factory and distribution centre which sold over 600 different technical aids; a benefits rights office handling over 6,000 cases a year; and many other direct services.

In addition RNIB ran a wide range of *indirect* services aimed at other people who are impacting on the lives of blind and partially sighted people. So, for example, there were consultancy and training services aimed at social services departments, health authorities, local education authorities and even the world of commercial producers and service providers. Contained within those indirect services were campaigning and pressure group activ-ity where there were eight staff working, including parliamentary officers covering Westminster and Brussels/Strasbourg.

It is also important to note that 7 per cent of paid staff were blind, spread across all levels right up to top management. The majority of the RNIB executive council and its main standing committees comprised blind and partially sighted people in which they held the leadership positions; and the majority of these were elected representatives of organisations of blind and partially sighted people. In other words RNIB's end beneficiaries decided who represented them, and it was these people who helped to proposed policy and monitor implementation.

The organisation's structure in the mid-1980s is laid out in Figure 5.1.

Where should marketing management be placed?

The structural question was where to insert the marketing management. Each of the main service division directors had between five and seven managers accountable to them, and RNIB created a marketing manager post at this divisional second-tier level (M). In addition it created a marketing manager post in the second tier of the External Relations Division (CM), together with support, with the aim of facing in two directions, one inward into the division providing marketing for external relations, and the other facing the marketing managers in the three other service divisions to give them support and advice. A crude comparison would be to regard the three main service divisions as being separate companies, and the marketing manager at divisional second tier being the equivalent of a marketing director. RNIB considered placing all these marketing posts in the corporate division, i.e. the External Relations Division, but on balance concluded that there would be greater ownership of marketing if it was located in the individual divisions.

In the Technical and Consumer Services Division (500 staff and 600 products) there were three product managers, one for Talking Books, a separate one for Braille magazines and a third for technical equipment. At the divisional level there was also the marketing 'director' (M) responsible for line-managing the product managers, but also responsible for the actual and potential product areas for technical and communication products. Thus the divisional marketing 'director' not only had responsibility for delivering targets on the existing product lines, they also had responsibility for identifying any gaps in the market which RNIB should fill in the technical and communications products area. The division also had a market research manager who commissioned market research and wrote interpretations of the research to make them particularly relevant to technical and communication products.

RNIB also had marketing managers in its two other divisions (Education and Leisure with 550 staff, and Vocational and Social Services with 450 staff) both located at the divisional centre (M). In both divisions the marketing manager was at head office level and had an advisory rather than a line management function. In one division there were two other marketing staff associated with operational services. In each of these cases the marketing

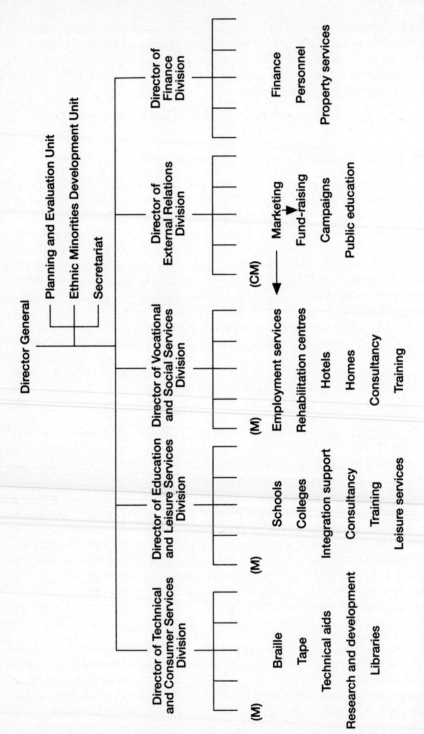

Figure 5.1 The organisation of RNIB

function at the operational service level was accountable to the operational manager, who in each case was a technical professional (e.g. teacher).

The marketing function in the External Relations Division (CM) was planned to provide marketing planning support to the other divisions and marketing services to them. In particular a publications unit provided large numbers of professionally produced leaflets, brochure and prospectuses for the other divisions.

While this pattern may not have been ideal, it showed that the three structural possibilities described at the beginning of this section could coexist in one organisation, i.e. the corporate centre, the main operational areas and the product level. The description also showed how marketing structure developed on the basis of specific characteristics of the organisation or parts of the organisation. For example, the reason that the marketing managers in the Technical and Consumer Services Division were line managers of the communication products was that, by and large, they had many of the attributes of physical goods, whereas the marketing managers in the other two divisions were advisory, in part because they were dealing with services and ideas rather than physical goods. As we saw earlier in this chapter, marketing line management responsibility is easier to implement for physical goods than it is for services and ideas.

It is important to emphasise that these structural insertions did not take place until there was a cultural commitment among staff, supported by senior management and committees.

How successful?

How successful was the introduction of a marketing approach? After five years RNIB brought in an external consultant to evaluate its marketing effectiveness across the agency. Although his evaluation was largely a qualitative one, the subsequent description detailed percentages because it gave a simple, clear picture. The consultant crudely estimated that RNIB was about 60 per cent of the way towards becoming a truly marketing-orientated organisation. However, this was an average which masked differential rates of implementation in the four divisions.

In the External Relations Division, comprising fund-raising, publicity and campaigning, it was judged that RNIB was almost completely marketing orientated. In the Technical and Consumer Services Division the estimate was put at around 75 per cent marketing effective. The marketing 'director' had a staff of around 40 people – the combined total of customer services and customer sales staff. The majority of the products and product groupings such as Braille magazines, talking books and technical aids have marketing managers or product managers line-managing them; and these staff are in the driving seat in comparison with production. However, marketing plans and their implementation were still problematic. In addition there is a market research officer who undertakes considerable research for various product managers.

In the Education and Leisure Division and the Vocational Social Services Division the picture was less advanced – only about 40 per cent effective. These divisions made extensive use of market research, promotion and segmentation but marketing plans were not well developed and implemented, and in many cases were not even in existence. Pricing policies that took full account of the external market were only implemented recently. The divisional second-tier marketing managers' posts were problematic. In one of the divisions the post-holder stayed for four years but had a major uphill battle. In the other division the post was empty for half of the four-year period.

So why were two divisions more successful in implementation than the others? First, the overall heads of these two divisions had a professional marketing background. Second, each of these two divisions had, in the main, products that were either physical goods, non-professional services (in a sense of not employing social workers, teachers, etc.) or ideas, either for fund-raising or for campaigning. Third, the divisional second-tier marketing managers had line management control over reasonably sized staffs, and had either direct control or a controlling interest over the production side of their business.

The two divisions where a marketing approach had not come as far were divisions where the heads had necessarily been professionally qualified in non-marketing fields (e.g. education) and therefore had much less experience of marketing. Second, the majority of output activities of these two divisions were professional services (such as education and social work) and, as in the commercial world of professional services, marketing was harder to apply. Third, the divisional second-tier marketing managers had advisory posts, rather than line management posts with relatively little budget and staff support.

These two divisions had also suffered because the corporate marketing planning support anticipated to come out of the External Relations Division had not in fact been given the necessary resources or authority to do this work. Rather this post had been responsible for encouraging the External Relations Division to be the most marketing-orientated division in RNIB. The originally allocated resources for corporate marketing had quite understandably been drawn into supporting the fund-raising, publicity and campaigning requirements within that division. There was also a case which said that the corporate marketing planning coming out of one of the five operating divisions was not regarded as 'neutral' (and should be a staff function responsible to the chief executive). The exception to this lack of outreach into other divisions was that of certain marketing services such as public relations, corporate identity, publicity, publication and advertising material which came from the External Relations Division and were widespread across the whole of RNIB.

Now, some three years further on, there have been further developments. First, a senior corporate marketing manager has been appointed in the Planning and Evaluation Unit who has had direct accessibility to the chief executive. This, it is argued, has two advantages. The marketing function and marketing planning can be integrated into the wider RNIB planning process, i.e. each will strengthen the other. Also the new senior marketing post is not to be located in any one of the five operational divisions, and has more direct backing from the chief executive. This senior corporate marketing manager has also, with senior management support, introduced a structure for a marketing plan, called service plans, which is utilised in all 120 service delivery units (SDUs). These SDUs are also all budget centres so that financial and marketing planning can be integrated. In order to take account of different divisional needs some differences in terminology have been used, but the structures of the plans are similar.

Second, a process of core competency analysis involving representative groups of staff has identified marketing as one of four core management competencies required of all RNIB managers. This has been the jumping-off point for comprehensive marketing training as part of managerial development in the organisation and has put marketing 'in the line'. The training has half-a-dozen modules developed jointly between RNIB and the Open College and, completed in full, gives a Certificate in Marketing. However, most managers and customer facing staff only need complete two or three modules to gain a firm understanding of the marketing approach.

Third, the two second-tier advisory marketing management posts in the two professional service divisions have been abolished and more marketing support and responsibility pushed down to the level of operational management in the education, employment and social services parts of the agency. A marketing approach has been fully adopted in the Technical and Consumer Services Division and the External Relations Division and more brand or product managers have been appointed.

Fourth, a second strategic review of the whole organisation and its services has fed into a new corporate strategy which, like its predecessor, confirms a marketing approach as 'the way we do it round here'. A greater concentration appears in this new strategy on improving the quality of services to beneficiary customers, and the need to be more customer focused. In other words, rather than fall back on imperatives couched in marketing jargon, the strategy goes to the core of marketing, namely customer-focused, quality products.

This case study shows that in a large charity where the senior management and committees are committed to a marketing approach, this can be implemented effectively over a relatively short timespan (three years) in those parts of the charity delivering physical goods, high turnover non-professional services, and fund-raising and campaigning ideas. But it also shows how difficult it is to implement fully a marketing approach in the area of professional services even when the senior management and committees are committed, and even when many of the operational managers (e.g. heads of schools) are also committed and are natural marketers! While the external environment in which such professional services operate remains stable, the marketing approach has been successfully embedded in the line for some years in the way that Baker (1987, p. 9) says is ideal. However, when the external environment changes quickly or radically, this is the time when RNIB service (marketing) plans have been crucial and have been a vital tool for development and evaluation.

Conclusion

Most medium-size and larger British charities have a reasonable marketing approach installed in their fund-raising and publicity functions aimed at supporter customers (Arbuthnot and Horne 1997). However, very few have a formalised marketing process installed for the offerings they deliver to their beneficiary customers.

Those charities that are experimenting with introducing a marketing approach can make fairly rapid headway where the products are physical goods and fund-raising or campaigning ideas. There has been less development of formal marketing approaches in the field of services in general and professional services in particular.

This pattern reflects the commercial world although developments are almost certainly less well advanced, except perhaps in certain areas of fund-raising.

The relative lack of progress of instituting a marketing approach in the field of services to beneficiaries are various and have been identified in the preceding pages. The main reasons are that charity services to beneficiaries still operate in an environment where demand massively outstrips supply; the multiple customer groups are extremely complicated to deal with; and professional services and associated professional workers play a leading operational management role.

Factors that are likely to propel charities further into a formalised marketing approach are their normally very different and quasi-legal commitment to their beneficiary customers (in comparison to commercial marketing organisations); the fact that the majority of charity chief executives recognise the importance of understanding the needs of customers as part of a managerial structure; the fact that the charity market is becoming increasingly competitive both on the fund-raising side and on the service-giving side through statutory organisation competitive tendering procedures for the contracting-out of services.

Charities would benefit from more research and writing on the successful and unsuccessful attempts to introduce marketing into commercial professional services and similar work in their own sector.

Key points

☐ A marketing approach must permeate the whole organisation if it is to succeed. Encourage acceptance by showing that marketing has the needs of beneficiary customers as its *raison d'être*.

☐ Appoint a limited marketing resource, supplemented by external marketing advisers if need be. Initially, do not leave marketing to existing staff who are already hard pressed.

☐ Train internal staff and/or bring in expertise from outside.

☐ Make sure that money is available for marketing and/or promotional activity.

☐ Encourage communication between the marketing person and their internal customers.

☐ Establish marketing plans, keeping them simple at first.

☐ Establish where the marketing function fits into the organisation structure.

6

PHYSICAL GOODS: WELFARE GOODS, PUBLICATIONS AND FOR- PROFIT GOODS

While services dominate voluntary organisation activity, physical goods are much more widespread than might at first be thought. The provision of information products is probably the most ubiquitous role of voluntary organisations, with publications in particular providing a massive output. The development and provision of physical goods aimed at disadvantaged groups is much more widespread than casual observation would suggest: for example, technical aids for many different groups of people with disabilities; medically orientated aids; appropriate technology goods for the developing world; environmentally friendly products, etc. Selling profitable goods in order to raise funds occupies a very significant part of many charities' fund-raising activity. All of these areas need a marketing approach if they are to be effective.

Physical goods for the charity's main beneficiaries

Some marketing texts suggest that marketing is only applicable in situations where supply exceeds demand (see pp. 92–93 above). But I would argue that it is *more* important to adopt a marketing approach with disadvantaged customers. Voluntary organisations might get away with less marketing expenditure, especially in the area of promotion, but they still need a marketing philosophy and a marketing approach. Perhaps the most dramatic illustration of the negative consequences of a non-marketing approach is where inappropriate food provided by aid agencies to people in famine areas is rejected by the indigenous people because of cultural or religious traditions.

Offerings of physical goods to beneficiaries play an important role among charities. A significant part of the output of overseas agencies is still the provision of food and equipment, although technical advice has rapidly grown in importance. Among home charities, many working in the disability and health fields provide physical goods to their primary beneficiaries. For example, 15 per cent of RNIB's expenditure is on such products going to blind and partially sighted people; the Scout Association has a major trading subsidiary selling equipment, clothing, publications and other articles to people in scouting; some sports voluntary organisations sell equipment to members; and voluntary organisations in the broad environment field sell environment related products to their members, although these have some of the attributes of physical goods sold for profit, which are considered in the next section.

Price

It is in the pricing of physical goods that the comparison of roles between commercial and voluntary organisations is at its most striking. Where the target market has enough profit in it, commercial companies will be dominant. McDonald's serves burgers to the relatively affluent and the Salvation Army serves soup to the homeless. The waters get very muddy in niche markets where charities providing goods free or at subsidised rates cannot satisfy consumer demand but subsidisation has driven out commercial suppliers; or where commercial suppliers, normally of high-tech equipment to disadvantaged groups, charge very high, perhaps unreasonable, mark-ups. An example of the latter has been the hearing-aid market where the high prices and profit margin of commercial suppliers encouraged the RNID to move into the market in its own right. However, it has suffered all the difficulties of the new, late market entrant.

It is quite difficult to understand the impact of charities providing free or subsidised physical goods in what commercial operators might regard as potential niche markets. At its simplest, if a charity is meeting the vast majority of demand for a particular product or product grouping with subsidised prices, then there is no dilemma. However, if the charity is not meeting market needs, especially in volume terms, but through its subsidised pricing is squeezing out commercial competitors, then there is a moral and practical conundrum. To allow commercial providers in, the price of products must go up, to the detriment of existing purchasers who are already disadvantaged. However, if the charity prices are heavily subsidised on each unit sold and there is low market penetration, then there is a huge disincentive to the charity to increase its volume output and market penetration even though there are potential beneficiaries going without help. At its simplest, the more it sells, the more it drains limited charitable income.

This pricing dilemma becomes even more complex in markets where the statutory authority purchases on behalf of the charity beneficiary. This can distort the market in two directions. If the charity is selling goods at a subsidised rate and the state is purchasing on behalf of a charity beneficiary at the subsidised rate, then effectively the charity is subsidising the state which is hardly what donors had in mind. Where the state is purchasing on behalf of disadvantaged individuals and there are only commercial suppliers, this can easily lead to distortion in the other direction, i.e. unreasonable profit margins. However, this situation is outside the primary purpose of this book.

An example of this complex interaction around price is the RNIB Talking Books service. Until 1985 the subscription rates were very heavily subsidised, which inevitably inhibited the charity's ability to expand the service without undue drain on its charity money. Further, the vast majority of the subscriptions were paid for by local government on behalf of individual blind people in their locality. So in effect the RNIB low price was subsidising local government in its responsibilities to provide a library service to the wider community. Research showed that many more blind people wanted the service and so expansion was planned. In order to avoid the financial 'losses' (through the subsidy) of a major expansion of its talking-books service and in order to stop further subsidy of local government in its duties, RNIB raised its prices quite significantly on memberships paid for by local authorities. But it kept an artificially low rate for individuals paying with their own money. Until 1990 this pricing policy worked like a dream. Membership, previously static, almost doubled because of increased promotion. But the amount of donor income RNIB had to put into this service expansion remained relatively constant at just over £1 million. By 1990 things began to change dramatically. Through the recession and central government policy, local government had less to spend. More and more local authorities began to cash limit the budget head for talking-books memberships and only raised them year on year at a nominal inflation rate. Thus membership expansion from this source ceased. Even worse, the difference between the individual purchase rate and the local government purchase rate was sufficiently large to encourage some local authorities to manipulate the system by giving grants to individuals to purchase at the individual rate – something which was formally forbidden by RNIB rules, but was very difficult for the charity to police. RNIB's response in April 1993 was to raise the individual subscription rate to equal that of the local government, but only for new individual members.

I would suggest that the following conclusions can be drawn on pricing policy for physical goods provided by voluntary organisations:

☐ If a charity is aiming to be a high-volume supplier of physical goods then a necessary, but not sufficient, condition is to have a price that covers or is close to costs.
☐ The greater the subsidy a charity puts into physical goods, the greater the disincentive to expand the volume of output. The only exception to this

would be where the charity has a very restricted brief and a very high voluntary income.

☐ Where a charity is heavily subsidising goods, it should satisfy itself that this action is not inadvertently depressing supply and preventing other players coming in to meet unmet need.

☐ Charities need long-term pricing strategies which take account of the social and economic policies of governments as well as their responsibilities to their beneficiaries.

Subsidised pricing of physical goods provided by charities is an under-acknowledged and extremely complicated area. Pricing and subsidy policies have traditionally developed in a very haphazard way. Decisions are sometimes made by committees, or sometimes by traditional evolution of decisions made decades ago. In fact pricing decisions have to be taken from a strategic (i.e. long-term and taking account of social policy) as well as a tactical (i.e. short-term) viewpoint.

Distribution (place)

After price, distribution is probably the least carefully thought-out area of the marketing mix in the voluntary sector. Elation at having developed a new product, or having obtained substantial goods as donations in kind, is often rapidly followed by depression about how to get these items through to the beneficiaries. In the early stages of the crisis, charities trying to help in Yugoslavia rapidly had warehouses in Britain filling up with goods which they could not deliver. Free gifts of computers to charities often stick at head office for far too long before being distributed around the network. Geographic patterns of homelessness are created by the fixed location of soup kitchens. Technical aids for disabled people have low turnovers because the centres where people can try them out are few and far between; perhaps fifty miles away or more from the potential beneficiaries.

Of course, it is not always like this, but it can be at the start because the charity normally gets much more enthusiastic about the physical goods themselves rather than thinking about the nuts and bolts of how they are going to be delivered to the end consumer. Many charities have a complicated set of intermediaries between them and their beneficiaries. As with intermediaries in the commercial supply chain, they can have subtly different, or substantially different, objectives which can undermine or even destroy the distribution process. To be effective, it is necessary to regard these intermediaries as customers in their own right, identifying what their needs and wants are. Getting the support of intermediary distributors is arguably more difficult in the voluntary sector than it is in the commercial sector. In the latter, financial incentives by way of margins and fees are universally applied. In the voluntary sector this is far less usual, acceptable or even in some cases legal. All too often we assume that intermediaries will at best have common objectives with us to help the end customers, and at worst will do it out of the 'kindness of their hearts'. But intermediaries are equally as busy as the supplying voluntary organisations. Distributing charitably donated food gifts by a community worker on a high-tension estate may be desirable, but may be of much lower priority than other work they want to do, leaving aside the difficulty of decisions over who gets what and whether these decisions may actually hinder or undermine the community worker's role. The last thing the local fund-raising group might want will be the delivery of 500 newsletters from head office for onward distribution, arriving just two weeks before they organise a local house-to-house collection.

In summary, charities delivering physical goods to beneficiaries need to think very carefully about distribution. Recognising the needs and wants of intermediary distributors to establish joint action as well as common cause can be helped by a variety of methods. These can range from fees or percentages such as the commercial sector uses, through to relying only on personalised thank-you letters. What is certain is that if voluntary organisation providers do not systematically plan and monitor their distribution networks, the number of beneficiary recipients will be well below target, and significant amounts of physical goods will simply 'rot' somewhere in the supply chain.

Promotion

At first glance, voluntary organisations would appear to be very effective at promoting the physical goods they supply. Regular news items appear in the press, on radio and even on television covering a genuinely revolutionary new product from a charity, or featuring the departure of a convoy of food lorries, or describing extra feeding arrangements for homeless people at Christmas. In their ability to gain editorial coverage, voluntary organisations are the envy of their commercial counterparts.

However, closer inspection from a marketing standpoint often reveals that these are very often promotional activities towards the general public rather than to potential beneficiaries. How many homeless people just before Christmas are watching television? How many deaf people will absorb media coverage about a new hearing aid? These promotional efforts have a valid role in creating a greater public awareness, understanding and donations, but they need a lot more thought and planning if they are to be effective in reaching potential beneficiaries. Effective voluntary organisations plan their promotions as professionally as a commercial company, considering a variety of questions first. How best can one reach the beneficiary target groups? Can one reach disabled people directly through radio programmes such as 'Does He Take Sugar?' or deaf people through the television programme 'See Hear'? Given the fact that most blind people in this country are over retirement age and simply regard themselves as having weak eyesight, is it better to try to reach them via appearances on the Jimmy Young show, rather than the Radio 4 'In Touch' programme aimed at visually impaired people? Or do you go for both with different content approaches for each? What are the take-up rates for different forms of media exposure? For example, promoting a new large-print newspaper for visually impaired people on the Jimmy Young show produced 700 requests for sample copies, whereas a similar piece on the 'In Touch' programme aimed at visually impaired listeners only resulted in 110 requests. But the conversion rate from enquiries into subscribers was only one in four for Jimmy Young and one in two for 'In Touch'. In terms of total numbers of new subscribers, far better results were obtained through advertising in a magazine aimed at older people, but whereas the cost per new subscriber via the two radio programmes was £1.50, the cost of the new subscriber via the magazine advertisement was over £10. Now that the subscription base of the large-print newspaper is more substantial, the latest promotional activity is peer group recruitment. The large-print newspaper is aimed primarily at older people where as many as one in four people over 80 years old, and many people over 70 years old, find large print much easier to read. Therefore encouraging people to recruit friends is clearly a potentially effective way forward.

This section on the promotion of voluntary organisation goods has attempted to show that while the high-profile one-off editorial splash coverage can be useful for general public awareness, promotion to beneficiaries needs a well-thought-out plan and promotional mix. Unless beneficiary target groups are extremely large, there is often nothing to beat steady, relatively low-volumed methods of promotion.

Goods and their target groups

As we saw in Chapter 4, the attributes of a physical goods product are features (and more importantly the benefits they give to purchasers), quality, name, services and associated guarantees.

Each of these attributes needs to be planned. For example, a production-led rather than a marketing approach can easily result in a product being given more features than the customer either wants or can use. The name looks straightforward but can be problematic, especially on new products. In development they tend to be given tag names which stick, and which may be far easier for scientists to understand than the end beneficiary. The area of associated services and guarantees can also be problematic for a charity. Supporting services for high-turnover, widely distributed products can be difficult to arrange even when there is the potential to use volunteers. Guarantees are an important area of development, especially with increasing legal requirements. It is helpful to divide physical products into two categories: existing and new. Long-established physical products in charities often do not get enough attention. Rather the excitement and concentration is on new physical products. Good marketing requires a concentration on both.

As we have seen, it is all too easy for very useful charity physical goods to have a very low market penetration. In other words, the products can be very useful to a small percentage of the potential beneficiaries, leaving the vast majority of beneficiaries without the help of the product. It is therefore very important to assess the potential size of the target market and to measure what percentage the product is covering. If the market penetration is small, it is important to find out why. Is it because of promotion or distribution problems? Or is it because the product itself still is not quite right? This can be found out through marketing research among purchasers and potential purchasers.

The area of new physical products provided by voluntary organisations has become a very exciting one over the last ten years or so. This is primarily because of the increasing expansion and accessibility of high technology, especially computer-based technology. Charities are virtually in the position of having too many new physical products from which to choose. In a situation where disadvantaged people have too few choices, these statements need explaining.

Commercial companies have known for decades that for every twenty interesting new product developments, only about five will get tried out, and only one will succeed. Even these figures may be optimistic. In the commercial sector, at its crudest, the question is quite simply 'Are enough people going to buy this new product to make it viable and profitable?'

However, in the voluntary sector 'success' is defined much more broadly and is more difficult to judge. For example, if resources are not a problem, then developing a new product for just one person in difficulties is justifiable. Of course resources are constrained, but in charities there is enormous pressure to develop more new products than can be promoted, distributed or, even more importantly, piloted and market evaluated. Consequently there is more danger than in the commercial sector of new physical products being developed, put in the sales catalogue and then left to languish. The best interpretation that can be put on this process is that it means that the product is available for those few beneficiaries who want it. However, the worst interpretation is that many people who want/need the product are not getting it. In the absence of piloting and marketing research the product, while good in many ways, may be significantly flawed. For want of minor adaptation it is not wanted by the majority of the target market. This latter situation is by far the most insidious, because it provides incorrect evidence that a particular product line is not wanted, when in fact, given minor but significant changes to the product features, it might be invaluable.

There are no easy answers to deciding the balance among new product development, new product launch and existing product expansion. It is important that the charity discusses the balance in their own setting, and with an understanding of the target beneficiary markets. For example, it is not uncommon for a voluntary organisation gradually to realise that it is not serving a major segment of its population – the very elderly or the very young, women as opposed to men, urban rather than rural, newly disabled as opposed to congenitally disabled, etc. If a major under-attended segment is discovered, and if no other organisation is serving it, then that obviously has important pointers for new product development.

If a particular product line has become relatively high volume (in the charity's terms) but is still only serving 10 per cent of the potential market, then this product line deserves much closer attention. If it has gained 10 per cent of the market despite being under-promoted and with serious distribution problems, could it be that investment in these areas would lead to a doubling or trebling of volume?

If the charity has an active research and development arm and is producing a fair number of new products which may be gaining high media attention but do not seem to be of much interest to the end beneficiaries, then the research and development processes need closer examination. Is there over-investment in this area? Or is there under-involvement of the ultimate beneficiaries in new product selection and too little pilot testing with marketing research?

Another crucial area for attention is the purchasing power of the targeting market. If the target market wants the goods but cannot afford them, the charity can consider two disparate solutions. One that can be implemented quickly but may have very difficult consequences is to increase subsidy. The other, which takes much longer, is to use argument and persuasion for some or all of the costs to be borne by the state, or for additional state cost allowances to be distributed to the disadvantaged purchasers.

Conclusion

This section has looked at the marketing of physical goods from the point of view of price, place, promotion, product and target groups. Philosophy, even for goods, is an important part of the mix, but will be dealt with in more depth in the next chapter; as will people, physical evidence and processes, which are less important here. However, most charity physical goods, such as bicycles for health auxiliaries in Mozambique, or wheelchairs for physically disabled people, have a significant service component. So people, physical evidence and processes should not be ignored.

Publications

Publications in the voluntary sector are a nightmare to the marketer. Voluntary organisations produce far more publications than equivalently sized organisations in the statutory and commercial sectors. Several large charities produce so many publications which change so frequently that they cannot even give a list of them, let alone produce a publications catalogue. For one large charity it took one person working full-time for six months to identify all its publications and produce a partial print catalogue containing over 250 items.

The more important charity publications are usually overseen or produced by a hard-pressed publications officer or department. This results in the larger, longer-run publications generally being of a high standard of design, print and content with well-thought-out target readerships. But distribution and promotion are too often ill-researched and carried out.

However, the majority of publications pop out of organisations, with a good core purpose but often with little thought given to target group, language, design, distribution, promotion and price. These documents either languish in large piles on shelves or get scattered around like confetti with no one knowing whether they are even read, let alone acted upon.

Six questions need to be answered before a charity publishes. These are: who? why? to whom? how? and how effective?

☐ *Who?* The commissioner of the communication is crucial, and should have the final authority for signing off on the message and its form. For example, leaflets promoting the charity's various services may be written by an internal or freelance copywriter and be finally signed off by the senior manager of a large service group. But the head of the particular service about which the leaflet is written has to have ownership otherwise they will not actively distribute it. In this situation the commissioner is effectively the individual service and service head. The role of the senior manager of the group of services or the corporate centre is to check for acceptability rather than be the real commissioning agent. This still allows for corporate requirements, e.g. on design, house style and families of publications. But the final signing-off/acceptance of the copy should take place where it really matters.

☐ *Why and what?* The why and what of a publication are inextricably linked. In essence, what do you want to say, and why does it need to be said? The objectives (why) of the communication exercise are of central importance, as is being absolutely clear about what (the product) needs to be communicated. For example, is the aim simply to help the recipient identify a problem area, and indicate where they can go for help? Or is the object of the publication to do that and to help people to help themselves more directly? Is the idea to create sympathy for the cause and recruit volunteers to help, or is it to elicit donations, or (with more difficulty) both? Answering these kinds of questions makes decisions on the actual content (the what) much easier to determine.

☐ *To whom?* Being clear about the target audience is a prime requirement because it will predict to a large extent the message both in terms of particular content, language and style. If the target audience is too broad it will lead to far too many objectives for the document, and to a style that will either appeal to one subgroup and not to another, or attempt to be acceptable to all and convince none.

☐ *How?* This deceptively simple question covers several very important parts of the marketing mix, namely distribution (place), promotion and price. The target audience and the budget will largely predict the medium through which to get the message across. It might be a leaflet, a more substantial pamphlet, a mass-mailed letter, a book, etc. However, it could well be that a publication is not the right medium at all. These considerations are not the end of the matter. The *distribution* decisions are also of fundamental importance. For example, will the charity use inserts into newsletters or distribute multiple copies to local groups for onward distribution? If so, how will the charity encourage the groups to do so rather than leave them on the shelves? If they are to be distributed via doctor's surgeries, how will they get there and how will the medical secretary be encouraged to display them? Good *promotion* is also critical. If the target market actually asks for the publication, this is halfway towards getting the recipient to act, rather than simply to be passive. Good promotion to the end receiver can partially overcome poor distribution and reinforce good distribution, e.g. patients asking their general practice for a particular leaflet. *Price* of publications is always a tricky issue and, not unreasonably, is related to cost and who pays the costs. If the costs are coming out of the central publications budget, then the service manager usually wants it to be free. If the document is free, how can the enthusiasm of intermediaries who ask for more copies than they can distribute be dampened? If the document is priced, will this stop it reaching its end recipient? Or could it be that for some customers (e.g. social services departments) a charge would be affordable and might actually enhance the value with which it is perceived?

☐ *How effective?* Trying to assess how effective a publication has been is extremely difficult. The most basic performance indicator of how many copies have been sold or distributed is easy to keep track of. If that can be combined with a record of which subgroups of the target audience are taking the publication up, then the information begins to have more evaluative use other than knowing when to reprint. If the purpose of a publication is to encourage action, then a prompt on the lines of 'for more information write to us on ...' can be a partial indicator of how many recipients are actively taking up the ideas. These supportive calls for action can be constructed in such a way that audience response can be coded so as to learn more about the active responders. Where the publication is a regular one, such as a newsletter or magazine, or even on occasions for a one-off publication, a questionnaire enclosed with the publication can give useful information. Because the readers of charity publications are often highly motivated and committed, it is not unusual to be able to achieve anything up to a 30–40 per cent response rate, and exceptionally as high as 70–80 per cent. Completed questionnaires, suitably aggregated, can give a lot more information about the customer group and what they find helpful and unhelpful about the publication. This attempt at quantification is more effective and reliable if it is combined with some form of depth discussion with a smaller number of assumed 'typical' readers.

Conclusion

Perhaps with the exception of organisations set up exclusively as publishers, charities are among the most prolific distributors of information, particularly in the form of printed documents. These publication products, where they are large in size or high in circulation, tend to be well thought out and well produced, using professional publication staff input. Nevertheless even in these instances it is quite normal for most attention to be devoted to the product and insufficient attention devoted to price, promotion and distribution.

However, except in the most professional and best-endowed charities, the majority of publication products such as information sheets, duplicated advice sheets, practice guidelines, etc., are produced with far too little attention to the six important interrogatives of who? what? why? to whom? how? and how effective?.

For-profit fund-raising goods

This section could just as easily sit in the chapter on fund-raising. It is included here for two reasons. First, there are commonalities (as well as differences) in the marketing of physical goods, whether they be for profit (to supporters) or loss-making (to beneficiaries). Second, marketing approaches and techniques have become much more pervasive in the acquisition and selling of goods for profit than they have in the provision of physical goods to end beneficiaries. While this is ironic, juxtaposing the two areas in this chapter may provide additional lessons and comparisons for marketing of goods to end beneficiaries.

While comprehensive data are hard to come by, partial surveys suggest that charity trading for profit has increased quite significantly over the past ten years, and is likely to continue to expand in the foreseeable future. Hiscock (1991, pp. 5–9) surveyed the 200 largest fund-raising charities as listed by the Charities Aid Foundation; of these 200 charities, 157 (79 per cent) said they were trading, and of this number 110 had set up one or more separate trading companies. Of the 120 trading companies identified, 26 had been established in the previous five years, and of the total only 6 were dormant. The most prevalent trading activity was Christmas card and small gift sales (25 per cent), followed by promotional items, e.g. T-shirts, pens, mugs, badges, etc. (20 per cent) and charity catalogue sales (19 per cent).

Trading for profit is a proportionally small contributor to total charitable income. Hiscock (1991, p. 21) reports that 18 per cent of the top 120 traders were losing money according to their declared accounts. In reality, this is likely to be an underestimate given that almost another 30 per cent were hovering around the break-even point. In those circumstances true attribution of the cost of trading to the accounts has to be suspect.

If trading is not very profitable, why is it so widespread? Two of the main reasons are Christmas cards and charity shops.

Charity Christmas cards

Charity Christmas card activity exhibits some of the best and worst practice of charity marketing.

As a concept of added value, charity Christmas cards must be one of the neatest and most brilliant ideas ever developed. They combine to be simultaneously attractive to Christmas card senders, card manufacturers, retail distributors, the Post Office and obviously to charities themselves, both trustees and staff. Charity card senders feel good about having done so; card manufacturers arguably gain increased sales or at least defend themselves against decline; retailers benefit; similarly the Post Office protects its volume; and charities feel it is good public relations and sometimes make a profit out of it. Everyone wins – or do they?

My guess is that the majority of charities with their own Christmas cards only make a profit through the associated donations which come with the card orders. If those donations could have been secured by other means, then the majority of charities are actually losing money on their card operations. So why do the smaller charities carry on with this activity? There is tremendous pressure on charities to be in this market. Charity trustees and senior staff somehow feel that they are not significant charity players if they do not have a card operation. Their family, friends and neighbours will continually be asking them why they do not do Christmas cards. In so far as the card operation is wobbling around the break-even point, or even making a loss, justifications (or rationalisations) about the importance of the public relations aspect of the Christmas cards will be trotted out.

So what distinguishes the more successful from the less successful? As one would expect, it is down to a good comprehensive marketing approach, once again concentrating particularly on the Cinderella areas of the charity marketing mix, namely distribution and promotion. The less successful charities are essentially production orientated and spend hours debating, or even arguing, between and among trustees and staff as to whether the right designs were chosen. Then the vicious self-justification spiral starts to dominate, i.e. we are in the charity Christmas card market because it is good PR and the 'done thing'. In other words, narrow public relations objectives begin to dominate. Cards are chosen because the senior managers, trustees and sometimes their spouses like them, and consequently fewer and fewer other people ever buy them.

It is probably not over-simplifying to say that the two 'Ps' of *product* and *price* are not the reason for success or failure. As far as product design goes, it would take a thick-skinned aesthete to distinguish between the myriad charity card designs. They all seem to have skaters wearing muffs against the backcloth of a baroque city, or robins in various poses on gates, or doves of peace. There is little differentiation between charities on price – it is a highly price-competitive market even among the high-price business card end of the range. What makes all the difference are the two 'Ps' of promotion and place.

In essence, it is distribution and promotion that gets a charity the volume, and volume gets the cost price down which gives the profit. This is achieved with a great deal of difficulty because the major charities have now commandeered an enormous volume in the market.

The key to successful *promotion* is the list. This involves how many names and addresses the charity has of existing supporters who might be interested in purchasing cards. If there are 50,000 or more, then diligent marketing will bring success. If there are fewer than 10,000, success is possible but the risks are high. Such a loyal database of customers will give breathing space while the charity tests promotion elsewhere. Purchasing segments of lists from agencies, swapping them with other charities, putting inserts into regional sections of magazines, etc., all allow test marketing to establish profitability. Coding leaflets and analysing subsequent sales can, in the space of one season, establish profitable areas for expansion. Timing of promotion is also critical. Small, relatively unknown charities are wise to promote their cards at the end of August or in early September.

The other key area of promotion is sales promotion. A whole range of possibilities exist. Are there any corporate donors who send a relatively high volume of business Christmas cards? If so, talking with them, arranging a special (but profitable) price and letting them choose their design can bring success. Has the charity got local groups who will sell actively, either for a share of the margin, or for a share of the public relations (which will involve overprinting the local group's name in high-volume situations or providing stickers in low volume ones)? All these activities and others like them require assiduous attention to comparative profitability and comparative donations, which in turn require pre-coding of brochures and post-receipt analysis.

Distribution is important, especially linked with sales promotion. If it is a popular cause, national and regional retailers are increasingly taking on individual charities' cards. The profit margins for charity may be small, but the volume is very large and so therefore is the public relations benefit. While managerial responsibility of in-house volunteers may be too much in the early stages, significant costs can be taken out by a charity handling packaging and distribution itself rather than using a company. Access to loyal and competent volunteers, providing there is space, improves efficiency and cuts costs.

However, the real key to success in Christmas cards is 'shops'. If a charity has its own shops, or can negotiate sales through national retailers, then volume follows. A relationship with a national retailing chain will add enormous card sales, but not a lot of profit. If a charity has its own shops, then it can get volume *and* profit.

Charity shops and trading

The number and growth of charity shops is startling. Corporate Intelligence on Retailing (1992, p. 7) estimates that there are 4,700 charity shops. This is almost certainly an underestimate because they only list those under the umbrella of national charities and their networks. However, just twelve national charities control 77 per cent of these 4,700 shops. For example, in 1992 Oxfam had 850, the Sue Ryder Foundation 460, the Imperial Cancer Research Fund 460 and Barnardo's 290. In the three years to 1992 the twelve largest charity operators had added over 800 shops to their total (+ 23 per cent). In 1993 Marie Curie were opening a shop a fortnight (see Figure 6.1).

There are three main reasons for this sudden expansion: the search for additional income; the publicity presence offered; and the market and location opportunities offered by the early 90s recession. Of these three, new net income can be the most challenging. Harker (1993, p. 9) reports the Cancer Research Campaign and British Heart Foundation having net profit margins of 12 per cent and 14 per cent respectively. However, in comparison the most successful, Oxfam, is reported as turning in a net profit margin of 36 per cent, Save the Children 31 per cent, the Children's Society 31 per cent, and Imperial Cancer Research Fund 28 per cent. By almost every measure the outstanding player is Oxfam which not only has the highest net profit margin, it has three times the absolute net profit of any other charity, turning in £18.3m net in 1991/2.

Publicity and public presence provide a further push towards expansion. Voluntary fund-raising of all types is heavily dependent upon, at least as a prerequisite, high public awareness. Charity shops, strategically located in

Figure 6.1 Charity shops' high street presence gives public awareness as well as additional income, and numbers are expanding dramatically – Marie Curie Cancer Care opened one shop every fortnight in 1992/3

high pedestrian volume areas, make a major contribution to public awareness. It is no coincidence that Oxfam has the highest level of spontaneous
awareness among the general public of any charity, and also has the largest
and most long-established shop network.

There is no doubt that the recession on the 1990s has provided the
conditions for expansion in at least two important respects. First, more shop
sites are available either free or at reasonable prices. Second, the majority of
customers are from the socio-economic groups C2, D and E, i.e. they are less
well-off and the low prices of second-hand goods are all the more attractive
in times of recession and increasing relative poverty.

But this does not account for some charities being so much more successful
than others, e.g. Oxfam, Imperial Cancer Research Fund and SCOPE. The
answer is quite simply a professional marketing approach. The product
range is well thought out in relation to target markets. Pricing is effective.
The various elements of promotion are very carefully attended to. Corporate
style is particularly crucial.

Most important of all, place receives a great deal of attention. The operational nuts and bolts of distribution, location, inventory/stocks and transport assume a massive importance if profitability is to be maintained and
extended.

Most of the largest fund-raising charities have a substantial trading arm
although net trading profits only provide a very small percentage of total
charity income. Hiscock (1991, p. 14) reports an average of only 1.4 per cent.
However, any average on a disparate sample contains surprises! For
example, two of the very largest charities, Oxfam and The National Trust,
receive up to 5 per cent of their total income from trading activities. Perhaps
more interestingly a handful of lower-ranked charities feature in the list of
top ten traders. For example, Hiscock reports that in 1988 the following
lower-ranked charities out of the top 200 fund-raising charities were in the
top ten as far as covenanted profits from trading were concerned: Prince's
Trust (91st), MENCAP (88th), East Kent Hospice Project (168th), MIND
(199th). In MIND's case nearly 12 per cent of their total income (i.e. from
voluntary and statutory sources) comes from trading and as much as 25 per
cent of their total voluntary income.

Profitable trading which also helps beneficiaries

Some charities manage to achieve profitable trading activity which also
helps beneficiaries at the same time, for example Age Concern and Oxfam.

Age Concern Insurance Services

The trading division of Age Concern England exists for four reasons: to
provide products and services relevant to older people; to enable the Age

Concern network to provide 'commercial' services to older people along with advice and practical services; to enable Age Concern groups to build up a source of independent income; and to generate income for Age Concern England.

In Age Concern's case the product is largely a service rather than a physical good, but it is included in this chapter because of its profitable trading objective. Age Concern Insurance Services was started to help older people insure their homes at competitive premiums. In the early 1980s home contents insurance from the majority of companies had minimum sum-insured levels which were significantly higher than many older people wanted. For example, many older people only had £3,000 worth of contents to insure and the minimum sum that companies would insure was £6,000. This meant that, to be insured, older people were paying a premium higher than was required. So Age Concern developed a product that was more in line with older people's needs. Initially the insurance brokerage activity was handled in house and, as it grew, was contracted out to an external broker. Gradually the range of insurance products has increased both in range and quantity.

The products offered include pet insurance (e.g. for the cost of veterinary treatment, or for the cost of kennel fees during an older person's hospital-isation), holiday travel, home and contents, private car insurance, etc. Beneficiaries (older people) benefit by receiving a low-cost product which has been specifically designed to meet the needs of older people (e.g. low sums insured, instalment payments at no extra cost, hospital cover under pet insurance policies, etc.). Local Age Concern groups that promote the policies benefit by receiving commission for the business they generate. For some of the more active groups this can result in many thousands of pounds per annum. Age Concern England also benefits by participation in the service. As long as Age Concern continues to negotiate insurance packages that are relevant and represent value for money for older people, this form of practical marketing combines the best of all worlds for the national charity, its local groups and its beneficiaries.

Oxfam Bridge Programme

Oxfam undertakes profitable trading activities in a way that benefits beneficiaries, not as consumers but as producers. Oxfam Trading has an arm, the Bridge Programme. Bridge buys products, at fair prices, from producers who are 'the poorest, especially women, refugees, the landless, slum dwellers and vulnerable minorities' (Oxfam 1992, pp. 12–15). Nearly 85 per cent of Bridge sales are made through Oxfam shops, and the commis-sioned goods obviously have to be able to compete in the UK charity shop market. Oxfam claims that an additional benefit of the Bridge Programme is that it helps to distinguish Oxfam shops from other charity outlets.

In addition in 1991/2 Oxfam Trading collaborated with three other UK alternative trading organisations – Equal Exchange, Traidcraft and Twin Trading – to develop a fairly traded coffee, Cafedirect, which pays an above-market price to small-scale producers in Mexico, Costa Rico and Peru but is also sold at a profit in the United Kingdom.

These examples show the potential for charities to become involved in the marketing of products that benefit beneficiaries, provide the charity with 'profit' and may also serve supporters. The sophistication of the marketing model developed would leave many FMCG brand managers gasping for air!

Conclusion

In this chapter we have looked at the application of marketing to charity publications, charity goods aimed at end beneficiaries, charity goods sold to the general public for a profit and charity goods sold at a profit but which aid beneficiaries.

The provision of physical goods to a voluntary organisation's end beneficiaries is more widespread than many commentators have presumed. In the main they are subsidised, which brings a complex series of interactions that are unique to the voluntary sector. To the libertarian right, this results in unhelpful distortions of the market. For those supporting a mixed economy of welfare, such an approach can make provision which would stimulate the commercial market or provide additional goods where the commercial market cannot operate. In general, marketing of physical goods to end beneficiaries is poorly developed and is more akin to a production-orientated approach to commerce in the 1950s without the benefits of mass production techniques. Voluntary organisations owe it to their end beneficiaries to become more effective in marketing their physical goods.

In each of these areas the more effective charities are increasingly applying a marketing approach. As a generalisation, however, marketing strategy is ignored. Target markets are not well thought out. Pricing is unsophisticated. Place is largely ignored.

For these reasons profitability, when it is sought, is low; market penetration, especially into beneficiary customer groups, is low; and publications are wasted and unread. Most charities have a lot to learn.

Key points

Physical goods
Voluntary organisations owe it to their end beneficiaries to become more effective in marketing their goods.

Price
- [ ] Be aware of the consequences of subsidising, or over-subsidising, goods. If the organisation is aiming to be a high-volume supplier, prices must cover, or almost cover, costs.
- [ ] Pricing strategy should take account of the social economic policies of government (which is often the purchaser) as well as responsibilities to the beneficiary.

Place
- [ ] Planning and monitoring how physical goods are going to be delivered to the end customer is essential.
- [ ] Get the support of intermediaries by understanding their needs and priorities.
- [ ] Consider using incentives, however small.

Promotion
- [ ] Promotion to beneficiaries needs to be carefully and regularly targeted in spite of the seeming attractiveness of obtaining high-profile coverage generating only general awareness.

Target groups
- [ ] Assess the potential size of the market and measure how much is covered by the product.
- [ ] Do not let the organisation be distracted into developing new products which cannot be promoted properly.

Publications
- [ ] *Who* is responsible for the publication, its content, message and style?
- [ ] *Why* is it being produced, *what* is it going to say and *to whom?*
- [ ] *How* will it reach its target audience? Consider distribution, promotion and price.
- [ ] *How* will its effectiveness be measured?

For-profit fund-raising goods
Common pitfalls
- [ ] Pressure to be seen to be trading in a particular market, e.g. Christmas cards, causes bad decisions by smaller organisations who may not have the resources to enter the market in sufficient volume.
- [ ] Promotion and distribution are often badly handled.
- [ ] Although recession of the 1990s has helped and prompted expansion of charity shops, the most successful still demonstrate that effective pricing, promotion and distribution are key.

7

SERVICES TO BENEFICIARIES

Introduction

Applying a marketing approach to charity goods, as with any physical goods in the commercial sector, is relatively straightforward. As we shall see in the next chapter the application of marketing approach to pressure group work is also reasonably straightforward. However, marketing of services in general, and in the charity sector in particular, is very challenging. Chapter 4 on the marketing mix explored some of the difficulties involved. Services are less tangible; they have a complicated interface with beneficiaries and have beneficiaries' active participation on many occasions; production and consumption are often simultaneous; the service is an activity extending over some considerable length of time; and the attitudes and behaviour of service providers as well as users can make or break the quality of the service.

These differences between service marketing and goods marketing are arguably different in kind, and are certainly different in extent. This has led some writers to modify the traditional marketing mix to make it easier to apply to services. Booms and Bitner (1981, pp. 47–51) have added three extra 'Ps' in the form of people, physical evidence and process (see Chapter 4). Cowell (1984, p. 69) states that in the absence of any empirically based scheme, this modification of marketing mix appears to make good sense. I argue in Chapter 4 that for charity and public services a further 'P' of philosophy is required. The explicit or implicit philosophy adopted by a charity has a significant impact on how a charity's services operate, especially in relation to customers.

Direct and indirect services

Direct charity services

The vast majority of service output by charities are those delivered direct to end beneficiaries. The array of such direct services is vast in range and quantity, e.g. schools, colleges, libraries, holiday hotels, play schemes, visiting schemes, social work in a variety of forms, museums, galleries, theatres, feeding programmes, education and development programmes, social and employment rehabilitation, employment training, bird sanctuaries, stately homes, housing, financial aid, etc. In fact the majority of the activities coming from the voluntary sector is in the form of such direct services.

Indirect charity services

The majority of charities have very broad-based objectives which are far more interventionist in the external environment relating to their cause than might at first be expected. For example, Age Concern's mission is 'to promote the well-being of all older people and help make later life a fulfilling and enjoyable experience' (Greengross 1993, p. 76).

Save the Children Fund makes it clear in its mission statement that in order to achieve lasting benefits for children within the communities in which they live, it will attempt to influence policy as well as practice (Hinton 1993, p. 11). These examples are typical of a vast range of charities in the United Kingdom, and almost certainly for not-for-profit organisations across the world.

These broad-based objectives mean that charities do not rely exclusively on direct services to their end beneficiaries. In addition, through indirect services aimed at intermediaries, they attempt to influence the policy and practice structures impacting on their end beneficiaries. For example, if the Royal Society for the Protection of Birds (RSPB) can encourage statutory authorities through advice and guidance to be more assiduous in their anti-pollution responsibilities, this might do more to protect birds than setting up several new bird sanctuaries.

The Wolfenden report (Wolfenden 1977, pp. 22–7) usefully divided the world in which voluntary organisations operate (and all of us for that matter) into four sectors which arguably cover all areas of human activity, namely the commercial sector, the statutory sector, the voluntary sector and the informal sector (of family, friends and neighbours). A moment's thought will establish that the end beneficiaries of any voluntary organisation are going to be affected considerably more by the combined attentions of these four sectors than they are through any direct services by a particular voluntary organisation or charity. Therefore, increasingly, charities and other voluntary organisations are using the full interventionist potential of their broad-based objectives. They are achieving this by adding activities to their repertoire which can influence those parts of the statutory, commercial, voluntary and informal sectors that are important to their end beneficiaries. So, for example, in the early 1970s Age Concern England started an active advisory service to the major retailers on the small package requirements of elderly beneficiaries. Oxfam has long given advisory support to government departments, voluntary and commercial organisations in other countries on a whole range of humanitarian issues and programmes. The Disability Alliance runs training courses for statutory authority social workers and others on the benefits available to disabled people under social security.

As a proportion of financial turnover, these indirect services form a very small part in comparison to the turnover of direct services.

The structure and relationship of direct and indirect charity services

While the distinction between direct and indirect services is a helpful analytical tool to marketers and providers of services, each may have some of the attributes of the other. For example, a school catering for disabled children is clearly a direct service. However, the placement process will involve the local education authority's professional expert visiting the school, where they might pick up a few ideas for application back in their own local education authority setting. Cancer Relief Macmillan provides and funds nurses to care for cancer patients in their own homes which is clearly a direct service. But in many instances these nurses are outposted to the National Health Service (NHS) and are funded only for the first three years, after which the NHS agrees to take the post on to the full-time establishment – a very clear example of how a direct service impacts on and changes the attitudes and behaviours of a statutory service provider.

This last example begins to reveal a continuum (see Figure 7.1), with one end being the provision of direct services to end beneficiaries, plain and

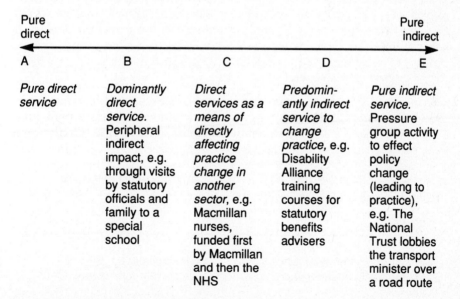

Pure direct				Pure indirect
A	B	C	D	E
Pure direct service	Dominantly direct service. Peripheral indirect impact, e.g. through visits by statutory officials and family to a special school	Direct services as a means of directly affecting practice change in another sector, e.g. Macmillan nurses, funded first by Macmillan and then the NHS	Predomin-antly indirect service to change practice, e.g. Disability Alliance training courses for statutory benefits advisers	Pure indirect service. Pressure group activity to effect policy change (leading to practice), e.g. The National Trust lobbies the transport minister over a road route

Figure 7.1 Direct/indirect service continuum

simple; moving along the continuum towards the other end, the proportion of direct service provision decreases and the significance of indirect service provision increases, to the point where indirect service provision shades into 'pure' indirect services or pressure group activity, i.e. working indirectly to achieve a policy change.

However, before reaching the pressure group end of the continuum, we find the location of the most common form of indirect service, i.e. activities such as advice, consultancy and training aimed at groups of people who, in turn, impact on the charities' end beneficiaries. For example, the National Centre for Volunteering provides advice, training and consultancy services to voluntary and statutory organisations who wish to involve (more) volunteers in their work. The Children's Society runs similar activities aimed at statutory health, social and education services encouraging them to be more effective with children and families.

Running along the continuum in Figure 7.1, there are four vital but changing attributes, as laid out in Figure 7.2.

So what does such a model contribute? For the marketing or charity manager, it can be a useful analytical tool in understanding and guiding the positioning of a service both within the charity, outside it in respect of other charities' services and outside it in respect of activity in the other sectors. For example, in the 1960s and early 1970s the legitimacy of charities (rather than the state) running so many direct services (positions A and B) was questioned. Charities continued to run them, but they tried to do so more from position C, i.e. to influence policy and practice in statutory services, for example by pioneering services (new product development) which would be taken on by the state (e.g. family planning). At the same time position E became more attractive as we shall see in Chapter 8. Recent government policies to encourage contracting-out have re-legitimised areas A and B, i.e. direct services in their own right.

The model also begins to help to predict the particular opportunities and challenges that will be met from any one position. It can also make the process of effective service development more conscious and logical. for example, for the school for disabled children which only provides direct

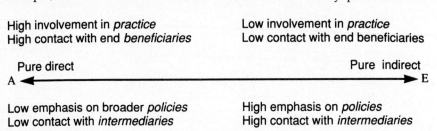

High involvement in *practice*   Low involvement in *practice*
High contact with end *beneficiaries*   Low contact with end beneficiaries

   Pure direct   Pure indirect
A ◄──────────────────────────────────────► E

Low emphasis on broader *policies*   High emphasis on *policies*
Low contact with *intermediaries*   High contact with *intermediaries*

Figure 7.2 Changing attributes in the direct/indirect service continuum

services, it prompts the question, 'What about indirect services that could be added on?' Who are the other target groups that impact on the children in the school, and how can the school services be modified/added to in order to impact on these relevant indirect target groups? The answer to the question of 'who else' will almost certainly initially be parents/family and/ or local authority professional workers in the child's home area. Where the disabled child has a close family, the family is likely to be extremely influential on the development of the child. What can the school do to share and exchange with the parents, particularly in knowledge and skills? In the case of local authority professionals (who may not be familiar with the particular disability in which the school specialises), what can be shared with regard to knowledge and skills?

This discussion leads naturally into service positioning.

Positioning and other-player (competitor) analysis

Chapter 3 looked at the component parts of other-player analysis and positioning and some of the strategies that charities can follow.

Throughout this book the term 'other-player analysis' has been used rather than 'competitor analysis', which would be the normal commercial marketing term, as the latter description sits uncomfortably in the charity market, especially when considering services to beneficiaries. I could not possibly count the number of times that people have said to me (particularly people from commerce and industry) 'Why don't you all get together and merge into one charity for such and such a cause?' While superficially sensible, such proposals, especially coming from commercial entrepreneurs bred on the merits of competition, always strike me as a bit rich! Nevertheless the arguments for cooperation between charities in the field of service provision seem invincible – in theory at least. In my experience charities do try quite hard to cooperate on such activity either through formal processes such as cross-representation on each other's boards, or through informal groupings of service managers, sharing information. In comparison to the commercial world, it probably has been quite cooperative and well ordered. For example, Age Concern and Help the Aged have an understanding as to who does what, albeit somewhat uneasy at times. The RNIB and Guide Dogs for the Blind have clear activity boundaries. Similarly the National Federation of Women's Institutes and the Townswomen's Guild have reasonably clear geographic, if not functional, boundaries.

If and when competition breaks out between two or more charities, it is important from a marketing point of view to have the affected services positioned properly. For example, Help the Aged services are largely positioned out of its high priority for fund-raising, while Age Concern services are positioned largely on its strength of being able to gather together at national and local level all the parties interested in older people into a cooperative effort.

However, this can change, and there are some indications that there will be increasing competition between charities in the field of service provision over the next decade or so. While the arrival of new 'dynamic' service managers or chief executives can increase the amount of competition, in general growth or decline in competition occurs for broadly structural reasons. For example, declining numbers of disabled children going into residential schooling will up the competition stakes between such schools. Similarly structural changes such as new commissioning policies by (normally) statutory funds bring change. While the current moves towards many statutory authorities introducing a purchaser/provider split offer charities opportunities, the simultaneous introduction of competitive tendering for work has increased competition. The statutory purchasers are actively encouraging competition to gain keener tender prices.

Certainly in the present economically stringent times, with changing government, trust and company funding policies, charities that provide services would be wise to undertake a careful other-player analysis, comparing strengths, weaknesses, opportunities and threats between themselves and significant other players.

Needs (marketing) research

Needs research has long had a legitimacy in the charity sector although the quality and frequency leaves much to be desired. The insufficiency of research can be explained in a number of ways. First, as in general, demand outstrips supply; there is no impelling business reason to understand the end beneficiaries' needs better. Second, even sensitive professional workers in charity services dealing with disadvantaged groups often develop the 'I know best' syndrome. This is not exactly akin to the 'production-orientated' approach in 1950s manufacturing industry because the charity service professional is much more closely in touch with the end beneficiaries, but it has some echoes of that way of thinking. Third, charities have a tradition of policy-making committees having fairly large numbers of 'the great and the good', who are somehow meant to know the answers. Fourth, the more progressive charities have been involving increasing numbers of their end beneficiaries, or organisations representing them, on their policy-making committees, e.g. National Association of Youth Clubs, Age Concern, SCOPE, RNIB, etc. Ironically such representation can lead the organisation to feel that it is taking on the beneficiary voice. In one sense it is, but these are not typical beneficiaries. They are the ones who are confident enough, able enough and available enough to join committees. In other words, they are seldom typical. It is wholly good to have increased beneficiary representation, but not as a substitute for needs research. Indeed beneficiary representatives can often be the first people to acknowledge that they cannot know all the needs of their group and, for this reason, can be some of the strongest supporters of marketing research.

Needs research can have a very significant impact on a charity's services. For example, RNIB spends in excess of £200,000 per year on needs research among beneficiaries, a figure which would rise to nearer £500,000 per year if service take-up and quality monitoring were to be included. In particular a major one-off piece of research among 600 blind and partially sighted adults (Bruce *et al.* 1991) and 300 children and their families (Walker *et al.* 1992) has had a significant impact on the organisation's services. Interestingly it has also been rated among the top three most important RNIB initiatives by a clear majority of RNIB stakeholders – showing that policy-makers welcome marketing research as much as service managers. Cancer Relief Macmillan Fund is another charity that spends considerable sums on marketing research among people with cancer, their carers and friends, relatives and colleagues. Its major 1992 MORI survey revealed needs not previously fully acknowledged, in particular difficulties with non-medical day-to-day tasks such as shopping, child care, etc. As a result it has amended its services.

Such needs research is particularly valuable to a charity's indirect services. Externally validated, quality research among existing and potential bene-ficiaries first describes the situation of the client group which can be compared with others; second, indicates the areas of priority need within the client group; and third, indicates what needs to be done. This informa-tion provides a powerful and credible ammunition to the indirect services trying to make an impact on relevant intermediary groups of professionals and managers, such as social workers, doctors, environmental heath officers, etc.

Market segmentation and target markets

Chapter 3 described the reasons for segmenting the charity market (e.g. to allow prioritisation of groups to be served; to allow higher quality services to be delivered via homogeneity; to identify under-served groups, etc.). It describes in more detail the criteria that can be used for segmenting the market (e.g. geographic, socio-demographic, psychographic and behav-ioural).

One of the key differences between professional companies and charities is that the market for the charity is more likely to be prescribed, even to the extent of being identified in the legal charity registration document. It could be argued that this gives charity service managers a flying start, i.e. we are here to serve deaf people/children/theatre-goers in Coventry/fencers/ people/animals suffering pollution, etc. However, as Chapter 3 described, this is only the start if real need is to be met effectively when resources are in short supply. Unfortunately few charities analyse their market much further than that outlined in their charity registration document by asking and answering such questions as how many; what ages; where do they live; what characteristics are most relevant to our cause; which subgroups are we serving and which not; among those we are serving, are we reaching a high percentage or a low percentage within that group, etc.

For example, a charity serving people with learning difficulties might segment its beneficiary market by age, severity of learning difficulty, and presence or absence of parental support under the age of 40 years. Following that segmentation, needs research and other-player analysis might indicate that children and young people up to the age of 25 across all severity groups are relatively well served and are likely to have younger parents. The charity may identify potential beneficiaries in middle to late middle age with aging parents as a particularly vulnerable group, *under-served* by statutory services which have relied for too long on parental support. Such targeting does not predict how this group might best be helped and a final decision on whether to go ahead with this particular priority group would depend on further needs research, review of existing services capable of adaption and potential new services, identification of additional or sub-stitute resources, choice between direct and indirect service intervention, etc.

But because a group with some degree of common need has been identified, this will allow a *higher quality service* to be introduced in that the recipients have certain common characteristics, and will therefore to an extent be a source of *efficient allocation of resources*; and if the segmentation and needs research have been efficient, there should be a strong case for *attracting funding*. (The words emphasised are a repeat of the list of reasons that segmentation can be helpful to decisions on service delivery, as outlined in Chapter 3.)

Service design and construction (the product)

Under the first 'P' of the marketing mix, the list of elements to be considered consists of 'quality, features, name, packaging, services and guarantees' (Doyle 1991, p. 275).

Let us use the example of the voluntary visiting service quoted in Chapter 1. What is the quality of the visiting service – are the volunteers trained well enough to be sensitive to the needs of the elderly person to be visited? What are the features of the service – can the elderly person decide in principle and in practice how often they would like a visit? Has the service got a name that is attractive? Is its reputation in the neighbourhood good? Is it generally believed only to be provided for people who are mentally confused, and if so, is it unlikely to be attractive to people who are simply lonely? Are the volunteers invariably polite, reliable and punctual? Do they seem able to refer effectively any problems the older person may have? Is there a clear procedure for the older person to indicate that they would like to try an alternative volunteer visitor? Is there a regular assessment meeting every six to twelve months with a social worker so that the visiting relationship can be reviewed, and a more fundamental but associated assessment be offered? All these characteristics of the service need to be thought out before the service is launched, and monitored throughout its existence, otherwise many of the failures enumerated by the research of Shenfield and Allen (1972, pp. 159–69) will become apparent.

The service marketers Berry and Parasuraman (1991, pp. 15–76) introduce some very useful concepts in everyday language. They argue that delivering the top criterion of service quality presumes 'doing the service right the first time'. How much more true is this for a charity service? How many patrons of an orchestra will be lost if the first performance they hear is a bad one? If an older client has a bad or poor experience with their visitor or social work assessor, then their confidence in the service will be shattered, far more than if the gasman turns up on the wrong day (to use a commercial service comparison). If the worst happens, Berry and Parasuraman then talk of 'doing the service *very* right the second time': in our case bringing in an alternative volunteer or assessor whom we know is one of our best and going to great lengths to listen and repair the damage as perceived from the client's point of view. They argue, and our own everyday experience would confirm, that taking a great deal of trouble to rectify a bad experience has a very convincing impact on an upset customer.

Chapter 4 introduced the five dimensions that influence a commercial service customer's view of the quality of a service which, in order of priority, are as follows:

1. Reliability (delivering the service dependably and accurately).
2. Responsiveness.
3. Assurance (confidence in the service).
4. Empathy.
5. Tangibles (physical clues to the service).

Except for the last, all these features were found to be critical by Shenfield and Allen (1972, pp. 159–69) and would seem to translate into almost any charity service to beneficiaries. The older people being visited want the visitor to be dependable. 'Accuracy' is perhaps too narrow a term for many charity services, especially complex ones, but it conveys the necessity for a thoughtful, high quality professional service. Responsiveness of the scheme towards the client in the service and empathy towards the client are clearly both service attributes that are vital. Figure 7.3 of a VSO teacher illustrates, in one photograph, four of the five dimensions – responsiveness, assurance, empathy and tangible clues.

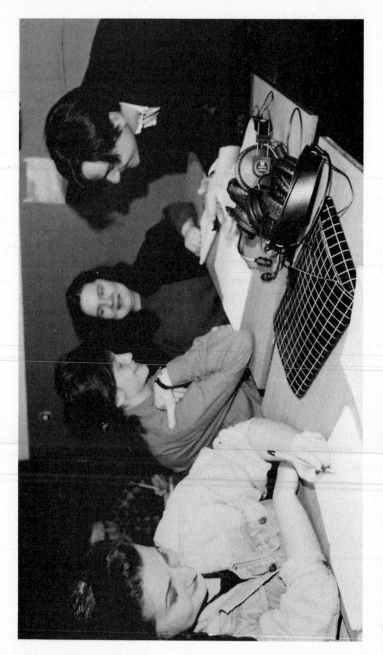

Figure 7.3 For customers to regard services as successful they want reliability, responsiveness, assurance, empathy and tangible clues – VSO English teacher in Poland (VSO/Jeremy Hartley)

New service development and service closure and (new product development and deletion)

Adding to or closing services to a charity's range of products are often given too little thought and analysis. For example, new services can be added into the portfolio almost unilaterally by an enthusiastic staff member or group of staff in response to needs they have identified from their beneficiary contact (e.g. staff in social work advice unit add in advice on social security, which is very complicated and individualised work – this results in neither service being done properly and clients being turned away). In one sense this staff initiative is what charities are famous for, i.e. quick, flexible, innovative responses to newly identified need. But then demand becomes greater than existing staff and/or volunteers can supply and more resources are requested. If these are granted it is often outside a new product analysis (i.e. still not thought through) and, hey presto, the service has grown like Topsy. If extra resources are refused, either the new service has to be closed, resulting in accusations of bad faith, or more likely it stumbles on, making little penetration into the market and providing poor quality through being under-resourced and stretching staff and volunteers to breaking point.

While this 'try it and see' method can be akin to informal test marketing, it needs to be more efficiently handled. Dibb *et al.* (1991, pp. 243–54) describes the process of new product development as idea generation, followed by screening, followed by business analysis, followed by product development, followed by test marketing, followed by commercialisation (commercialisation is essentially planning the full launch and the first year's activity plan). This process is probably not as linear as described, but it does provide a rough and ready cross between a checklist and a process to be followed. In the example quoted above, idea generation was good but virtually no screening or analysis of the resource/business implications took place and it shifted from idea generation through to service development and straight into the market-place in a form that was halfway between a test market (without any evaluation built in) and a full launch.

New product development can be a disorientating term, encouraging a concentration on the product as opposed to the whole marketing mix. Johne (1996) emphasises the importance of developing the whole marketing mix calling this development 'product augmentation development'. Development of the whole mix is particularly useful with a mature product range. For example, community service as an alternative to custodial sentencing is well established with several variants, many focusing on remotivating disillusioned young offenders and trying to get them into jobs. Product augmentation development as an approach concentrates on what marketing mix changes can add value. In this example several community service schemes have concentrated on the people elements of the eight-point service marketing mix and introduced volunteer 'buddies' to the young person –

these buddies (or mentors) being successful, employed people (rather than social workers) who can help the young person through example, through mentoring and through introductions, i.e. the core community service product is retained but is augmented by attention to one or more of the marketing mix elements, in this case the 'P' for people.

Johne (1996) also argues that in the commercial world new product development is often simply incremental change which avoids failure but does not maximise potential. Not-for-profit organisations not required to achieve business success and often required by their funders to innovate (e.g. by trust grants) can exhibit the opposite characteristics, i.e. innovating for the sake of it and dropping the new product the minute the (three-year) grant ends. Nevertheless the growth of contractually funded services (government as purchaser and charity as provider) may make the commercial comparison more apposite. Competitive bidding between charities with the cheapest quote winning may encourage a climate where genuine innovation is forced out by the requirement from the purchaser for the successful bid to be cost-effective, recognisable and low risk, i.e. 'more of the same'.

Cutting out services can be even more rough and ready, verging on the amateurish. It is not uncommon for a service area of a charity to be effectively in terminal decline but largely ignored by charity decision-makers until the service becomes 'critical'. This criticality can be triggered by an overall financial crisis in the charity which engenders analysis of major subsidy areas, and the realisation that the subsidy per client in service A has become untenable. Another way in which a service area can become critical is when a major funder decides either to withdraw funding completely or cut it back to levels where charity subsidisation appears unreasonable. A subsequent decision to close a service often then gets made hastily, almost under panic conditions, with a lot of blame being spread around. Also unexpected opposition to closure can be engendered.

An example, rather better thought out than the one outlined above, occurred in relation to residential homes provided by RNIB. RNIB's needs research revealed that the vast majority of older blind people were in ordinary residential homes. Market analysis showed that RNIB's four residential homes occupied less than 5 per cent of the charity market of specialised residential homes for older blind people. In addition, they were heavily loss-making with high subsidies per older person accommodated. This led to the proper question of 'why are we providing this service?' As a major provider of nationwide services, it was decided that there was no justification for such a small contribution to need in this area, as it was limited to four fairly narrow geographic locations and provided for only 140 blind people out of 150,000 blind and partially sighted people in other homes. Closure plans were developed. However, this triggered an unexpected and vigorous campaign in the four localities against closure, led by relatives and engendering the support of local political and social services leaders. sound argument and thinly veiled threats to develop a fairly n publicity campaign (one of the relatives was a senior executive PR agency!) persuaded RNIB to review the plans. The organisa been thinking of providing a national advisory service to integrated resi- dential homes (where approximately 150,000 blind and partially sighted older people live with their sighted counterparts) to advise on the special needs arising from visual impairment. Second, two of the homes had developed special expertise in accommodating deaf-blind older people. Third, the Housing Corporation proved very sympathetic to requests for substantial investment of capital improvement monies; and fourth, a Department of Health inspection had made a number of recommendations for improvement which RNIB felt could be made. Consequently these four homes are now being upgraded, as centres of excellence and as 'shop windows' for an RNIB national advisory service to mainstream residential homes on the care of blind and partially sighted residents, especially those very many who also have hearing impairments. Because physical and service facilities have been improved it has been possible to raise fees and occupancy, and subsidy has been dramatically reduced.

In short, while the outcome was unexpected, this process showed the stages of idea generation, service and business analysis, proposal (to close), public announcement and consultation, review of decision, reformulation, testing, and final and full planning. The difficulties of such an analytical approach, especially in a service as opposed to a physical product, are clear. The temptation is to make a snap decision ('we cannot keep shilly-shallying around') which avoids a lot of investment of staff time in the analysis of options. But the snap decision may not be in the best interests of the broader client group, let alone the narrower one directly affected.

Price – overt and hidden

The list of price elements (Doyle 1991, p. 275) is price, discount, allowances and credit. Even Booms and Bitner's list (1981, pp. 47–51) does not look much more encouraging for the charity service manager, namely level, discounts, payment terms, customers' perceived value, quality/price and differentiation. However, charity service managers are learning fast. The swing away from grant aiding and simple fees paid to charities, towards charities having to tender competitively against commercial companies as well as charities, has made the 'P' of price a major point of the charity service marketing mix.

Size and structure

Fees and charges (largely for services) are enormously important to char- ities, eclipsing even donations as a source of income. Posnett (1992, p. 12) reports that in 1990 fees and charges gave charities 54 per cent of their total income in comparison to only 20 per cent coming from donations. Table 4.3 in Chapter 4 showed the ONS study estimates (Hems and Passey 1996) which are lower. However, even ONS show fees and sales contributing 33 per cent of general charity income. The main purchasers are statutory bodies such as central and local government, the NHS or the Benefits Agency (either directly or indirectly). In certain circumstances, individuals will be charged, almost always at heavily subsidised rates (e.g. holidays, technical aids, gardening, etc.). Some of the fees will surprise the casual reader, e.g. £35,000 paid by a local education authority for a 32-week residential school year for a multi-handicapped student (e.g. someone with severe learning difficulties, severe sensory impairment, unable to walk and doubly incontinent). On top of this fee the charity might well be adding in a further £5,000–£10,000 charitable monies to top up to the full cost. At the other extreme, a charity might charge a nominal amount of 5p for pamphlets in order, simply, to control unusable over-ordering by local groups.

Gabor (1980, pp. 168–76) and Cowell (1984, p. 147) argue that the pricing of commercial services has received too little attention. Gabor divides pricing into either 'cost-based pricing' or 'market-orientated pricing'. In cost-based pricing, services will be either profit orientated or government controlled. In market-orientated pricing, services will be either competitive (the going rate) and/or customer orientated (set with regard to consumers' attitudes and behaviour).

Except in the minority of cases, none of these categories fit usual practice in the charity sector where the most common pricing policy is last year's price plus inflation. Because services, by definition, have a cost structure where salaries and wages form the largest component, this formula was a recipe for near disaster for several charities in the 1970s and early 1980s when wages rose faster than inflation.

The resulting growing subsidy of many charity services during the 1970s and 1980s combined with the recession of the early 1990s has led a significant number of charities to review their pricing policies, especially where statutory bodies are paying. In short, this has meant putting the prices up by as much as the market will stand where there is a multiple purchaser base (e.g. national services paid for by local government social services departments, education authorities, area health authorities, etc.). This policy has been remarkably effective where the local purchaser can see no obviously cheaper method of provision. However, increasing central government funding restraint of locally delivered statutory services has introduced a predictable but unhappy consequence. It is now more usual that, if charities raise the price of services higher than inflation, the local statutory purchaser will pay but will reduce the number of individuals for whom they are prepared to pay in order to stay within a cash-limited local budget. Some central government purchasers such as the Department for

Education and Employment have been operating harsher cash-limited purchasing budgets for almost a decade (Bruce 1991). So attempts by charity services to reduce subsidy levels are meeting problems.

Price and statutory purchasers

The policy that most charities would like to adopt is a fee of 'cost minus X per cent' where X is the percentage subsidy that the charity can afford/judges right from its charitable donations. In practice this policy is constrained by what (in the main) statutory purchasers will pay, and what sister charities with similar services are charging. In short, the most common policy is 'cost minus charity subsidy with a market eye on what other producers are charging', i.e. three of the four methods quoted by Gabor (1980) above.

Particularly critical in charity service pricing is whether there are multiple purchasers or a single purchaser. Single purchasers (e.g. the Department of Education and Employment nationally, or a local authority to a local charity) are not dissimilar in their purchasing behaviour to Marks & Spencer with its suppliers – i.e. tough verging on unreasonable! Traditionally in these situations there have been detailed discussions between the statutory purchaser and the charity provider, with the provider declaring a detailed breakdown of costs for authorisation/clearance by the unitary purchaser.

However, we are seeing a changing trend which looks set to continue. This trend is being caused and encouraged by significant shifts towards competitive tendering. Charity service providers are finding competitive tendering very difficult for a number of reasons. First, it forces them into a much more competitive stance with sister charity service providers with whom they have been trying over the years to cooperate. Second, there are widely varying charity subsidies being put into bids which may or may not be declared to the purchaser. Third, as is not uncommon in the commercial service world, it is hard to cost individual units of service accurately – and given that purchasers are strongly pushed towards accepting the lowest bids, incompetent bid construction by charities could very badly affect the charity services market over the next few years. Fourth, there is an unclear interaction between lower priced bids and whether or not these are attempts to build volume savings.

While much of the charity service pricing is amateurish, thoughtful discounts and/or innovative sales promotion techniques do exist. As with, say, contract catering in the commercial world, loss-leader contracts are entered into by some charities at national and local level, in the hope that price reviews (i.e. rises) will be in both purchaser and provider interests after a set period. An example would be a local charity setting up a voluntary visiting scheme for local older people at a loss-making rate, but with a realistic price review built in after two years. It is unlikely that the local authority is going to want the major upheaval of re-letting the contract to another organisation, therefore the charity assumes/hopes that a more realistic price will be negotiated at the two-year break point.

One the most creative discount/loss-leader schemes is undertaken by Cancer Relief Macmillan where the charity provides, free to the NHS, nurses who are specialists in cancer treatment, but only for three years. At the end of that time, by previous agreement the NHS takes over the cost of the post.

Price and beneficiaries

So far the discussion of service price has concentrated primarily on situations where a statutory body or some other third party is paying for a service to a beneficiary. This is the source of the majority of charity service income. However, there are two situations in which beneficiaries can be said to be paying. The first is in the non-monetary *impact price* (see Chapter 3) which the beneficiary pays regardless of whether a third party pays the cash price. The second is those relatively few situations where the beneficiary also pays the cash price.

The non-monetary impact price can on occasions be critical. For example, certain forms of rehabilitation may require a child or adult to go to a residential centre away from home. Even though a statutory body may be prepared to pay the fees, the impact price may be too high for the child, adult or their family. In Kotler and Andreasen's terms (1991, p. 477) the psychological costs and the costs of dislocation of social arrangements may be too high in relation to the potential beneficiary's perception of the benefits they will get from the rehabilitation. Therefore the charity has to try all avenues to *reduce the impact price* through arranging transport home at weekends, having accommodation available for the family to visit at weekends, arranging part of the rehabilitation course at the beneficiary's home, etc. Another complementary approach is to increase the *perceived value* of the rehabilitation course to the beneficiary and their family so that the impact price becomes worth paying. Ways of doing this might be offering the potential beneficiary and the family a trial weekend to meet the staff and other previous beneficiaries who will have greatly benefited from the course.

Cash payments by individual beneficiaries are often a very small part of the charity service income. This is partly pragmatic and partly philosophical. Pragmatically, fees for services are usually high in relation to individual means. Philosophically, charging (high) fees to individuals goes against the charitable ethos. However, there are exceptions and there are some signs that things are changing. For example, it has been common for social services departments to charge clients some or all of the costs of local authority home care. As the home care service becomes, to a greater or lesser extent, contracted out, charity bid winners will almost certainly have to charge clients also. Instances where service charges to beneficiaries might be made are where the service is relatively low cost and/or the service activity is something the beneficiary might have expected to pay for, e.g. a holiday. However, almost without exception the service price will be subsidised by charity voluntary income and/or will provide benefits not available on the commercial market, e.g. the Age Concern Insurance Service quoted in Chapter 6.

Variable discounts are in operation in some charity services depending on who is paying. There may be one rate if a statutory authority is paying and a lower rate if the individual or family is paying. However, this variable discount system is open to abuse in that some local authorities in particular will develop complicated systems of grant, aiding individuals to take out individual purchases at the lower rate. This has led some charities to withdraw these variable discounts because of what it believes is the unfair dealing by some local authorities. Variable discounts are common among arts charities and relate to the status of the customer (student, unemployed, retired), to the volume of purchase and to the popularity of the timing of the performance.

Conclusion

Service pricing in the commercial world is underdeveloped, and is in an even more embryonic state in the charity services sector. This is changing rapidly as charitable income has been squeezed by the recession, statutory service fee income has been similarly squeezed, and competitive unit-price tendering has been introduced increasingly by central and local government. In the commercial world, losing a customer to a competitor is, at its worst, a loss of market share and potential profit. The moral tensions of losing a potential charity service beneficiary because of too high a price are significant. Charity services managers feel moral and personal tension when pricing policies result in them losing beneficiary 'custom'. This is because customers of charity services are not often lost to a comparable 'competitor': instead, although the need of the beneficiary has been established, rejection on the basis of price results in no service being provided or, at best, a substandard alternative service being taken up (e.g. a home care two hours a week for a 90-year-old housebound person as compared to a residential home place). Charity service pricing has moral and practical implications that are seldom, if ever, found in the commercial service world.

Promotion – getting through

The commercial subheadings of promotion, namely *advertising*, *public relations*, *personal selling* and *sales promotion* and *publicity* all make immediate sense in the charity services market-place even if the words and concepts are not always attractive to professional service providers such as teachers, social workers, health workers, etc. However, *word-of-mouth recommendation* and *professional referral* assume far greater importance and acceptability in the promotion charity services in the same way that they do in the promotion of commercial professional services (as opposed to non-professional services).

Advertising is important, especially against a background of difficult market conditions described in the previous section and generally low penetration levels of charity services into their target markets. Advertising to end beneficiaries is sometimes problematic (e.g. advertising aimed at blind people, deaf people, non-English-speaking ethnic minorities, homeless people, etc.). Often the advertising is aimed at intermediaries or is via unusual channels (e.g. tape-recorded newspapers, soup runs, newsletters to massage parlour owners, etc.); nevertheless with these exceptions advertising is similar to the commercial world.

Public relations and associated *publicity*, however, is massively more important in the charity services field. First, charities seldom have the money for large effective advertising campaigns, so public relations is much more attractive. Second, they have a product which is far more likely to get onto the editorial pages. Third, charities have developed a professionalism in this area which probably outdoes their commercial counterparts. While it is infrequent, it is not unusual for charity services to feature on prime-time television news (e.g. overseas aid programmes, Braille services, services for homeless people just arrived in London, etc.).

Personal selling sometimes to beneficiary customers, or more likely to intermediary beneficiary customers, has become much more unusual since contracts have become more common. Many voluntary organisation personnel feel uncomfortable about 'selling' their services but two reasons should encourage them, one altruistic and one self-interested. Statutory services purchasers have too little money to purchase all the required services. If you do not sell-in your services, on too many occasions no services will be purchased at all and the end beneficiary will be the loser, receiving no services. More self-interestedly if you do not sell-in your service there will be less service income and the service unit that much less viable.

Evans and Schultz (1996) in the USA found four factors that are regarded as crucial by the purchasers: reliability; effective communication; good follow-up; and help with specification construction.

Cowell (1984, pp. 176–7) quotes seven guidelines for the *personal selling* of a service (based upon George, Kelly and Marshall 1983). The guidelines were derived from empirical data looking at the differences between selling goods and services. They provide an extremely useful checklist of the factors that are likely to be in the services purchasers' mind when they are considering whether or not to take up the service, adapting them for charity service:

1. Orchestrate the service purchase encounter. This needs to pay particular attention to the purchaser's needs and expectations; the service representative needs to put across technical expertise and represent the service.
2. Facilitate quality assessment. The representative needs to establish with the purchaser what might be reasonable levels of expected performance so that the purchaser can subsequently judge quality after the service has been used.
3. Make the service tangible. Here the representative 'educates' the purchaser as to the things that they should be looking out for generally in the service field, comparing alternative services, but particularly emphasising the strengths and uniqueness of their own service.
4. Emphasise organisational image. Here the service representative needs first to assess the beneficiary's understanding and appreciation of the charity in general and, while taking account of this, to present the positive realities of the charity and its general benefits.
5. Utilise references external to the organisation. Here the charity tries to encourage satisfied previous users to promote the service.
6. Recognise the importance of all public contact personnel in the service. Given that production/delivery of the service is simultaneous to its consumption, it is important to sensitise and train all personnel in their direct role in contact with customers; and it is also important to minimise the total number of people interacting with each customer.
7. Recognise the customer's involvement during the service design process to generate customer specifications by asking questions, showing examples, etc. Unlike a physical product, the beneficiary can have an impact on the detail of the service provided which will not only make for a better service, it will also increase beneficiary commitment.

Where high fees are involved for a charity service (e.g. schools, colleges, residential homes, employment rehabilitation centres) it can be particularly effective to encourage the end beneficiary (disabled person, frail person, homeless person, etc.) and/or the intermediary purchaser (local education authority adviser, Department of Employment official, housing benefits manager, etc.) to visit the physical location of the service and so I would add an eighth guideline:

8. Where high-value/high-volume purchasers of service are involved, encourage the person to visit the service location.

Professional referral as a means of promotion is critically important to most charity services. Unlike the world of commercial services where brokers expect commission, statutory service professionals and charity professionals (even from 'competing' charities) regard it as an ethical requirement to refer clients on to the most appropriate service source. This includes charity services. This puts a premium on promotional work by charity services to such intermediary professionals as doctors, other health workers, social workers, educationists, police, embassy officials, newspaper critics, etc. However, charity services managers, as opposed to the charity PRO, are often (but not always) reticent to push their services to these intermediary groups. It is almost felt to be improper or unprofessional. These attitudes need to be talked through against a background of low charity service penetration and the prospect of charity service closure as a consequence of falling numbers of beneficiaries.

As with commercial services and products, beneficiary *word-of-mouth* recommendation is a very important method of charity service promotion. While this method cannot work among socially isolated individuals or permanently institutionalised groups, it is effective in many settings. Among relatively numerous beneficiary groups such as old people, hearing-impaired people, homeless people, etc., peer group interaction is very significant – more colloquially, the grapevine is very active.

Place – how beneficiaries participate

Issues such as where the service is located, how accessible it is, how it is distributed to the beneficiaries and how widespread its coverage is, are all crucial to effective charity service delivery. For example, as social policy has changed and residential provision in a whole range of service areas has given way to day provision, physical location has become paramount. Residential services in out-of-the-way places have closed in favour of day services in high population areas and near motorways and railway stations. Location within communities rather than out in the country is more attractive because of the element of normality. Accessibility for wheelchair users, sensorily impaired people, etc., and those from ethnic minorities is now a virtual requirement if statutory contracts are to be achieved. Unhelpful geographic location can be mitigated, for example, by providing transportation services to and from a client's local area.

The geographic distribution coverage of a service has a very real impact, but one which is often underestimated by charity service managers. Most services have a heavy geographic bias, e.g. national services based in London have disproportionate numbers of beneficiaries in the South East. National schools in Leeds have disproportionate numbers of students from the North. Even services in local communities can be geographically circumscribed either by the presence of community boundaries or main roads, or simply by walking distance.

Distribution channels for charity services can throw up surprises. A combination of the Freepost facility which is available for blind people and the fact that the majority of blind people are old and housebound means that the postal service is an ideal distribution channel for libraries for blind people, rather than the local library. Turning to franchising as distribution the voluntary sector has been effectively using this distribution method for 50 years or more. The majority of local charitable groups are independent charities even though they may be fully integrated into a network such as Age Concern, MIND, MENCAP, etc. Services from these national charities are distributed via these independent local groups which undertake to deliver services to a certain standard and be subject to (informal) inspection. That there is such effective cooperation between independent local groups and the national charitable body suggests that the commercial world, becoming increasingly interested in franchising and devolution, has quite a bit to learn from its charitable service counterpart.

If the voluntary sector has been leading (but it is arguably now behind) the commercial world on franchising, it also has some track record in a commercial growth area of distribution which Cowell (1984, p. 189) calls, in the commercial world, 'service integration'. This is where a charity does not simply provide one service, but services that relate to each other. Berry and Parasuraman (1991, pp. 137–41) argue that successful commercial service organisations run a range of services and, using positive customer experience of one service, cross-sell to another. Larger service-giving charities certainly do this, although sometimes unconsciously rather than by design. SCOPE will refer clients, say, from their social services on to the employment rehabilitation arm. However, there is an important distinction between the commercial and charity experience. In the commercial instance, the more referrals made, the more advantageous financially it is for the company. In the latter case, the more cross-referral of clients from one service to others in the charity, normally the greater the loss! Given the overall shortage of charitable donations to make up the shortfall, this is a significant inhibition to cross-referral, especially as fee income often comes tied to the first service and either cannot or is insufficient to be shared with the second charity service. To take account of this, charity service referrals can, on occasion, require reference back to the original (say) local authority referring professional, or the Department of Education and Employment referral agent, in order that fees can be agreed for the additional and separate service provision.

People in service delivery

This is the first of the three elements (people, physical evidence and promotion) that Booms and Bitner (1981, pp. 47–51) (see pp. 48–51 and 77–79) argue need to be added to the traditional marketing mix to make it relevant to services.

Staff and volunteers

Recruitment, selection, training and support of staff and volunteers are crucial in delivering a charity service of quality. While a charity manufacturer of goods also wants good staff, in the event of poor work, quality control should identify a poor product *before* it reaches the beneficiary. In services, especially charity services, where there is a high interaction of staff and customers, one has to get it right first time because the product is the service and poor quality impacts immediately on the beneficiary. So commitment to quality and to beneficiaries is essential in charities.

The section on services above (pp. 55–57) defines what beneficiaries are looking for in judging quality, namely reliability, responsiveness, assurance, empathy and tangible evidence of effectiveness (Berry and Parasuraman 1991, pp. 15–21). This list makes it immediately apparent that the role of staff in contact with beneficiaries is crucial. If they are not delivering all of these attributes, the service will not be excellent.

Because conventional quality control in a (charity) service only picks up problems *after* they have impacted on a beneficiary, effective quality control and a commitment to a marketing approach has to be embedded in the service personnel themselves. Expectations need to be set high because operational staff *are* the quality control.

If things do go wrong, speedy rectification is essential; once again this comes back to operational service staff and their immediate managers who need to have sufficient delegated authority to put things right. If rectification is not speedy, the whole customer service experience will be over (and ruined) before matters are put right (e.g. changing the seat of someone who cannot see the stage, or changing a person's tutorial group when the rehabilitee is unhappy).

Other customers

In a charity service, especially to beneficiaries, customer-to-customer interaction is a crucial element of the marketing mix which has to be handled with care and sensitivity. There is something distasteful and unethical about 'managing beneficiary interaction', especially where they are adults. But the adage that 'one person's freedom is another person's prison' applies. If the attitudes and behaviour of one or more beneficiaries upsets or, even worse, destroys the confidence of another, then the service experience and the service quality for the latter will be poor. The boundary between legitimate intervention with a beneficiary group and interference with a beneficiary's independence is a fine one. Successful charity services require staff who are well trained, professional and sensitive. Beneficiaries need processes of appeal, in some cases with the help of advocates, for those instances where they feel that staff or volunteer actions were unreasonable.

Putting the customer-to-customer interaction into a positive mode, there is no doubt that successful peer group interaction among beneficiaries adds to service quality. Careful segmentation of the beneficiary target market helps by bringing together people who are likely to have more similarities than differences. Then sensitive service personnel, subscribing to the philosophy of the charity, can encourage a setting of personal development where beneficiary peer group support can improve the beneficial impacts enormously.

Physical evidence – making the service tangible

Charity services are less tangible than physical goods such as technical aids. While the potential beneficiaries may not be paying for the service, or at least not paying the full cost, they may still have reservations about taking up the service. They may take a lot of information about the offering on trust, but still not be reassured enough to sign up, simply because the service is in the future and is intangible; they may feel nervous about being trapped into a process that they think they may not like; they may not be convinced that the benefits will outweigh inconveniences.

Commercial services marketing has found that physical evidence experienced beforehand can encourage people to take up a service. In our field, some charities offer the opportunity to sample a service (especially where significant beneficiary commitment is involved, such as being residential, significant travel or long course commitment) prior to the beneficiary taking advantage of it; for example, residential homes will encourage potential residents to stay for a week, schools will invite young people and parents to look around the building and meet staff, or rehabilitation staff will have open days attended by previous rehabilitees who have gained from the experience and attest to this.

In these settings the physical environment of the service and its ambience are vital. Are facilities clean and tidy? Are they well equipped? Are they well furnished? There is some evidence from the commercial sector (Sewell and Brown 1990, p. 122) that staff confidence in their service, which they will ideally exude to potential beneficiaries, is enhanced by good physical settings for beneficiaries.

Processes which impact on the customer

There is an argument for saying that in many charity services, such as schools, theatres, holiday schemes and group work, the process is all. How well people are educated, entertained or empowered is crucial. Many of these activities are really part of the service product (see pp. 136–141).

But particularly vital is customer involvement. There is the well-known dictum in education of the importance of being 'active in your own learning' to be successful. This is true of charity services aimed at beneficiaries. Any service that metaphorically pours its service down the throats of clients or other beneficiaries is doomed. Constructing service processes that give beneficiaries the opportunity to influence service delivery will not only be more likely to enthuse them, but it will also give higher quality interaction and benefit.

Philosophy matters most

In charity services marketing this eighth 'P' is the beginning and the end of the mix. The section on pp. 51–54 looks at this in more detail. It is likely and logical that the starting point of philosophy will be the same for each service that a charity runs, to ensure a consistent and cumulative approach. The philosophy to be adopted will depend on the current era (compare Victorian charity values with today's), who runs the organisation (both volunteer and paid leaders), the extent to which beneficiaries are part of this leadership, the area of charity activity, and so on. But what is certain is that without an explicit philosophical position for the charity as a whole, and hence for each service, things will become muddled and contradictory. If independence of beneficiaries is explicit, even nursing homes for disabled 90-year-olds will create choices for residents. If empowerment is part of the philosophy, then carers in a school for multi-handicapped youngsters will sit patiently while a pupil with cerebral palsy, severe learning difficulties and poor hand/eye coordination spends one hour feeding themselves.

However, the complexities of achieving consistent translation of philosophy into practice are considerable. The British Parachute Association is, rightly, totally committed to safety. Yet the journal of the association, as with many voluntary organisations, has a quasi-independence and has the usual disclaimer 'the views expressed in *Sport Parachutist* ... are not necessarily those of the BPA'. Its December 1993/January 1994 issue printed a picture showing a skydiver in mid-air drinking from a can, with the headline 'Yorkshire Bitter can seriously improve your skydiving' and the caption 'Tandem master enjoys a swig' (Pentreath 1994, p. 9)! A stark example of contradictory safety philosophies.

Charities such as Shelter, British Red Cross, Friends of the Earth, Save the Children, Birmingham Royal Ballet, Christian Aid, Barnardo's and others have developed clear philosophies which are transferred more or less explicitly into their services. A marketing approach in a charity requires this if potential charity beneficiaries or their advocates are to be able to choose a service and have their expectations met.

Conclusion

Voluntary organisation services currently provide around 3 per cent of the United Kingdom's gross domestic product, and that excludes the contribution of volunteers. With the shift in the welfare state responsibility from provider to purchaser, the role of charity services is growing. Given charities' poor record of reaching only a small proportion of their potential beneficiaries, charity services need to adopt a marketing philosophy and practice with increasing rapidity if they are not to fail potential and actual beneficiaries.

The language of commercial services marketing is not attractive in the charity sector but many of the ideas and practices, suitably adapted, work much better than might at first be thought. However, certain important differences between charity and commercial services (e.g. permanent commitment to a particular customer group regardless of loss, the impossibility of hostile takeovers, the legal commitment to the objectives of their cause, etc.) require commercial marketing concepts and practices to be adapted. This need for adaption provides particularly interesting challenges to marketers, whatever their background.

Key points

Positioning
☐ Distinguish between direct and indirect services and identify the relationship between them so that the service can be positioned effectively in the market.
☐ Understand your position in the market in relation to other players providing similar services.
☐ A programme of needs (marketing) research can be invaluable in terms of ensuring that service provision keeps up with demand and adapts as needs change.

Product
☐ Examine the quality, features, name, reputation and guarantees of the service being provided and monitor it regularly.
☐ Think from the service customer's point of view. Is the service reliable and responsive; does it have empathy?
☐ Avoid rushing into decisions to add to or close a product.

Price
☐ Service income has been squeezed by the recession, and by competitive unit-cost tendering imposed by central and local government.
☐ Charities need to be able to respond to this by understanding clearly the cost of the services they provide and structuring their bids accordingly, for example discount/loss-leader schemes.

☐ If the perceived value of a service can be improved, it may be possible to alleviate the impact price to the customer.

☐ When pricing policies result in a charity losing beneficiary 'custom' the moral, personal and practical implications are far more significant than in the commercial world.

Promotion

☐ While public relations and publicity are vitally important as means of promotion, personal selling can be highly effective. Use Cowell's seven guidelines which focus on the potential purchasers' point of view.

☐ Professional referral is critically important, so effective promotional work to intermediary professionals such as doctors, social workers, newspaper critics, police, etc., is essential.

People

☐ Encourage staff and volunteers to 'get it right first time' and give them the authority to rectify the situation if it is not.

☐ By targeting sensitively, make sure that interaction and relationships between beneficiaries and between beneficiaries and staff is positive. Provide mechanisms for appeal.

Physical evidence

☐ Offer beneficiaries the opportunity to sample a service before taking it up.

☐ Make sure that the physical environment and its ambience are appropriate.

Philosophy

☐ Ensure that the philosophy of the service is consistent with that of the charity.

8

PRESSURE GROUP ACTIVITY

As we saw in Chapter 4, product is a marketing term to describe physical goods, services and ideas. Commercial companies are seldom in the business of marketing ideas (e.g. patents), but voluntary organisations market ideas very frequently either in their pressure group and campaigning work or through fund-raising. In this chapter we look at pressure group activity and campaigning.

Background

In my experience charities go about their pressure group work very differently to commercial interests, and fairly differently to powerful interest groups such as doctors and lawyers. In essence it is because charities (and most voluntary organisations for that matter) are not seen as sufficiently powerful or cohesive to be brought into the early stages of local or central government decision-making. It might surprise many people to learn that the gross domestic product of the voluntary sector is larger than that of the car industry: but voluntary sector interests span literally hundreds of disparate causes, compared to the interests of motor manufacturers which arguably span one, or only a few at most.

As charities are not automatically brought into the early stages, they tend to use the media earlier and more frequently to try to inflate their perceived importance in a decision-making process. By doing so they try to create a climate where decision-makers will judge it wise to do some 'cooption' work, e.g. agreeing to meet and discuss points of concern to defuse and dilute opposition and to provide opportunities for cooperation, agreement and compromise.

So for reasons of lack of power and cohesion, charity pressure groups tend to be more public than their more powerful commercial counterparts.

This widespread public face of charity pressure group activity is a fairly recent phenomenon which began in the late 1960s and early 1970s. Indeed a number of dramatic things were beginning to happen in charities during that period. They were maturing as policy-proposing organisations that wanted to press their case. They were gaining new confidence in a putative pressure group role, even if the post-war consensus on the role of welfare state services had downgraded the charity service-giving role. But their access to, and influence on, government was very restricted (Field 1982) and did not compare with the power of the industrial lobbies (Miller 1991, p. 49). Increasingly charities realised, through research or direct experience, that welfare state services in their broadest guises were not reaching the ideals set for them, and felt powerless to intervene effectively. But the tinder-like atmosphere in which pressure groups operated was warming up. In particular, government was becoming more consultative during the late 1960s and early 1970s (Miller 1991, p. 50). Then came the launch of Shelter as a charity, which was the spark that lit the pressure group fire. While other voluntary organisations either worked quietly as pressure groups (e.g. Child Poverty Action Group and the then National Council for Civil Liberties, now Liberty) or noisily to the same end (the Campaign for Nuclear Disarmament), Des Wilson and Shelter, launched via the television film 'Cathy Come Home', rewrote the rules of charity pressure group activity. Just three years later David Hobman woke the sleeping giant of the National Old People's Welfare Council and turned it into Age Concern; David Ennals did the same with the National Association of Mental Health, transforming it into MIND. In 1971 Sir Keith Joseph, then Secretary of State at the Department of Health and Social Security, acknowledged charities' legitimate pressure group role by saying 'constructive criticism must always be welcome by the government. Strident or shrill criticism should not be necessary unless the government refuses to enter into a dialogue ... I welcome guidance and constructive, widespread criticism' (Joseph 1971, p. 2).

And so the 1970s became a decade of vigorous pressure group activity which was modified by the new climate of the 1980s. Narrow parliamentary majorities of the second half of the 1970s, which inflated the importance of backbench and charity influence, gave way to massive government majorities and so put the focus back on civil servants and ministers. The radical reappraisal in the 1980s of government policies in almost every area, gave significant opportunities for charity pressure groups to bring their influence to bear. However, radical policy reviews combined with an overall requirement to cut public expenditure produced a heady cocktail which some charities were very nervous of drinking. There was at least one occasion when disability charities actually refused the offer of a ministerial meeting, so concerned were they that their views might fuel what was seen as certain regressive policy developments.

After the 1992 election charity pressure groups were having to live even more dangerously. Both the major parties were worried about the extent of public expenditure. Radical new policies which were only on the drawing board in the 1980s were being implemented, in particular community care, education reform, NHS reform, the remaining public utility privatisation and significant deregulation. These reforms were being implemented at a time of massively increased public expenditure deficit. This meant that the charity pressure group positions were largely defensive, trying to protect the gains of earlier years from cuts and reorganisations, and only seeking gains at the margin of change. As one cause or client group gained, another lost.

The position on the resource front did not change with the election of a Labour government in 1997 and so gains to one group still nearly always resulted in losses to others. The increased emphasis on 'community' and stakeholders is giving many charities, especially social welfare ones, a creative backcloth to policy development and proposal but the more 'radical' the government manages to be, the more charity pressure groups have to ride a policy roller-coaster. As far as methods and target groups are concerned the large Labour parliamentary majority swept away much of the power of backbenchers, so useful when majorities were slim. As in the 1980s, ministers, their advisers and civil servants once gain has become the key focus of attention.

So, all the generally accepted conditions for successful pressure group activity (Coxall 1985, p. 142) remain in place. For pressure groups there is the opportunity for the following:

☐ valuable advance information;
☐ the chance to influence policies.

For government there is the opportunity for the following:

☐ advice and information;
☐ gaining acquiescence in, or even assent to, their proposals;
☐ and, quite often, gaining assistance with the administration of policies.

Pressure group campaigns: case studies

Adapting Ansoff (1965, p. 109) there are four kinds of pressure group campaigns that can be waged:

1. Defending established gains to existing groups.
2. Promoting existing gains to new groups.
3. Promoting new gains to existing groups.
4. Promoting new gains to new groups.

At times of recession and/or government determination to cut public expenditure, there will be heavy emphasis on type 1 campaigns. Insofar as campaigns on 2, 3 and 4 are waged to the point of implementation, there is a high risk that this will set off a process whereby other gains are eroded to provide substitutional budget. Therefore in times of recession and/or government expenditure cuts, campaign types 2, 3 and 4 need to be undertaken cautiously and are most likely to be used as further defensive outposts to type 1, or as a ground-breaking exercise to establish fertile soil to grow the campaigns effectively when a more propitious public expenditure climate returns.

In times of plenty, but with a cautious government, campaign type 2 is more likely to be successful. In times of plenty, but with adventurous government policy-making, types 3 and 4 are particularly attractive.

The typology laid out above, is just that – a typology. In other words, pressure group campaigns do not always fit neatly into one type, but most do. In the examples that follow, the Articles for the Blind campaign and the free eye test campaign are both type 1, i.e. defensive; the attendance allowance extension campaign is type 2; the disability income cost allowance campaign is type 3; and the campaign for lead-free petrol (CLEAR) is type 4. Examples give a first-hand feel as to how pressure group campaigns actually run in practice and they provide exemplars to which I will refer in the following sections of this chapter. With the exception of CLEAR, they are all ones in which I have been involved. This gives the advantage of intimate knowledge but the disadvantage of involvement, and thus I have tried to guard against subjectivity. They all started under Conservative governments but three continue under Labour. While the policy context is now different the processes and techniques remain the same.

Freepost for blind people (Articles for the Blind)

This 1992/3 campaign was to preserve a long-established concession which allows post and parcels of Braille, tape and technical aids to go to and from blind people free by first-class post. In 1992/3 prices it was estimated to be worth in excess of £30 million; and to RNIB alone, it was worth £3 million per annum, i.e. the cost of sending over three million talking books to blind people each year, let alone the £3 million it would cost them to return the tapes.

So why did RNIB feel that the concession was under threat? At the time of the campaign there had been several ministerial statements to the effect that they wished the Post Office to be privatised. While at that stage no decisions had been made, government policy on privatisation and its lack of cash meant that the privatisation proposal was a distinct possibility. RNIB reasoned, partly on the basis of the erosion of concessions to British Rail on the build-up to proposed privatisation, that freepost concessions under a privatised Post Office would not be inviolate. These worries were taken quietly to the relevant civil servants at the Department of Trade and Industry (DTI) and talked through. In essence, they said that there was nothing to worry about because the long-established concessions would be passed on to any private contractors as a requirement. On enquiring how this requirement could be guaranteed, the answers became less precise, but seemed to be limited to civil service contract drafting, or ministerial regulation at most. RNIB asked civil service colleagues for the requirement to be put into primary legislation, but they said that this was unnecessary and were not prepared to recommend this to the minister. A ministerial meeting was requested and readily offered. The presenting team consisted not only of RNIB, but of blind representatives from the National Federation of the Blind and the National League of the Blind and Disabled. The minister welcomed us but in his opening remarks said that if it was decided to privatise the Post Office, he did not see the necessity explicitly to include the freepost concession in the bill. We said we hoped to persuade him to the contrary, describing how important the concession was to individual blind people. We outlined our worries that the concession, if it was not guaranteed in primary legislation, would be eroded, if not abolished, over time because of the pressures on a privatised Post Office to make maximum profits. When we had finished presenting, the minister politely thanked us and said that he had not been convinced and, while he would do everything he could short of primary legislation, he was not prepared to include the concession on the face of any bill. We had failed.

With nothing left to lose, I decided to do something which can easily backfire, i.e. point out the consequences of continuing disagreement. We said that his initial view (i.e. not his final decision) was a pity because it was going to involve everyone around the table in a great deal of extra work and annoyance. Blind people were extremely angry about what they saw as a possible loss of the concession. We had persuaded them to hold back from launching a public campaign, and that so far we had resisted attempts to be co-opted into anti-privatisation coalitions. However, we then said that most of the extra work would be during the various stages of the bill through parliament. We quoted the experience of the recent Education Bill where only 10 per cent of the face of the bill was on special educational needs, but almost 50 per cent of the debate and amendments were on this subject because of an effective pressure group coalition, led by Paul Ennals, RNIB's Director of Education and Leisure. Where there is only a parliamentary majority of twenty or so, many concessions can be achieved on the floor of the House. For a moment, you could have heard a pin drop. Then he suddenly turned to a civil servant and asked if this description was true, which the civil servant confirmed. The reply was short and incisive: 'We can't have that.' (While the narrow majority was unusual the ability of a pressure group to get a 'disproportionate' emphasis of the debate on a relatively narrow point is a bargaining tool with House business managers, especially if backbenchers are sympathetic.) The rest of the meeting was devoted to his questioning the civil servant to see whether primary legislation guaranteeing the continuance of the concession was feasible. When he had established this, he said he would write to RNIB.

This he did, giving a ministerial undertaking to put the concession into primary legislation, should a privatisation proposal go ahead.

As our part of the bargain, we did not join any coalition against privatisation. We talked directly to all the various organisations of blind and partially sighted people and they asked their members not to mount any further campaigns on this subject.

Loss of free eye tests

Another example of a type 1 defensive campaign was the attempt to maintain free eye tests. The government in the mid-1980s was out to dilute what it saw as the opticians' excessive profits on spectacle provision. Part of the government's proposals included the abolition of the free eye test which was RNIB's main concern. Approximately 25 per cent of the eye test is looking for signs of abnormality in the eye which would indicate disease, not infrequently blinding disease. It was RNIB's belief that if charges for eye tests were introduced, fewer people would have them. Several irreversible and potentially blinding eye diseases (such as glaucoma) have no painful symptoms, therefore the individual would be largely unaware of any deterioration before significant visual impairment had set in.

There were three main allies opposing the government proposals: the Association of Optical Practitioners (AOP), i.e. the trade association; the British College of Optometrists (BCO), i.e. the professional group; and the Federation of Dispensing Opticians (FODO). RNIB had an easy and relaxed relationship with BCO but was much more cautious with AOP and FODO, being essentially trade interests.

BCO, the professional association, provided the neutral ground on which we then met for the loose coordination of campaigning activities. To give them their due, the trade associations never sought to compromise RNIB, and we were very cautious about ever quoting their statistics, although on balance they were pretty reliable.

One powerful group which did not join in the coalition was the professional grouping of opthalmologists, and in particular one of their influential leaders. This is not to say that we did not have the support of eminent individual opthalmologists. It is true that there are far too few opthalmologists in this country and some felt that if opticians 'stopped trying to pretend they were opthalmologists' by undertaking a certain amount of inspection for disease during the eye test, then their case for larger numbers would be better made. It is hardly an exaggeration to say that there had been a covert antagonism between these two professional groups for some years.

The government put forward its legislative proposal which, it argued, would not reduce the numbers of people going forward for eye tests. First, they said that charges would not deter people – which seemed a strange claim coming from a government supportive of market forces, and which gave us a fair bit of counter publicity ammunition. Second, the government said that it would introduce exemptions, although initially it seemed that these were very narrowly cast. RNIB responded by arguing that fewer people would go for tests and that eye disease would go unchecked as a result. However, our difficulty was that the majority of the general public did not realise that the eye test checked for eye disease – they simply thought that it examined whether one was becoming long or short sighted. Therefore we checked our facts carefully with sympathetic opthalmologists (as opposed to opticians or optometrists) and felt that we would be absolutely correct in the claim that fewer people going for eye tests would mean more people going blind. This provided us with much tougher news copy and we appeared on radio and television to make these statements. We then ran out of newsworthy material, but through academic contacts came across a research write-up of an experiment in a province of Canada which had introduced eye test charges. As a result, the numbers of people going for eye tests dropped dramatically. With this new research information we regained the media offensive.

Even though the government had a massive majority, the coalition worked hard on backbench Conservative MPs, arranging frequent meetings with key backbenchers, especially those on the committee stage of the bill. However, none of them voted against at that stage. As the drama reached its climax, MPs of all parties were using RNIB briefs extensively and ministers were having to respond to allegations point by point. In the final vote, the new Secretary of State, Kenneth Clarke, got the bill through by a majority of only eight. At one level that was a major achievement, considering the massive majority of the Thatcher government. However, you either win or lose in a pressure group campaign, and we lost.

Several years later a civil servant who was only indirectly involved told me how close we came to winning. They told me that the civil servants had become pretty demoralised by our successful public campaigning: 'you were always one step ahead of them'. This person went so far as to say that if Kenneth Clarke had not arrived as the new Secretary of State, the campaign would have won. Apparently he called all his civil service team in and made it clear to them that if he had initiated the bill, he would have kept eye tests free, but given that the government was now so far committed to this line of action he was damned if he was going to be beaten. Apparently this pugnacious leadership raised departmental morale and the result is history. However, I am inclined to believe that, but for his arrival, another five members would have gone into the opposition lobby!

The campaign was relaunched in 1996/7 first because the build-up to the 1997 election offered opportunities and second because it fitted in with a broader RNIB initiative to pursue one of its mission statements 'to prevent blindness'. The campaign idea product was refined to propose free eye tests for older people, among whom undetected eye diseases is most common. In March 1997 a Labour shadow health minister 'brought' this idea 'paying' for it out of the bottomless £100 million planned efficiency savings. Unfortunately the shadow Treasury opposed and the proposal from the cancer charities for increased cancer screening won through and took its chance in the post-election resource bargaining. I make no comment on the relative merits of the *service* products of eye disease screening among older people versus cancer screening among the middle-aged. But the *idea* product aimed at the politicians, of offering the hope of more screening among the electorally more volatile middle-aged was more attractive to politicians than screening for firmer-intentioned older voters.

Disability income and cost allowance

This is an example of an offensive pressure group campaign which primarily took place between 1984 and 1990, but arguably has lasted from 1970 to the present day. I shall keep this description to the six most germane years. It is an example of a type 3 campaign: new gains to existing groups.

Disabled people are among the poorest in our society. Some 70 per cent of them have to live on 75 per cent of the average wage or less. But not only are their incomes very low, they have additional costs arising from their disability: for example, medical requirements to keep the house warmer than average; significant extra transportation costs; higher laundry bills through incontinence, etc. Research which we undertook in 1987 showed that the majority of blind people were living in households where the net income was less than £70 per week and where more than half had savings of less than £500.

For around 20 years, organisations of blind people have been arguing for what they call a blindness allowance to cover the extra costs that blindness brings. In the 1970s they fought this campaign alone and were successful in getting it into the Labour Party manifesto in 1979. However, by the early 1980s other groups of disabled people had pressed their needs forward, and even the Labour Party was likely to renege on the earlier manifesto commitment. As a result RNIB, the National Federation of the Blind and the National League of the Blind and Disabled made a policy decision to drop their public claim for a blindness allowance, join more actively in a coalition of all disability organisations and support the call for what became known as a disability income and costs allowance. This would be determined on a functional rather than medical test of need and should be self-assessed by the individual disabled person.

In the disability world there are well over 250 different national and local organisations representing different groups of disabled people. There are four groups particularly concerned with disability benefits: the Royal Association of Disability and Rehabilitation (RADAR), the Disability Alliance, the Disability Income Group (DIG) and the British Council of Organis-ations of Disabled People (BCODP). However, most of these four umbrella groups are not members of the others. Thus by dint of an earlier initiative by Amanda Jordan, then of the Spastics Society, in 1984 a loose coordinating group was brought together. The goodwill that this engendered rapidly enabled us to set up a formal overall coordinating group called the Disability Benefits Consortium (DBC) which had the four aforementioned groups as primary members, and five of the major individual disability charities on the steering committee, namely RNIB, SCOPE, MENCAP, Age Concern and the RNID.

The impetus for setting this group up was the announcement by Norman Fowler, then Secretary of State at the Department of Health and Social Security, of four major benefits reviews, plus the establishment of a major research survey into the income and circumstances of disabled people. We argued, logically, that if we did not 'get our act together' it would be a case of the government dividing and ruling. Blind people's representatives had enough evidence of that from the 1970s.

The aim of the coalition was to persuade the government to institute a comprehensive disability income and cost allowance which would be based on a functional need rather than medical condition, and would be awarded on the basis of self-assessment by the disabled applicant. The coalition gave us power and cohesion – just! Keeping a coalition together of organisations representing blind people, deaf people, physically disabled people, deaf-blind people, people with learning difficulties, diabetes, cystic fibrosis, motor neurone disease, spinal injuries, etc., is extraordinarily difficult. Every organisation knows that there will not be enough new money to go around. Indeed in the end there was less money.

This kind of coalition was strong in two ways: first, on what the coalition wanted in principle, i.e. the comprehensive disability income and cost allowance (CDI); second, it could be strong in exposing the inadequacies of the existing disability benefits system. What it could not be strong on was detailed proposals for a new system with a realistic cost (as far as the government would see it). The CDI proposal was going to add between £4 billion and £5 billion to the then estimated £7 billion already being spent to help disabled people. In terms of need, that was a perfectly realistic request. In relation to a government wanting to restrain public expenditure, it was unreasonable. Matters were also made worse because of the demographic shifts going on. The majority of disabled people in this country are over retirement age, and the number of older pensioners was and still is rising rapidly. Therefore government expenditure on disability benefits had to rise rapidly in real terms just to leave an individual disabled person no worse off.

The other very difficult thing to do in pressure group work involving a disparate coalition is to think tactics through clearly. The consortium managed to identify what it wanted to challenge, namely the arbitrary and inadequate means-tested Special Additions available to (mainly) disabled people under what was then called Supplementary Benefit. In essence, people on Supplementary Benefit who had additional requirements for hearing, nutrition, laundry, etc., were eligible for, and normally given, additional payments on top of the basic Supplementary Benefit rate. The system was a complicated nightmare, had developed incrementally over the years, and was not well understood by disabled people.

With the benefit of hindsight, it turned out to be a tactical error to attack the additional payments on Supplementary Benefit. Referring to the typology above, the consortium was pressing for a new, better benefit reaching more people, and to support this it attacked the *status quo*. At a time of public expenditure shortage, this left the way open to the government of the day to give the consortium a new benefit but offer much less money than was being sought, which is what happened. In crude terms, the government swept away the anachronistic system of special additions and replaced it with what it claimed was a simpler, more comprehensive system of Additional Premiums. The Disability Alliance, which was the analytical powerhouse of the Disability Benefits Consortium, estimated that this made one million disabled people (out of six million) worse off. What was worse was that this new simplified system did not have the flexibility to give the relatively larger sums of money which very severely disabled people needed, and to an extent received, under the old Supplementary Benefit Additional Requirements system. New Labour have learnt fast!

The massive outcry and organised protest, plus the substance of the argument, persuaded the government to act in two ways. First, the minister, Nicholas Scott, proposed what he called an 'Independent Living Fund' which had a very strange legal constitution but essentially had the flexibility to pay out relatively large sums of money to very severely disabled people. The second initiative which ameliorated the situation somewhat was the offer of a new benefit, the Disability Living Allowance (DLA). The attractiveness to many groups of this new benefit was that it was to be awarded on the basis of self-assessment by the disabled person (for which the consortium was calling); it would go to groups of disabled people who had previously had relatively poor access to existing disability benefits (in particular, people with learning difficulties and people with visual impairments); and as a costs allowance it adopted the consortium's principle of being non-means-tested and non-taxable (i.e. it was money to repay disabled people for the extra costs that they have to pay out because of disability). The downside of the new benefit is that it is only available to people of working age, and the majority of disabled people are over retirement age. The primary consolation is that, if the consortium and its constituent members had not been so active, analytical and vociferous, the results of the government's review might have been very much worse.

There are four other points to be drawn from this mini case study. The first is the extent to which any government will use information tactically in public argument with a pressure group. For example, in this case study, and consistently since, the government stresses heavily the very large real increases of expenditure on disability benefits over the last ten years or so (which is true) but in such a way as to allow the general public to form the view that individual disabled people are getting a lot more money (which is untrue). The only reason for the large real increases in expenditure on disability benefits is that the economic/demographic structure of our society has changed (many more older disabled people). Individual disabled people in general are no better off.

The second point to emphasise is that timing is crucial, especially related to economic cycles. The review of Supplementary Benefit (1985/6) was under-taken not only at a time of public expenditure constraint, but also before the boom at the end of the 1980s. Government cuts were therefore inevitable and the only question was how big they would be. However, the subsequent review of disability benefits (1988/9) effectively took place in the middle of the boom and dropping public sector borrowing, and arguably this positive economic background might have persuaded the Treasury to put back into the system some of the money it had taken out during the Supplementary Benefit review decisions.

Third, well-thought-out substantial research, especially when it is the government's own, does actually have an effect and leads to better decision-making. The major government disability research undertaken by the Office of Population Censuses and Surveys during the mid-1980s was crucial to the consortium (and probably also to the Department of Social Security) in being able to hold a fairly solid defensive line against a voracious Treasury. It was also very helpful in the design of the new benefits, even if they were not sufficiently well resourced.

The fourth point to emphasise is the importance of luck – good or bad. One important aspect of the campaign over the five-year period was the active involvement of individual disabled people in writing to and lobbying their local MPs and joining in demonstrations. Our largest demonstration was a linking of arms of disabled people across Westminster Bridge and a major rally in Trafalgar Square, which was very successful. It gained a great deal of media interest, especially from TV news crews. Despite being filmed, it was not aired on either national television or radio news; also virtually no press coverage was obtained. Why? Because that was the day the Berlin Wall came down!

Campaign for lead-free petrol (CLEAR)

This campaign is an example of type 4, i.e. new gains for new beneficiaries. Like the first of these four case studies, this campaign was an unequivocal success story. There is no doubt in my mind that one of the key reasons for the success was that it was directed by Des Wilson who is an outstanding exponent of applying a marketing approach to pressure group work.

The aim of the campaign was to get all lead taken out of petrol. The reason for attempting this was that there was growing evidence that lead in petrol reduced the IQ levels of young children so exposed, and was inexorably distributing three million tons of non-degradable lead across our land each year.

As well as having Des Wilson, the campaign had over £150,000 in 1982/3 for what turned out to be a fifteen-month campaign, which was nine months in the planning.

Because the minister and his civil servants had recently made a decision to reduce lead by two-thirds on the recommendation of an expert working party, CLEAR decided that the internal corridors of power would be highly resistant to a change of tack to a complete ban. Rather, the tactic should be for a high-profile public campaign to enlist mass support from the general public. One of the many advantages of this approach was that the campaigners could promote the straightforward case on their chosen ground – in this case the health of children and long-term environmental damage. It was judged that grappling with the technical complexities of achieving lead-free petrol and a debate over costs would result in CLEAR being out-manoeuvred. It was enough to say that Japan and America were doing it. If the campaign had gone into the corridors of power, it would inevitably have had to argue in these two areas where civil servants and the various commercial interests would have been much more knowledgeable.

Another advantage of keeping the campaign relatively simple was that it enabled it to build up quite a powerful coalition in favour of banning lead even before the campaign had been launched. The launch in January 1982 was, at first sight, conventional; an exclusive to a Sunday newspaper prior to the launch on the Monday. The main features of the launch were two studies to give a news hook. The combination of careful planning, good research and good prior media hustle meant that the newspapers, television and radio turned out. However, now come the professional and technical add-ons. On the same day, copies of a specially prepared handbook and a newspaper summarising the main points of the campaign were mailed to all members of parliament and other influential organisations. Then Des and two others set off on a provincial tour, hitting Coventry, Birmingham, Manchester, Liverpool, Leeds, Newcastle, Bristol, Southampton and Cardiff in a very short space of time. These places were chosen because they had TV stations as well as local radio. This is a technique that he calls 'barnstorming', after the American methods of political campaigning.

Des Wilson (1984, pp. 54–5) describes a typical 'hit' of a city. He and two colleagues would arrive in the designated city in the afternoon, give an interview with the local morning newspaper for the next day and then an interview with the local evening newspaper for the following evening, then go in to the local radio station and record the news programme for 6 p.m. They went across to the TV studios to do a recorded interview with one of the two local stations and one or two regional stations for an insert in the 6 p.m. news, and then went off to do a live interview on the other station. At 7 p.m. they met potential leaders of local groups along with local personalities, ideally the MP and the leader of the council, and went into a public meeting which the advance guard would have organised and ensured was going to be full. A reception followed and possibly an appearance on a late evening radio chat show. The next morning, there was another local radio appearance followed by breakfast in a hotel with local leaders, perhaps a newspaper editor, leader of the council, local church leader, etc. They then went to the assembly of the most important local secondary school, followed by a special period with the sixth formers; a late morning meeting of local women's organisations followed and, with a bit of luck, a chat with the local Rotary leaders. In the hands of a skilled operator like Wilson, this barnstorming gained enough critical news mass for the news story to achieve blanket coverage and to start regenerating news. It is the equivalent of 'burst' advertising as opposed to a steady 'drip' of consecutive smaller stories and, as such, is much better at generating awareness.

It was towards the end of this tour that Wilson played what he called his 'trump card', which was a confidential letter from the Chief Medical Officer at the Department of Health and Social Security confirming that, in his view, lead should be completely banned from petrol. Now it is possible to argue that getting hold of such a letter is a matter of luck, and indeed it is. However, it is also the case that leaks only tend to go to those whom the person leaking thinks is going to (a) do something effective with the document and (b) protect the source. Nevertheless it was mainly luck. However, what cuts Wilson out as a master tactician is the fact that he did not release the letter until well into the campaign – even though it was available from day one. He knew that the campaign could easily lose momentum after the first three or four weeks.

So what did he do with the letter? For reasons I do not fully understand, he no longer had a copy of the original letter, only a typed-out version. Therefore wide distribution to newspapers and television might create a challenge to its authenticity. So he chose to leak it to *The Times* and convinced Harold Evans, the then editor, that the letter was genuine (which indeed it was). *The Times* then printed the letter in full, attributing it to CLEAR and putting it on the front page. All these were conditions that Des

Wilson laid out (and probably were only agreed to because it was one journalist speaking to another). Because it was front-page news in *The Times*, it was then picked up widely by radio and television, and within twenty-four hours the Leader of the Opposition was challenging the Prime Minister in the House on it.

News momentum was building, but how could it be kept going? Wilson then produced a Coopers & Lybrand report on lead-free petrol which Godfrey Bradman, the main funder of the campaign, had commissioned back in 1981. Because it contained conclusions damaging to the government's position, once again it got good coverage; not least because it came from such a reputable city firm.

To keep the momentum going, the campaign then felt confident enough to commission an opinion poll among the general public as to their views on the issue (remember that there had been major national publicity on three occasions over a five-week period as well as a great deal of local and regional coverage). If the results had been hopeless, they could have been ignored – but they were not. Seventy-seven per cent of the general public said that they wanted lead out of petrol even if the price went up by 'a few pence per gallon'. Once again this report provided significant coverage and, more importantly, the *Daily Telegraph* headed its story with the fact that the government was 'losing the argument'.

Des Wilson (1984, p. 167) also points to the inept response of the oil and motor industries. Carefully crafted, polite letters to the oil companies and their trade association resulted in a brush-off. This gave the campaign another powerful weapon. They could claim that they had tried to engage in a dialogue with the oil companies but the companies had refused, which left the campaign with no option but to go public. It allowed Wilson and his colleagues to paint a picture of the oil cartel being uncooperative, secretive and only interested in their own commercial profits.

Later the campaign was helped by major research studies from the United States and Italy which once again gave more media coverage. In addition, Des Wilson (1984, p. 173) reports that the Associated Octel Company, manufacturers of fuel lead additives, gave a considerable boost to the campaign by spending over £100,000 on major newspaper advertising under what he calls the 'absurd heading' of 'the health and wealth of the nation'. He argues that this was totally counterproductive because it was unbelievable and in many detailed respects inaccurate, and gave the impression that the only way the company could be heard was through buying space. This allowed him to build more newsworthiness in countercharges.

Meanwhile the campaign had commissioned two more surveys which produced damaging results for the pro-lead lobby. The first survey found significantly high levels of lead in dust outside schools all over the country. This not only achieved national publicity, but it was also obviously covered very significantly in the local press. The second survey found that 40 per cent of the land in inner London and 20 per cent in outer London was unsuitable for growing vegetables because of lead. This study also got extensive coverage.

In fact, it was of great significance that the campaign involved increasing numbers of people from the scientific establishment to support the case. Des Wilson (1984, pp. 169–70) argues that the Conservative Government and the commercial lobby could arguably have fought off the pressure group campaign if it had not had the support of the scientific establishment. Similarly, the scientific establishment could have been squashed or at least ignored if it had not been reinforced by such an active public campaign. He argues that the coalition together was unbeatable.

Two last points are worth mentioning in this brief résumé. First, the Royal Commission on Environmental Pollution had decided to study the case and had finally concluded that the campaign claims were essentially correct. Second, the publicity was beginning to so damage the government that Prime Minister Thatcher became involved. The government could do without claims that it was damaging children's health in the run-up to an election! On 18 April 1983 the Royal Commission on Environmental Pollution published its report, calling for the elimination of lead from petrol. One hour later the Secretary of State announced in parliament that the government accepted the recommendation and would press for a Europe-wide ban on lead in petrol! The previous day the *News of the World* had announced 'Premier Margaret Thatcher has decided to respond swiftly to the Royal Commission report'. I describe this because, while Wilson and his colleagues did not engineer this 'honourable' way out, it was very important in allowing a favourable final decision to be reached. Any pressure group campaigning will be more successful, more quickly, if the decision-makers who have to change their mind have an honourable and face-saving way of doing so – in this case accepting a recommendation from a Royal Commission.

Conclusion

These case studies give four very different examples of pressure group work: two were successful, two failed; one was private, three were public; two were defensive, two were seeking new gains. The following sections will examine how marketing can be applied to pressure group work and will use the case studies as exemplars.

Analysis of other players and positioning

Competitor analysis and subsequent positioning is a critical success factor in pressure group work. Unlike charity provision of physical goods and services, the charity pressure group market is very busy and highly competitive. The charity pressure groups are competing with each other and the commercial and statutory sector interests for influence. Demand massively outstrips decision-makers' ability to supply. Every disadvantaged group quite rightly wants more and better resources and services. Every environmental charity has a distinctive priority of agenda points; if there are commonalities, they are still competing for the ear, the time and the money of decision-makers. Every arts organisation needs more money. Even if the interest of the more junior official (where the work is done) can be engaged, convincing the boss that time and effort should be committed to the issue is very difficult. A fair bit of pressure group work meets the ultimate bottleneck of the parliamentary legislative programme where competition is at its most intense.

So a charity decision to press an issue needs much analysis of other players. For example, in the 1970s when organisations of blind people pressed ahead with a demand for a financial allowance to overcome the extra costs of blindness, they did not anticipate being defeated by representatives of other disabled people. But in effect this is what happened. They got a commitment in the Labour Party manifesto at one election, but lost it later because of complaints from other impairment groups. Consequently campaigns in the 1980s were repositioned to be part of cross-disability campaigns.

Many of the traditional texts on pressure groups seem to regard them as unified organisations – almost an irreducible unit of common agreement. This is far too simplistic. External observers tend to see unanimity which is in fact a tactical pretence, covering a variety of points of view. Take something as apparently narrow and simple as the campaign for financial allowance for blind people. In the early stages of this campaign the National Federation of the Blind regarded itself as the owner of the idea, and was not 100 per cent convinced that it wanted other organisations in the field of blindness being active participants in the campaign, for fear they might hijack it. The National League of the Blind and Disabled backed the campaign in the early stages from the point of view of solidarity, but was not enthusiastic because it saw the leadership in another organisation of blind people. RNIB, in the very early stages, regarded the exercise as little to do with it, and disliked the methods used to promote the idea. So if those tensions can exist within an area that many people might regard as tightly bounded, with a proposition that is very precise, in a field in which one might imagine there are few differing voices – then just think what the situation must be like in pressure group activity in fields of greater economic and political significance!

In fact it is hard to think of many situations in which a pressure group operates unaffected and unimpeded by other related actual or potential pressure groups. It is possible to imagine two related continua. These two continua relate to each other vertically, and are consistent on the left-to-right plane (Table 8.1).

For example, the 1970s financial blindness allowance campaign started out as a solo campaign with reluctant acquiescence from associated groups, but over time moved to a solo one with active opposition. The pressure group work to preserve freepost for blind people was a solo campaign with associated groups being neutral; in other words, they had no strong position for or against maintaining this concession, or at least not one that they would mobilise. The CLEAR campaign was probably a solo one with positive acquiescence from associated pressure groups. However, Des Wilson would probably argue that it was a coalition. In reality it may have shifted between these two positions at different stages of the campaign, arguably starting as a coalition but shifting into solo with positive acquiescence as Wilson, and the resources he commanded, began to assume dominance. The free eye test campaign and the comprehensive disability income and cost allowance campaign are both coalitions with joint goals, but also with the individual organisations pursuing individual goals within the joint campaign.

In marketing terms, what does this model (Table 8.1) suggest with regard to positioning for successful pressure group work? It is possible for a pressure group to succeed in any position on the continuum, but clearly it would be much harder with associated groups only reluctantly acquiescing or openly opposing the individual pressure group's goals. So it is clearly important to try to avoid this situation either by modifying the pressure group goals to ensure that associated groups are at least neutral, or by building up better relationships with associated groups to explain how the individual campaign is not as competitive as it might appear at first sight.

Superficially the right-hand end of the continuum would seem to be the most attractive for success. Both coalitions and partnerships give the advantage of considerably increased resources. For example, the Disability Benefits Consortium has the combined strength of 250 disability organisations, including all the major charity players, with considerable lobbying resources at their disposal. However, the downside of a coalition or partnership is that the demands on the decision-makers tend to be much greater. For example, a satisfactory financial blindness allowance would cost the state less than £500 million, but a satisfactory benefit for all groups of disabled people as per the coalition would cost the state in excess of £7 billion. So if the magnitude of the demand increases with the size of the coalition, this goes a long way to cancelling out the impact of increased campaign resources. Another downside of a coalition is that, although there are joint proposals, the individual organisations are still likely to be pursuing individual goals. This takes a lot of time to talk through and involves the coalition leaders in endless meetings.

Table 8.1 Model of pressure group positioning options

	Solo				Coalition	Partnership
Approach of leading pressure groups	Opposition	Reluctant acquiescence	Neutrality	Positive acquiescence	Joint proposal	Partnership
Approach of related pressure groups	(active, competitive goals)	(relatively inactive, competitive goals)	(inactive but competitive goals)	(relatively inactive, cooperative goals)	(active cooperation on joint goals, relatively inactive pursuit of individual goals)	(active joint goals, inactive or nonexistent competitive goals)

Probably the most successful pressure group campaigns are those that are essentially solo ones, preferably with the positive acquiescence of associated groups, or at least their guaranteed neutrality. Such positioning allows the demand to be less costly to the decision-makers; it allows the demand to be well differentiated from other competing pressure group demands; it narrows down the number and range of decision-makers who have to be targeted; and it simplifies the advocacy work and message.

Analysis of the other players not only extends to allies who might become competitors; it very importantly concentrates on the opposition. Here the CLEAR campaign spent much analytical time. The commercial lobby of motor manufacturers, petroleum companies and lead providers was obviously very strong in the areas of technical competence and behind-the-scenes lobbying. Therefore Wilson chose what he called the 'moral high ground' of health and long-term environmental gains (D. Wilson, 1984 p. 160): he took the argument out into the public arena, and in particular the editorial arena. In an analysis of strengths and weaknesses of the campaign and the opposition this tactic made a lot of sense. Commercial companies are very powerful in their behind-the-scenes lobbying and in their technical resources, but they are often very uncomfortable under public scrutiny. The CLEAR campaign, although it had technical resources, could not compete in this area, nor did it have access to the corridors of power. However, it had the highly effective public representational resource of Wilson himself, it had excellent contacts in the editorial media and it had a sufficiently well-argued proposition on the moral high ground.

In summary, other-player analysis and subsequent positioning are crucial to any effective pressure group work. This analysis needs to concentrate not only on the obvious opposition, but also on allies who might become competitors. The well-established SWOT (strengths, weaknesses, opportunities and threats) analysis is ideal. The objective is to position the campaign both in terms of its contents, alliances and methods in ways that will support the overall objectives but concentrate on campaign strengths and opposition weaknesses. Pressure group work is an area where competition for attention and action is intense, and differentiation of the campaign is a necessary and often crucial requirement.

Targeting: beneficiaries, advocates, decision-makers and influencers

It is surprising how often charities do not think carefully about the target groups for their pressure group work. Instead, good ideas tend to spring out of charity knowledge and practice and become inscribed in the organisation's formal policy positions; everyone feels a lot better but nothing happens. Clearly it is not possible to promote every charity policy position, as it would be completely debilitating on resources to do so. However, even when a policy plank is selected for greater promotion, targets for the 'good idea' can be given little thought. Exhortations (such as 'GPs should do more of such and such', 'the Arts Council should spend more on such and such an area', 'overseas aid policies should be changed to do such and such' and 'pesticides in farming practices should be reduced') will only stand a chance of being effected if questions are asked along the following lines:

☐ Who are the beneficiaries?
☐ Who are the advocates of the beneficiaries?
☐ Who are the decision-makers?
☐ Who are the influencers of the decision-makers?

Beneficiary target group

Philosophically, and on most occasions practically, this is the group to start with. This is the group for whom the pressure group exists. It is the needs of this group that should be the primary (but not the only) determinant of the pressure group proposal. However, it would be disingenuous to suggest that there is not an important interaction between all four target groups of a pressure group campaign, i.e. beneficiaries, advocates, influencers and decision-makers. It is clearly no use spending significant resources on a campaign that will help beneficiaries but is unlikely to succeed among influencers and decision-makers in the long term, let alone the short term. Pressure group work should be judged on results, not on effort. Pressure groups often spend too little time identifying the key target groups among beneficiaries. Even in those relatively few instances where all beneficiaries benefit from a pressure group proposal, it is important to work out which groups benefit in what way, because the application of the proposal is seldom uniform. Establishing the differential benefits is important for two reasons. First, those members of the beneficiary group who are likely to gain the most are more likely to be advocates (see the next section). An example from the freepost campaign would be blind Braille readers of working age, who tend to be relatively heavy users of the freepost system (because Braille is very bulky and people of working age are more frequent users of the postal system) and hence were more able and willing to act as advocates.

Second, provided that the pressure group has a clear idea about the differential benefits of their proposal, concessions to opinion-formers and decision-makers can be made in ways that appear to be significant, but in reality result in little diminution of the benefit. For example, in the free eye test campaign, proportionally more eye disease is picked up in tests of the over-40s than the under-40s. If the government wishes to make concessions on its hard line 'charging for eye tests' position for political or economic reasons, then it is more important to continue to demand free eye tests for the over-40s than it is for the under-40s.

The third, and most important, reason for targeting and segmenting the beneficiary group in relation to any proposal, is to test the proposal out. This can be done both through desk analysis and research. It is surprising how often pressure groups develop proposals for change which are on the basis of hunch or 'we know best'. A little desk analysis will show that a superficially strong demand will, in practice, only benefit relatively few beneficiaries. So the pressure group must ask, very early on, 'Who will benefit from this proposal?' Also the pressure group must have, especially for major proposals, strong evidence that the beneficiary group will actually welcome the proposal. If you are not clear about your target beneficiary group, this most basic question cannot be answered! (See the section on market research, pp. 178–180.)

Thus segmenting and targeting your beneficiary group is important for deciding and backing up the campaign proposals, for identifying advocacy groups, and for identifying areas where concessions can be made in ways that will minimise impact on the campaign objective.

Advocates

Identifying and targeting individuals and groups who can be advocates for the proposition, but are somewhat distanced from the pressure group, is a key tool for success. For all sorts of reasons, charity pressure groups themselves can easily be discounted. Even pressure groups such as Save the Children and Age Concern will meet the occasionally overt, and certainly covert, reaction from influencers and decision-makers on the lines of 'well, you would say that, wouldn't you'. Advocates somewhat distanced from the pressure group increase the credibility of the proposition enormously. For example, involving recent immigrants who have successfully settled in this country as advocates for a more sympathetic immigration policy, can make the campaign much more credible. Involving sympathetic employers as advocates for employing disabled people can make influencers and decision-makers sit up and review the situation afresh in a way that yet another meeting with the Royal Association for Disability and Rehabilitation cannot achieve. Influential independent scientists were crucial advocates for CLEAR.

Identifying advocacy groups on behalf of the proposition is not a well-developed art among charity pressure groups. When it happens it can too often be on the basis of the most important leader in this particular pressure group. It is important to identify advocates who are likely to be most credible to the influencer and/or decision-maker.

Decision-makers

The term 'decision-makers' is deliberately put in the plural; it is seldom that only one person makes a decision. There will be people above or below who have to sign up. Second, the real decision-maker is seldom the obvious person! The obvious decision-maker is already visible, e.g. the director of social services, or the junior minister in charge, etc. However, if the potential decision-maker is visible, it means that they are sufficiently well known to have a whole mass of responsibilities and rely primarily on recommendations coming to them from the bureaucracy. There has been an increasing trend for pressure groups to concentrate on local and central government political leaders as the objects of lobbying which Miller (1991, p. 51) argues is a mistake. Even when local or national government has a relatively small majority (and is therefore more open to influence at a political level), the majority of decisions are taken by the executive (i.e. civil servants, local authority officials, head officers of national associations).

But if the executive makes the decisions, at what level? Once again there is a tendency to assume that decisions are made at a much higher level than they really are. For example, the majority of work on a policy issue in the civil service will be undertaken at the level of what used to be called principal (now called 'number sevens'!) which is the fifth tier of the civil service hierarchy. Occasionally a higher-tier assistant secretary (number five) will be involved in shaping the policy and the decision on the basis of work done by the principal. However, these are the administrative civil servants, who have their equivalent in local government and other statutory organisations. The professional advisory arm, such as doctors, social workers, nuclear scientists, pesticide experts, construction engineers, etc., also plays a role. While the administrative part of the executive would claim, often rightly, that they make the decisions, the professional advisers will be influential to a greater or lesser extent. A good rule of thumb is that the higher the status level of the profession or the greater the complexity of the subject, the greater will be the influence of the professional arm.

If all this seems very complicated, it is relatively easy to find out who the key decision-makers will be on any issue. The charity simply writes to the health authority's general manager, the director of social services or the only civil servant known in the relevant department. The returning letter will give all the information needed. It may be signed by an official; the next stage is simply to find out who is above and below them, and this will identify the decision-making unit, i.e. the target group. If it is signed by the minister, or the director of social services, there will normally be a reference on the letter with initials, or 'for further information ring extension ...', which once again gives you the information as to the key decision-makers.

Influencers

The influencers also play a crucial role. They may have the authority, on occasions, even to overrule the decision-makers, but they will seldom do so. There are three stages when the influencers can have an important impact.

In descending order of impact it will be at the *start* of the consideration, *during* the consideration and *after* the decision has effectively been made.

If a charity pressure group can raise an issue right at the start with a senior influencer, e.g. a minister, a director of education or a chairman of social services, in a friendly cooperative way, then this can spark an important catalytic effect. The senior influencer will then pass it on to the people who will work on the issue on the lines of 'Age Concern Eastbourne has raised with me the problem of the crossing outside Marks & Spencer being dangerously placed – could you see if there is something you can do?'

Contact with influencers during the decision-making process has to be well judged, as it can make the executive decision-makers antagonistic because they will feel that the pressure group is looping over their heads to the top. However, a pressure group's role is not to please executive decision-makers! If it is judged that the shaping of the decision is going in the wrong direction, action obviously has to be taken. The contact with the influencers can either be friendly or adversarial. For example, in the freepost campaign example above, the civil servants were refusing to acknowledge the need for primary legislation. RNIB managed to engineer a situation where the civil servants were happy for matters to go on to the next stage of direct representation to the minister, i.e. this was a friendly and agreed 'looping over'. However, in the eye tests campaign, the civil servants were working to a brief for charges to be introduced – with that brief coming from the minister. Therefore the looping over to the minister was essential and adversarial. Because direct persuasion of the minister was not working, the pressure group work shifted into the public arena and 'advocates' were triggered to put pressure on the influencers, which in the eye test case were many and varied. These included the chair of the Conservative Backbench Health Committee, the Select Committee Conservative members of the committee stage of the bill going through Parliament, and influential government members in the Lords. While all this activity can in work terms seem impressive, the more activity there is and the more public it is, the more it is a signal that the pressure group is losing!

The least effective stage to approach influencers is just as, or just after, a negative decision has been made. This is normally the death throes of a campaign (although the CLEAR example above proves the lie of this) when the positions of decision-makers and key influencers are highly entrenched.

The distinctions between decision-makers, influencers, advocates and beneficiaries is at times hard to draw. One can imagine a continuum with decision-makers at the left-hand end, influencers next, then advocates and finally beneficiaries on the right (see Figure 8.1).

Figure 8.1 Relationships of key target groups in pressure group activity

As one shifts along the continuum from right to left, some beneficiaries become advocates, some advocates shade into influencers and some influencers practically become decision-makers. A minister in a government department has the authority to make the decision, but does not often have the power (i.e. the detail of the argument). For this reason the minister is closer to the influencing side of the divide rather than the decision-making side. However, if the decision is massively important and/or politically sensitive, then they will shift over into the decision-making end of the continuum to join the civil servants. In exceptional circumstances the civil servants may shift across into the influence part of the continuum in those cases where the minister makes the decision against the advice of the civil servant.

Conclusion

Segmenting and targeting the market in charity pressure group work is often superficial or even non-existent, yet it is essential to success. It is important to segment and target not only among potential beneficiaries, but also among credible advocates. Also it is important to segment and target not only among decision-makers, but among influencers. The relationship between these four groups is complicated but crucial. Not all beneficiaries benefit equally; some beneficiaries become advocates; some influencers can become advocates; some decision-makers can become advocates; and, depending on the stage of the campaign and its changing importance, people who were previously decision-makers may become influencers, and people who were previously influencers may become decision-makers! Nevertheless this four-category model is vital for laying out the chess pieces of any charity pressure group work. Such analysis allows a proposal to be truly beneficial to the ultimate recipients, allows the pressure group to marshal and deploy its meagre resources more effectively, and will impress and ultimately influence decision-makers who are generally dismissive of ill-thought-out, crude campaigning.

Market research

Market research is a key tool to effective pressure group success. It can help in four ways: first as a testing mechanism among beneficiaries to ensure that the proposal really does meet beneficiary needs; second, and in turn, as evidence to influencers and decision-makers of genuine and detailed needs of potential beneficiaries; third, in the form of opinion polls, as support to campaigns; and fourth, as a method of analysing opinions and positions of key influencers and decision-makers. The following paragraphs take these ideas in turn.

It is surprising and frightening how often charity pressure groups assume that their propositions are correct on the basis that 'they know best'. While it is understandable that charities believe that they know what is best for their beneficiaries from practical experience, it is still not good enough. A marketing approach requires that proposals are tested out among bene-ficiaries before they are launched. Elsewhere in this book the suggestion has been put that it is not enough that charity committees contain professional workers experienced in the field, and not even enough that a charity has representatives on its committees from the end beneficiary group. No one person can be representative of the full range of beneficiaries. Market research among actual and potential beneficiaries testing out alternatives can go a long way (but not all the way) to informing pressure group policy-makers.

This market research can have a double impact as use as evidence with influencers and decision-makers. For example, the Department of Social Security had long resisted arguments that blind people needed financial help with their mobility problems (which was available to physically disabled people). By bringing together the findings of the RNIB needs survey (Bruce *et al.* 1991) with government research among disabled people (Martin, White and Meltzer 1989, Table 3.5) it was shown that blind people were far less independently mobile than disabled people in general. This conclusion from market research transformed a proposal that had pre-viously been regarded as a self-centred whinge into a hard, credible piece of independent evidence (Bruce 1992, pp. 1–5).

Market research in the form of opinion polls can be a useful support, especially in media terms. Age Concern in the very early 1970s, and subsequently many other pressure groups, have used to good effect opinion poll findings on the lines of 'over 75 per cent of the general public would be prepared to pay higher taxes in order to improve services for . . .'. In the CLEAR campaign Des Wilson (1984, pp. 165–6) argued that opinion poll evidence of overwhelming public knowledge and support for the campaign increased their credibility with government negotiators. It is important not to over-emphasise the value of opinion polls, but they can be useful increments of influence.

Last, market research, usually qualitative, among influencers and decision-makers is crucial in assessing tactics. All too often pressure group leaders spend too much time writing and talking up their own case, and not enough time listening to the views of influencers and decision-makers. For pressure group representatives to allow these two groups to express opposing arguments in their presence is almost regarded as a sign of weakness and to 'stare defeat in the face'. Far from it – listening to counter-arguments from decision-makers in particular, assessing their individual validity and finding out how widespread that view is, is crucial in winning any pressure group initiative.

The proposal

This is the first 'P', i.e. product, of the marketing mix. The bedrock of the pressure group idea product is the 'P' for philosophy. Just as in services, the various campaigns will become contradictory if the common philosophy of the organisation is not clearly integrated into the pressure group idea. In some instances the philosophy element of the mix can be very visible (see Figure 8.2) with its example from the British Mountaineering Council's campaign for the freedom to climb difficult and dangerous mountains.

The proposal, i.e. the product one is trying to put across, has to be constructed with as much care as any physical good or service. The earlier sections have touched on the importance of having a high quality proposal which is well thought out, right down to the details. The detail may not initially be presented, but if the proposers are not aware of it, they cannot put the case in a way that will later stand up. What are the main features of the proposal? Where is the evidence that these are the most important ones that beneficiaries require? What is the proposition called (i.e. is it clear, as in 'disability income')? Is there a one- or two-sentence summary which makes it as plain as a pikestaff what is being sought and why? Keeping eye tests, taking lead out of petrol and saving a London orchestra are simple, memorable propositions.

Making all these decisions in developing the case, anticipating opposing arguments, is akin to new product development and requires all the stages of developing ideas, screening them in relation to target decision-makers, proposal development, 'business' analysis (cost of implementation, etc.), testing out on people and referring for launch. Des Wilson (1984, p. 53) talks of the phase of proposal development taking six months or so. This is ideal with a proactive proposal, but is impractical in defensive campaigns such as eye tests where the pressure group is likely to have days or weeks rather than months in which to act.

Price – it certainly has one

One of the more sterile arguments, especially on the other side of the Atlantic, is whether a marketing approach can be applied to charitable activities because the price is often absent or distorted. This is nowhere more so than in pressure group proposals. However, there most certainly is a price attached to any pressure group proposal which a decision-maker has to pay. What is more, the decision-maker is often more aware of the price

The only thing worse than falling off a rock face is not being allowed to.

North Wales Daily Post, 20th June 1990

The crags of Pen Trwyn in North Wales are home to some of the hardest rock climbs in the British Isles.

Attracting climbers from all over the world to a punishing test of strength and technique.

In summer 1990, the risk of falling rocks dislodged by climbers forced Aberconwy Borough Council to close the cliff.

Now Pen Trwyn truly was impossible to climb.

And so it would have remained if the BMC hadn't intervened.

Our Access and Technical Committees worked hard to find a solution which suited both climbers and the general public.

Using our Access and Conservation fund, we installed abseil stations on carefully selected routes on Pen Trwyn. Eliminating the danger of falling rocks at the end of a climb.

Thanks to the BMC, Pen Trwyn is once again open for business. And like many other threatened cliffs and rock faces, we believe it should remain easy to climb.

PROTECTING CLIMBERS AND THEIR MOUNTAIN ENVIRONMENT BRITISH MOUNTAINEERING COUNCIL

Figure 8.2 Organisation philosophy is important, and policy, campaigning and practice need to follow it – advertisement and leaflet from the British Mountaineering Council (BMC/Cheetham Bell)

than the manufacturer (the pressure group). In Chapter 4 it is suggested that the idea products have impact prices. Whether the target groups of pressure group campaigns respond positively or not depends on their implicit and explicit assessment of the balance of costs and benefits.

Price is a useful analytical and practical mechanism in pressure group work in two senses. The first is literally how much resource (not always money) the decision-maker will have to apply if the pressure group proposal is implemented. Sometimes this is money in the form of tax concessions, increased financing of local government or increased or direct grant aid to the charity, etc. However, often the resource is indirectly financial through demands for higher quality and more extensive services to a particular group. In my experience the impact on the decision-maker of the actual price of the demand is underestimated and under-discussed by pressure groups. At one level this is justified, legitimately, on the lines of 'it's our job to present to you unfulfilled needs, not to make decisions about cost of implementation, including where you will get the money from'. However, adopting the moral high ground as Wilson did in the CLEAR campaign is dangerous. Decision-makers are no longer (if they ever were) impressed by arguments that other countries are doing it. If the officials in the executive do a calculation of the price of implementation which proves to be far higher than that put forward by the pressure groups (if it is done at all), then the idea may be dismissed before the debate has even started. Or if the officials do a calculation of the price to be paid which is lower than the implications of the pressure group's demand and this is not made explicit until well into the campaign, then the latter stages of negotiation will get very bumpy as the (unanticipated) differences emerge. Even if the true price of implementation is not declared by the pressure group in the opening stages of the initiative, it is important to discuss it with officials no later than what might be estimated as the middle stages of the campaign. This gives time for all parties to adjust their demands/likely concessions in an ordered way rather than face a last-minute scrabble with plenty of recriminations. In particular if the price of the demand is seen to be too high, it does allow the pressure group, if it wishes, to re-phase and restructure its proposal in such a way as to set precedence for subsequent campaigns in their area. (It goes without saying that the officials will, unless converted, be very cautious about such restructuring!)

The second aspect of price which is seldom thought through is the price that decision-makers and, to a lesser extent, influencers will have to pay in personal terms. The decision-makers and influencers will be asking themselves how much aggravation they are going to get from other groups making demands if they are seen to support this particular one. This price therefore loops back to the construction of the proposal, preferably in such a way as to minimise the knock-on effects (unless this has been part of the agreement to gain, for example, positive acquiescence from other groups –

see Figure 8.2). The other more personal price which decision-makers and influencers will be considering is their popularity and standing with other important people in their work setting – with the treasury or department of finance in particular! Additional resources are hard to get at the best of times and will involve a great deal of debate, preparation of internal proposals, endless meetings, etc. If additional resources are refused after the decision-maker has in effect internally signed up to the proposition, the financial boomerang may come right back and hit the official doing the origination. This boomerang is in the form of a request for budget substitution – which in less bureaucratic language means that they are asked to find the costs of this desirable new initiative from elsewhere within their own budget, i.e. by cutting something else out of their area of responsibility.

In summary, calculating the price of a request and openly discussing it, not too far into the pressure group initiative, is important. I asked a minister with whom we had been dealing for some six years on initiatives to which we knew he was committed, what he felt were some of our less successful tactics. He described the situation in which we would troop in to him and make a proposal that his officials had advised him was a totally unrealistic price to pay in the medium term, let alone the short term. From his point of view we gave a really hard sell on behalf of the disadvantaged group we were representing and would leave, in his words, 'feeling good' and report back to our constituency to some degree of approbation. However, as far as he was concerned the whole meeting had been a complete waste of time, except that he had appeared 'reasonable' in listening to our demands! Even so, the minister's view was a partial one, and one would hope that presentation of just, but expensive, demands would over time have some impact. However, if I am honest, on several occasions we had not thought the detail of the price through in the way we should have done.

Promotion – much more sophisticated than media coverage

Promotion is something that charity pressure groups are particularly good at, but we do not always relate our public promotion to the impact we are trying to achieve. Within the confines of pressure group action, the only purpose of promotional activities is to influence decision-makers and influencers.

While mass publicity is very much the first love and expertise of charity pressure groups, we do need to learn a thing or two from our highly effective commercial counterparts. *Personal selling* of the proposal by liked and/or respected personal intervention is likely to be far more effective than stand-up, and superficially victorious, battles on Radio Four's 'Today' programme with ministers. Des Wilson (1984, p. 58) says 'contacts with people with the right skills, or people with the influence in the right places are crucial to any campaign'. Charities have an enviable list of contacts and should put them to good use. Clear, well-written and, above all, honest briefings are required. (Charity goodwill and trust is a valuable resource which cannot be squandered for short-term advantages.) If at all possible, charities enlist contacts through direct and personal requests, making it clear what they want the person to do. At the very least, most sympathetic people will write a letter, especially if the charity drafts if for them. Much better, however, is yet further personal intervention with influencers. Third-party approaches to influencers can have a major impact. First, the third-party advocate is more likely to be respected by the potential influencer. Second, the influencer cannot help but think 'if ... is sufficiently concerned to take up their cause, this is beginning to become a significant issue'. Commercial pressure groups have the resources for slap-up lunches and dinners. Luckily charities seldom have to use this method and can get contacts direct via meetings.

If personal selling of the idea is the most effective, *advertising and public relations* can play an important part in a pressure group campaign that requires public support. Environmental pressure groups, particularly Greenpeace, have made very effective use of advertising campaigns. However, these are obviously expensive and charities rightly tend to favour editorial channels. The CLEAR example above shows how coverage can be generated. The story itself should normally be strong enough to command some news coverage in the early stages. The difficulty is in maintaining momentum. The trick is to find ways to turn what is a continuing message into a news story. This requires some form of news hook. Here reports in general and research surveys in particular, when published at a specific time, give sympathetic editorial journalists from the various media the hook they need.

Both newspapers and television welcome graphic coverage in stills and footage. Once again successful charities can find visual events which are powerful and/or amusing enough to gain coverage. Dumping tons of non-recyclable drinks containers outside Schweppes headquarters; piles of bones representing slaughtered animals; disabled people linking arms across Westminster Bridge (see Figure 8.3); banners hanging from scaffolding up the side of Big Ben; street theatre outside the Arts Council – all these and more can provide strong graphic images for the media and remain true and relevant to the pressure group campaign.

Channels of communication – reaching decision-makers effectively

In classic commercial marketing this is place, the fourth 'P' of the marketing mix, and sometimes called distribution. In the activity of pressure group work, it is most easily encapsulated in the term 'channels of communication' and is perhaps the most crucial analytical tool in ensuring success. Having

Figure 8.3 Voluntary organisations are more public in their pressure group activity than their commercial counterparts – Disability Benefits Consortium demonstrating outside Parliament (Stephanie Henry/RNIB)

identified the target groups, the communications channel can be crucial in helping the message to be received positively rather than negatively. A vast array of channels is available. Personal communications (meetings and telephoning) always win over impersonal ones such as letters, radio and television.

Formal meetings with decision-makers and key influencers require not only a legitimate interest on behalf of the person or organisation making the approach, but also a very direct interest. However, contacts with more distant influencers such as government backbenchers when the majority is fairly small, can be more liberal in number and more informal. MPs and even members of the Lords are trapped in Parliament for quite lengthy periods and can be surprisingly ready to meet, providing it is in Parliament and at a time to suit themselves. Contact by advocates from their own constituency is a communications channel to be sought avidly. Building up constituency supporters of a particular pressure group proposal, especially in the constituencies of decision-makers and influencers, can be very effective. Charity pressure groups with service units in constituencies across the country are at a distinct advantage, as are those pressure groups that have local memberships. The Disability Benefits Consortium's campaign for a disability income was greatly helped by disabled people seeking meetings at MPs' surgeries and describing how lack of money makes their lives even more challenging than they would otherwise be. Also charities like Barnardo's, Save the Children, MENCAP and RNIB are major employers in many constituencies across the country, and as such have almost a guarantee of access to local MPs.

Last, influencing through relevant third-party organisations such as the Association of Directors of Social Services, local arts associations, sports associations, etc., indicate, rightly, that the issue is not simply one being dreamt up and supported by national pressure groups.

Conclusion

The idea that the pressure group proposal is sacrosanct, with the validity of the idea shining through without need of a marketing approach, could not be further from the truth. A pressure group proposal is as much a product in the marketing sense as a physical good or service. If anything it requires a greater degree of sophistication of market segmentation and targeting, competitor analysis, market research and positioning, as well as the remaining elements of the marketing mix of price, promotion and place. If these elements are attended to methodically and in advance of the launch, the chances of the pressure group proposal being accepted are enhanced considerably.

Key points

Positioning and other players
☐ Identify potential partners and, if necessary, modify your goals to ensure that associated groups are at least neutral and do not become competitors.
☐ Concentrate on campaign strengths and opposition weaknesses. Differentiation of the campaign is vital.

Segmenting and targeting
☐ To help set priorities, identify the beneficiaries, their advocates, decision-makers and influencers. How do they overlap and interrelate?

Market research
☐ To give credence to your campaign with influencers and decision-makers, support your proposals with evidence researched among your target beneficiaries. Use respectable independent research and opinion polls if they are available.
☐ Make tactical use of the most widespread opposing views, especially if they are shared by influencers and decision-makers.

Proposal
☐ Putting together the proposal is akin to new product development and equal care should be taken. Find a simple one- or two-sentence summary which clearly and memorably describes what is being sought and why.

Price
☐ Discuss at an early stage how much resource, directly or indirectly, the decision-maker will have to apply if the proposal is implemented. This gives time for all parties to adjust their demands or likely concessions.
☐ Consider the impact price to the decision-makers of supporting this campaign.

Promotion
☐ Personal selling of the idea is the most effective means of promotion, but can be helpfully supported by advertising and public relations.

Channels of communication
☐ Use personal communications (meetings and telephoning) as well as letters, briefs, etc.
☐ Find advocates who can make contact with influencers such as MPs, especially through constituency networks.

9

FUND-RAISING

The full charity income picture

Before concentrating on fund-raising it is useful to look at the full income picture of charities. This is difficult for several reasons, including problems of agreed definitions, poor primary data sources, insufficient research and the sheer size and complexity of the field.

It is not the purpose of this book to go into the variety of useful definitions of the sector and the impact these have on size and sources of income (but see Kendall and Knapp 1996, Appendix 1 of this book; and Hems and Passey 1996, Appendix 2 of this book). However, in order to indicate what we are discussing it is necessary to mention some definition in outline. Kendall and Knapp as part of the Johns Hopkins Comparative Non-profit Sector Project refer to the Broad Voluntary Sector (BVS) and the Narrow Voluntary Sector (NVS). The BVS includes not only charities as we recognise them but also such non-profits as cultural and recreational organisations, schools, universities, hospitals, housing associations, trade unions, trade associations, etc. The Narrow Voluntary Sector (NVS) is BVS minus recreation, education (schools, universities etc.), unions, trade associations, etc., but including housing associations and cultural organisations. See Appendix 1 (p. 241) for a detailed definition. They represent the findings in tabular form, repeated here in Table 9.1.

Hems and Passey (1996), reporting the Office of National Statistics (ONS) data interpretation exercise, use the term 'general charities' to cover registered charities (with the Charity Commission) minus those that are effectively part of government (such as the British Council, Arts Council, grant maintained schools, etc.) and excluding exempt charities such as charitable housing associations, universities, schools, places of worship. 'General charities' as a pragmatic collection probably approximates with what most member organisations of the National Council for Voluntary Organisations (NCVO) would think of as the charity sector, i.e. including all the 'household-name' national charities and all local charities. See Appendix 2 (p. 243) for a detailed definition. General charities equate roughly with the NVS minus housing associations and cultural organisations. More precision has been devoted here to Hems and Passey's 'general charities' because much of

Table 9.1 The UK voluntary sector, 1990

	Broad voluntary sector	Narrow voluntary sector
Full-time equivalent paid employment – total	946,000	390,000
– as per cent of whole economy	4.0	1.7
Total operating expenditure (£ billion)	26.4	10.0
Total operating income (£ billion)	29.5	12.3
Sources of income		
Government (£ billion)	11.6	4.3
Earned income (£ billion)	14.2	5.2
Private giving (£ billion)	3.6	2.9

Source:
Kendal and Knapp 1996, p. 109

the data in this chapter draws on this Office of National Statistics survey of these charities. One of the most descriptive tables of income from the ONS survey is shown in Table 9.2.

Broadly speaking the figures in Kendall and Knapp (1996) square with those in ONS (Hems and Passey 1996) when one takes account of the fact that (a) Hems and Passey's latter definition excludes housing associations and cultural organisations with their high fees/government income and low

Table 9.2 Gross income of general charities by income bands – percentages

	Less than £100K	£0.1m to £1m	£1m to £10m	£10m+	All
Sales of goods/ services	12	33	42	34	33
Grants and donations	54	49	34	31	40
Legacies	2	3	5	13	7
Investment and disposal income	32	15	20	22	20
Total	100	100	100	100	100
Per cent total sector income	11	29	30	30	100
Nos of charities (approximate)	110,000	10,000	1,350	174	122,000
Total income	£1.3 billion	£3.4 billion	£3.5 billion	£3.5 billion	£11.7 billion

Source:
ONS Survey, Hems and Passey 1996, Tables 3.1 and 3.2

donation elements and (b) Hems and Passey's fieldwork was five years later by which time the charities register had grown larger and average income had increased. While the figures shown in Table 9.2 are only associational, not causal, it is interesting to note that charities with turnovers of over £10m are more likely to have several, more equal sources of income (e.g. 34 per cent sales, 31 per cent donations, 13 per cent legacies and 22 per cent investments) whereas those in lower income bands are much more likely to be heavily dependent on one source of income (e.g. £1m–10m organisations in sales (42 per cent); under £1m in donations (50 per cent).

A quite different picture emerges if one values the resource put in by volunteers. The ONS survey (Hems and Passey 1996) report approaching 1.5 million Full-Time Equivalent (FTE) volunteers working in general charities comprising 0.75 million in fund-raising, 0.64 million in direct service and 0.06 million in administration. Even valuing these at £10,000 per annum gives a contribution in kind of £15 billion per annum, thus outstripping the total financial income of £11.7 billion. However, this 'in-kind' income via volunteers contributes disproportionately to the smallest charities as is shown in Table 9.3.

Table 9.3 Income of general charities including costed volunteer time*

	Less than £100K	£0.1m to £1m	£1m to £10m	£10m+	All
Financial income	1.3 billion	3.4 billion	3.5 billion	3.5 billion	11.7 billion
Costed volunteer time*	9.0 billion	2.4 billion	1.0 billion	2.75 billion	15.0 billion
Total	10.3 billion	5.8 billion	4.5 billion	6.25 billion	26.7 billion

* Each FTE volunteer costed at £10,000 p.a. and 1.5 m FTE volunteers distributed across income bands as per Figure 17 (Hems and Passey 1996, p. 60)

On this reckoning resources available to the '£100K or less' income band far exceed any of the others. (A significant 'health warning' needs to be applied to the volunteer estimator.) Nevertheless this interpretation challenges the commonly held assumption that the largest charities attract the majority of the resources.

Fund-raising – market sources and size

This chapter now considers voluntary income or fund-raised income.

The lay person's view of charity fund-raising fixes on activities such as rattling tins in street collections, sponsored events such as swims and walks, and the increasing amount of charity mail which drops through the letterbox. In fact this overt activity produces a minute fraction of net charity income. Fund-raising is much broader than this. The term 'fund-raising' is used in a variety of ways. Colloquially, even in many charities, it refers to donations in their most straightforward sense of individuals, companies or trusts giving money. However, among professional fund-raising charities it is synonymous with 'voluntary income' and covers all charity income (including gifts in kind) except fees/charges/sales of services and goods related to the charity's prime purpose; statutory income; and investment and rental income. Voluntary income or fund-raised income, therefore, covers such activities as company donations, gifts in kind (e.g. computers), sponsorship and secondment; charity and trust donations; and individual donations, sponsorship legacies, and charity goods (e.g. charity shops, raffles, etc.). Arguably, and some charities do it this way, statutory grants and the 'gift' of voluntary work should also be included. The approach required for company sponsorships and donations have many similarities to the approach needed to achieve statutory grants. Again recruiting volunteers has similarities with recruiting donors.

Figure 9.1 gives a graphical representation of the sources of giving (excluding fees and charges/sales, investment, rents and other income). Excluding the 'in-kind' giving detailed above and concentrating on 'cash' giving, Hems and Passey estimate this consists of £5.45 billion out of the £11.7 billion total financial income of the 120,000 or so general charities (1994/5) (see Table 9.4). Individual donations and government grants (i.e. not linked to a contract) are the two largest sources, followed by trusts and legacies. Company donations and trading provide relatively little income. However, looking at the position over time (1991–1994/5) a different picture emerges. Over this period government grants have expanded considerably on a large base. Legacies have shown useful gains on a medium base and company donations a high growth on a small base. Given Labour government policies, the state of the economy, and even bearing in mind pressures on legacies (greater costs in old age), I predict these trends will continue.

Statutory sector	*Commercial sector*
Grants	Donations
	Sponsorship
	Gifts in kind
	Secondment
Charity and trust donations	Donations
Donated profits of subsidiaries	Legacies
	Time and donations (e.g. sponsorship)
	Charity goods
	Voluntary service work
Voluntary sector	*Informal sector (individuals)*

Figure 9.1 Sources of giving

Table 9.4 Total fund-raised income 1994/5 and percentage change over 1991

General charities	1994/5 £million	Percentage change 1991–1994/5 in real terms
Individual subscriptions	117 ⎫	(4)
Individual one-off	1,591 ⎭	
Companies	234	47
Trading subscriptions	115	(29)
Trusts and non-profits	947	0
Legacies	766	9
Overseas	91	0
Government grants	1,582	21
Total	5,443	+26

Source:
Tables 3.1 and 3.7 ONS Survey, Hems and Passey 1996

The above figures do not take significant account of the National Lottery, launched halfway through 1994/5, i.e. no distributions were made to charities until 1995/6 and the impact on public giving would only just be making its mark. In funding opportunity terms the National Lottery's Charities Board (NLCB) gave £319 million to charities in 1996, i.e. adding around one-third to trust income. In addition, some entrepreneurial general charities will have been successful with one or more of the other four boards (Arts, Heritage, Sport, Millennium).

However, the debate is raging over what the *net* effect will be on charities. As punters put their disposable income into the lottery, will they put less into charities, particularly into collection boxes and street collections? The National Council for Voluntary Organisations through its research believes charities face a loss of £31 million per annum (NCVO Research Department 1997). It will take more time to be clear about the full impact. In the meantime the NLCB is providing a new source of funding with sophisticated application and evaluation procedures which all charities should consider (FitzHerbert and Rhoades 1997).

Details of the full voluntary income figure by charity size and the percentage change over 1991 for the larger charities are shown in Table 9.5 with some startling results. In the £1m–£10m band general charities lost income in real terms, especially voluntary income between 1991 and 1994/5, in particular on individual donations, trading subsidiaries and government grants. Whereas the large charities (over £10m) gained voluntary income from virtually every source. The one saving grace on voluntary income for the medium-sized charities compared to the large was significant legacy growth.

However, there are signs now that large charity income has stalled. The

Table 9.5 Gross income and income streams of general charities by income band (£million) plus percentage change 1991–1994/5 for larger charities
( ) indicates minus figure

	Annual Income (ONS based)							
	Less than £100k	£100k–£1m	£1m–£10m	% growth 91–94/5	Over £10m	% growth 91–94/5	Total	All over £1m % growth 91–94/5
TOTAL INCOME (all respondents)	£1334.7	£3402.6	£3542.0	(8.2)	£3496.9	31	£11776.2	26
Total sales of goods/services	£161.4	£1122.4	£1481.3	16	£1174.1	33	£3939.2	30
Total grants, donations	£726.1	£1678.9	£1190.3	(31)	£1082.1	8	£4677.4	2
* Total grants, donations from persons	£319.0	£494.4	£412.4	(29)	£482.5	0	£1708.3	(4)
* Grants, donations from companies	£26.7	£87.8	£68.8	(8)	£60.6	73	£233.9	47
* Grants, donations from trading subsidiaries	£13.3	£30.3	£33.0	(89)	£38.7	14	£115.3	(29)
* Grants, donations from charities	£152.2	£372.3	£252.8	15	£116.8	(2)	£894.1	0
* Grants, donations from non-profits	£0.0	£22.9	£20.5		£9.5		£52.9	
* Grants, donations from overseas agencies	£0.0	£14.2	£13.8	(88)	£62.8	2	£90.8	0
* Grants, donations from government	£214.9	£656.9	£388.9	(7)	£321.3	25	£1582.1	21
Legacies	£24.0	£112.6	£167.0	34	£463.0	8	£766.5	9
Total investment income	£404.4	£399.2	£492.2	(33)	£666.2	82	£1961.9	61
Gains (losses) on disposal of investments adjusted	£18.7	£89.5	£211.2		£111.5		£431.0	

* Using general charities surveyed in both 1991 and 1994/5, Tables 3.1 and 3.7, ONS Survey Hems and Passey 1996

Barclays/NGO Finance Magazine Top 100 Index (Nov 97) of voluntary income for the 100 largest charities has been relatively flat (i.e. no real growth) for several quarters in 1996–97. There are some signs of improvement but even if this is maintained it will be a welcome surprise if the last half of the decade is as good for the large charities as was the early 90s.

Individual methods of giving

The above tables come from money received by general charities and analysed through their accounts. Table 9.6 looks at how individuals say they give, as measured by an NOP public opinion poll commissioned by the

Table 9.6 Proportions donating by method and percentage of total donations

	Percentage of respondents making a donation	Percentage of total donations
Total givers	**70.3**	
Philanthropic givers	**62.1**	**58.8**
Door-to-door	27.4	7.0
Street collection	27.6	6.8
Sponsorship	10.5	11.8
Church collection	11.9	12.0
Shop collection	9.6	2.3
Pub collection	7.8	2.0
Appeal letter	3.5	5.2
TV/radio appeal	3.0	2.0
Work collection	7.5	2.7
Appeal advertisement	0.7	1.3
Telephone appeal	0.6	0.8
Buying goods for a charity	6.4	5.0
Purchase givers	**27.5**	**27.1**
Charity raffles/lotteries	18.2	6.1
Jumble sales	5.5	2.7
Buying in a charity shop	9.1	5.4
Buying from a charity catalogue	2.7	3.6
Attending a charity event	4.4	5.1
Subscriptions/membership fees	3.3	4.2
Affinity card	0.3	0.1
Planned giving	**4.8**	**14.1**
Covenant	3.2	9.8
Payroll giving	1.6	0.9
Gift Aid	0.4	3.5

Source:
Hems and Passey 1996

NCVO (1995). The second column should be approached with care because it records what people *say* they did which may or may not be what they *actually* did.

The second column above shows the percentage of individuals who gave by the method detailed in the first column, so 27.4 per cent of people gave via door-to-door collections but, in total, these only make up 7 per cent of individual giving, i.e. money. As a general rule the more personal the 'ask' the more likely people are to give, i.e. high percentages in column two. However, the average donation may be quite low. Planned giving is the ideal method from the charities' point of view for three reasons. First, the charity receives tax back in addition to the value of the gift; second, the giving is normally regular and predictable; and third, the donor needs less servicing in terms of prompts and thus it is much more cost effective.

Regardless of the reasons, charitable giving is in decline from 81 per cent of the population giving in 1994 to 68 per cent in 1996 with the average monthly donation dropping in cash terms from £10.08 in 1993 to £8.69 in 1996 (NCVO/NOP in Passey and Hems 1997). The coincidence of these declines with the launch of the National Lottery is a powerful associational argument for the damaging effect of the Lottery. However, as marketers we can help individual charities buck this trend, even though the trend makes this harder.

Methods of fund-raising

Fund-raising methods are as various as the ingenuity of fund-raisers and the volunteers who work with them. However, there are some broad categories of fund-raising methods which are widely understood. The previous section indicates how important the different methods of individual giving are in terms of the total volume of their contribution to charity voluntary income. In this section the main forms of giving from a wider variety of sources are listed in categories according to my estimate of the general cost-effectiveness of the method. The percentages are quoted to indicate the proportion of the gross income depleted by costs. In other words, a 20 per cent cost ratio means that every £1 of gross income raised costs 20 pence, i.e. the net income is 80 pence. As a generalisation, charities accept higher cost ratios on giving methods which contribute larger volumes of income, often via many smaller donations.

Legacies

These are by far the largest homogeneous income source for charities and are at the same time the most cost effective. Nearly one in ten legators leave a charitable bequest (Ford 1996). They provide 7 per cent of total charity income (or 14 per cent of voluntary income) and for the largest charities this rises to 13 per cent. It is surprising therefore that they have been the Cinderella area of fund-raising attention, except for a number of charities such as RNLI, Barnardo's, SCOPE, RNIB and the cancer charities. For these larger charities achieving 40 per cent or more of their total income from legacies, the cost of an active promotional programme is 1 or 2 per cent.

Nevertheless legacy marketing would seem at best to be a rather forlorn long-term hope, and indeed there is no certain, but plenty of anecdotal, evidence on why or how they get them (with the exception perhaps of the charities closely linked to the dying process, e.g. the cancer charities). The charities with large legacy incomes must be doing something right! For example, RNIB has been writing twice a year to every solicitor in the country for over fifty years, and almost 70 per cent of its voluntary income comes from this source.

Increasingly the larger legacy receivers, and some relatively new entrants such as SCOPE and the World Wildlife Fund (WWF) have been developing and implementing sophisticated legacy marketing plans. The hypothesis has been developed (but not yet proven) that loyal donors can be encouraged to make a final and substantial donation via a legacy. However, this hypothesis needs to be followed up with a great deal of care and sensitivity for the obvious reason that death is for most people quite a frightening prospect. A second hypothesis supported by disability and disease charities is that people who are beneficiaries or close to a charity's beneficiaries are more likely to leave a bequest.

Another approach that has been taken by certain charities for fifteen years or so is the promotion of free leaflets describing how people can make wills in general, in the hope that such a charity service might encourage the will-maker to remember the charity promoting the leaflet. While this service started by spreading leaflets like confetti, the process has now moved into the realms of sophisticated direct marketing. This means that cost per thousand of take-up of leaflets is measured, follow-up letters go to leaflet requesters and fairly sophisticated means are used to encourage people to pledge or declare to the charity that they have included the charity in their will. Charities can achieve a surprisingly quick return in the form of proved legacies in the bank. Several charities have achieved their first bequest in the bank in less than a year after recording legacy pledges. This is because the average length of time between making a last will and death is between two-and-a-half and four years.

Of the four marketing strategies (i.e. promotion to intermediaries such as solicitors, promotion to existing loyal donors, promotion to beneficiaries and promotion to people who want more information about will making) all seem to hold a good deal of promise.

Trust donations

Charitable trusts provide quick returns (six to twelve months) with low cost ratios of 10 per cent or less. Trusts provide 17 per cent of voluntary income ranging from 20 per cent for the smallest charities to 8 per cent for the largest – approaching £900m for the sector as a whole. However, the halcyon days (if there ever were such) of sending a standard request to all the large charitable trusts listed in a trusts directory are gone. An effective marketing approach requires the charity applicant to know the areas of interest of the trust and the typical levels of grant given; to arrange if at all possible a meeting, or at least a short telephone conversation with the trust administrator, and to produce an application form which has been obviously personalised to the trust itself. Any prior contact with one of the trustees can often be a tremendous help.

The big gift campaign

In its modern and sophisticated form, this is another highly cost-effective method which should achieve a cost ratio of 20 per cent or less. In its most usual form it consists of recruiting an active leader of industry, or a member of the aristocracy or acknowledged leader of the donating constituency, to chair an appeals committee of similar but lesser leaders. Each of these are used to make personal approaches to peers within their own particular area to seek donations. It is quite normal for a medium-sized national charity to raise £5 million by this method, and for a large charity to raise between £10 million and £20 million. Oxford University has recently raised £256 million!

The higher cost ratio is because of the extensive time involved in getting the campaign to the launch point. It will typically take two years of a full-time, fairly senior development director, plus the involvement of significant time from senior charity staff and trustees, to recruit a sufficiently senior and prestigious appeals committee. Tradition has it that you do not launch an appeal until you have secured one-third of the appeal target or more, but in times of financial pressure that is a luxury that sometimes has to be passed up.

While the sums may seem large, the combination of two years' planning and around two years to achieve the donations and pledges means that the sum is essentially covering a five- to seven-year cycle, if one is to leave a fallow period before starting the process over again. It is also fair to point out that some of the valuable sources of income will be the trusts mentioned in the previous section.

Corporate giving

Companies and their associated trusts have gained in popularity as a source of charitable income over the last fifteen years or so, not least through the leadership of some of the major companies in encouraging a corporate philanthropy. In pure donations of money they (only) contribute just over 4 per cent of charities' voluntary income. However, Table 9.4 (p. 192) shows this source is growing fast.

Broadly speaking there are four categories of corporate giving: first, *donations* which are very similar in form to those coming from charitable trusts (i.e. very few strings attached); second, *gifts in kind* in the form of goods, services or seconded personnel – once again with few strings attached; third, *company-specific sponsorship* activities, sometimes called cause-related marketing, where the company 'donates' money in a very public way, linked to its own business activity (e.g. 5 pence to the RSPCA for every returned pet food label, or royalties to a charity for the use of its logo because of the anticipated benefit to the product, e.g. WWF's panda on product labels). Cause-related marketing has grown quickly in the USA and is growing here although Sargeant and Stephenson (1997) report low penetration among local businesses; and last, *company-specific staff schemes* where the company sees morale and commitment advantages in involving their staff in charitable activities, e.g. British Airways staff sub-unit redecorating a charity school, or Asda store staff raising money for a charity over a year-long period, or a generalised policy of encouraging staff to become involved in local charitable activity with certain time-off arrangements – this being seen as an investment in the goodwill of the local community.

It will be immediately apparent that honing a proposal that takes account of the particular position of the company and its corporate needs takes up more time (and therefore money) than reasonably straightforward approaches to trusts. This is why this form of fund-raising can go as high as 20 or 30 per cent in cost ratio, not least because of the 'after-sales service' that has to be applied, especially in the last two categories. The company will expect significant publicity and public relations benefits to accrue which, once again, requires time and funds to be allocated by the charity.

Employee donations or payroll deductions

There can be an argument for this activity being a subset of the previous section except that it is specifically employee directed rather than company directed. In its formal tax-advantageous form, the total contribution of around 1 per cent of voluntary giving is small but the amount is growing significantly (CAF 1992, p. 71).

Some charities have had long-established programmes (50 years or more) of commercial company employees giving a deduction from their pay packet year after year to the charity (e.g. Barnardo's). This form of giving has recently been encouraged fiscally through the ability to make such donations tax advantageous to the charity. The costs in the first year can be quite high, in the 40–80 per cent range, but if the donations are sustained, they become one of the most attractive long-term investments, reducing to below 10 per cent per year. However, experience of the longer-established charities in this field shows what the commercial business sector already knows, i.e. donors need to be nurtured over the years, otherwise they will be lost.

Special events

This is the glamorous end of charity fund-raising: the film premières, charity balls, exclusive dinner parties, publicity-seeking awards, etc. Properly handled (and taking account of sponsorship), the cost ratio can be in the 20–50 per cent range, i.e. they justify this current positioning in the list. However, badly managed special events can, in truth, make losses even if the charity does not declare them as such. CAF (1992, p. 42) reports £139 million in income to the top 400 fund-raising charities via this method.

Special events often use all the organisational methods of big gift campaigns but the difference is that special events are speculative business activities. Take one of the most straightforward ones, that of the film première. Its success depends on the film having generated the relevant early publicity; the ability to attract a prestigious aristocrat and the stars; the ability to sell the cinema seats at a very considerable premium over normal seat prices; the ability to fill the seats with a majority of paying guests rather than complimentaries, etc. In short, it is a nightmare. For example, trying to coordinate the diaries of royalty and the stars is difficult; quite a few stars are unreliable as to whether they will turn up at the last minute; it is very difficult to predict how popular a film première will be, and a film première is one of the easiest special events to organise!

However, special events are here to stay, not only because they can be highly profitable, but also because influential people in charities, especially leaders of big gift campaigns (see above), like them. If a charity's volunteer corporate leader, who is raising £10 million, particularly wants a special event it can be hard to resist!

Local fund-raising

This is the least satisfactory heading because it can contain all of the above activities and many more (see Table 9.6, p. 194). However, local fund-raising in charities tends to be separately organised from the above methods and has significantly different cost ratios. Regional or national charities fund-raising locally will typically have cost ratios of 40–70 per cent. These percentages are seldom declared, and would not easily be understood by the public. However, for a charity a '50 per cent profit' on expenditure invested is still very attractive and contributes large sums of money in terms of volume for many charities – typically larger than any of the above methods with the probable exception of legacies. Also it is widely believed that local fund-raising leads to legacies as well as contributing to sustaining and increasing charity awareness – the lifeblood of the charity brand.

The stock in trade of local fund-raising consists of collecting boxes, street and door-to-door collections and raffles, church collections, sponsored events such as swims or walks, social events, lotteries, shops and special events. All these need a certain amount of paid staff involvement, but the trick is to maximise volunteer involvement to keep costs down. Virtually all large and medium-sized charities have some, or many, paid fund-raisers promoting, supporting and even organising fund-raising at the local level with volunteers heavily involved. The marketing sophistication of these fund-raising methods is shown by the burgeoning academic literature, e.g. Horne and Moss 1995 and 1996 on box collection schemes.

Volunteer recruitment is becoming increasingly problematic, not because people are volunteering less, but because there is more competition among charities.

Charity shops (considered in more detail in Chapter 6) are often an essential component of local fund-raising with a total number of 5,500 outlets, 50,000 volunteers and 2,000 paid employees.

Direct marketing

Direct marketing, as its name implies, is where the charity tries to go straight to the potential donor through direct mail, press advertisements, radio and even, on some occasions, television and telephone. There has been an enormous expansion in particular of direct mail activity, which every reader will have experienced. Direct response via press advertising probably reached its height in the 1970s and early 1980s and is used less now (for fund-raising purposes at least). The cost ratios involved are some of the highest of any fund-raising method, ranging between 60 and 130 per cent. Cynically one might say that the expansion of press advertising direct response in the 1970s and early 1980s and the associated direct mail explosion since then have in part been caused by aggressive promotion from the advertising agencies and direct mail agencies. However, that is not entirely fair, because it has been seen as reaching new fund-raising markets with new products. For a minority of charities it represents the major source of income.

Direct marketing certainly has provided a major flux of marketing information and expertise into the charitable sector via the advertising agencies and direct mail agencies. To support this direct response work, an encouraging amount of market research has been undertaken among donor groups. Terms like 'market penetration', 'cost per thousand' and 'opportunities to see' have become familiar ones to charity staff previously oblivious to such useful techniques. Direct marketing has also been the bridgehead for introducing relationship marketing into charities (see Burnett 1992 and 1996). However, it is important to recognise that there are a variety of strategies not-for-profits can use to relate to donors which depend on the competencies and the resources of charities (Saxton 1996b).

Market analysis: choice of method

There is tremendous pressure on charity fund-raisers to perform. Primarily this is because of the overwhelming requirement for resources to fund services to end beneficiaries. However, there are other more subtle pressures which can be equally powerful. First, unlike so much of the rest of a charity's activities, fund-raising is all about numbers. It has a bottom line which is measurable. It is almost possible to hear a sigh of relief from trustees and senior finance managers as the fund-raising items come up on the committee agenda – at last here is something they can measure and be hard-nosed about. At the same time everyone becomes an instant expert when it comes to fund-raising, even though this may be based on nothing more than personal views on receipt of charity direct mail letters or on Christmas card designs!

This primary pressure (the desperate need for more funds) and the three secondary pressures of measurability, measurability in contrast to intangible charity services, and amateur expert judgements, put enormous strains on fund-raisers to perform well in a very short space of time. The successful fund-raising charity has to resist pressures for instant success by giving fund-raisers time to prove themselves and for financial investment to be given time to work, but must still be objective in the analysis of success and failure.

'Time to prove themselves' must include some careful analysis of the fund-raising markets the charity is in and those it might go into, and the positioning of competitor charities. It is in this chapter that we can first use the term 'competitor charity' with an easy heart. There is no doubt that charities do, and by their very nature have to, compete vigorously for funds. (As an aside, this does not mean that charities do not cooperate over sharing fund-raising experiences – commercial companies would be amazed and pleased at the constructive way that this happens in the charity sector through organisations such as the Institute of Charity Fund-raising Managers.)

Methods of expansion

Once again we have the four-way marketing choice: existing donors with existing products, existing donors with new products, new donors with existing products, and new donors with new products. It is very important to be clear which of the four choices are being pursued in what combination and with what priority.

Unless there are strong contra-indications, priority should be accorded to the first choice, i.e. existing donors with existing fund-raising products. In my experience voluntary sector managers, especially the more dynamic ones, have a tendency to be too dismissive of a charity's traditional experience and activity and over-confident about the new things they will introduce – this applies particularly to fund-raisers, who as a breed are required to be optimists! As a generalisation, which is increasingly being supported and asserted in the commercial literature in relation to customers (Reichheld and Sasser 1990, pp. 301–7; Berry and Parasuraman 1991, pp. 132–5), it is more effective and profitable to encourage existing donors to give more and to reduce the rate of attrition of donors than always to seek new ones. For example, a significant proportion of donors would give more money if we asked for more and asked more frequently. This process would be greatly facilitated if we were more effective at thinking about and valuing our donors (or even keeping track of them!). All too often the key volunteer leaders of big gift campaigns are 'under-thanked' and given too little feedback as to the impact of their efforts on the charity's work; this is similar with trust donors and corporate donors as well as individual donors. Doing these things greatly enhances the chances of larger and more frequent subsequent donations. It may seem extraordinary that charities lose track of supporters, but we do. My guess is that two charities out of three would be unable to find the names, let alone the addresses, of supporters who attended a charity fund-raising dinner as little as five years ago. Reichheld and Sasser's research (1990, p. 301–7) shows that, depending upon the industry, profits can be improved from between 25 and 85 per cent by reducing customer loss by as little as 5 per cent. There is no comparable research for charity donors but I am sure it is the correct message for us. There is a very uneven equation between the high costs of recruiting a new (major) donor, be it an individual, a trust, a company or a legator, in comparison to the relatively small amount of gratitude, valuing and cost that is required to keep the loyalty of an existing donor for longer/forever.

There is one last major reason for looking initially to the first of the four choices, i.e. greater concentration on existing donors with existing fund-raising products. This is that the fund-raising products and the methods needed to deliver them are well known to the charity and, by using a marketing approach, they can be improved for little extra cost. In contrast the time, effort and failure rate of moving to new fund-raising products, methods and donors is high and should normally be a second choice.

Criteria for fund-raising diversification

So far the arguments seem like a recipe for the *status quo*. What are the conditions for expansion into the other three choices? The most important criterion is under-utilisation of one of the most cost-effective fund-raising methods with short lead times, e.g. trusts and companies. Second, the charity may be over-dependent on one form of support (e.g. legacies or employee fund-raising) and may judge that medium-term income stability requires diversification. Third, the fund-raising market changes rapidly and methods that were very successful a few years ago are no longer so. The key judgement is to identify when a method is waning. Fourth, competitor charity activity can be influential, crowding the market. There was a period when Action Aid was one of the few successful charities raising money via sponsored events organised within schools; it only maintained that position by radically amending its product and method as competitor charities moved heavily into this market.

Donor behaviour – why people give

Commercial marketing literature seems to me to be at its least scientific in the area of consumer behaviour, reaching its low point with services rather than products. The situation is even more problematic in the field of charity marketing, and donor behaviour in particular. For example, the likely difference between what one says one does, and what one actually does, must be vastly magnified in the field of donor behaviour over and above 'straightforward' commercial buying behaviour. Halfpenny and Saxon-Harrold (1991, p. 6) list five factors that make it particularly difficult to collect reliable information about individual charitable giving, namely:

1. Selecting a representative sample.
2. Different individual perceptions about what constitutes a charity.
3. Likely over-stating of donation behaviour.
4. Difficulty in remembering what was given to whom.
5. The distorting effects of national/international disasters on donor be-haviour.

In addition, Rados (1981, p. 203) argues that 'why did you' type questions are at best uninformative and at worst misleading, first because people do not really know why they give, and second because their reasons for giving are likely to be a complex interaction from any list of possible motives.

What the charity fund-raising market needs are the long-established con-sumer buying behaviour reports found in commercial sectors, but it is difficult to see how these could be replicated in the fund-raising field with its complex distribution channels.

We therefore have to fall back on opinion surveys and the experience of well-established fund-raisers and academics writing in the field. It is both extraordinary and at the same time completely understandable that, with a product that is essentially an idea, we have no objective understanding as to why people buy (give to) the product. Several thoughtful lists of motives for giving have been hypothesised (e.g. Lovelock and Weinberg 1984, p. 505; Kotler and Andreasen 1991, p. 283), but these are based on experience of the North American donor market which is different from the British one in many respects, not least because of the greatly superior generosity of North Americans towards charities and the different tax benefits of giving. Hibbert and Horne (1996) argue that 'the decision to give seems largely to be a response to a social learning and conditioning' and as a result situational stimuli are also very important in determining giving.

If we then overlay any list of likely motives with differing psychological, social and economic factors of the target market, one begins to despair of ever raising money at all! So how can we throw any light on this subject?

First, a charity fund-raising marketer should not be put off from undertaking their own market research among the charity's existing donors. Quantitative research of this kind can be very illuminating in terms of age segmentation, sex and marital status – all attributes easily obtained from mailed questionnaires. Once this is achieved, qualitative market research through depth interviews, and possibly group discussions, can begin to shed light on particular motivations of key donor groups towards your charity's cause. This approach has certainly helped many charities to identify the groups of people who are most likely to give to them, and the variety of reasons that lead them to do so goes a long way towards helping to frame the 'ask' (i.e. the proposition for which the charity is seeking funds and the manner in which help is asked for).

Finally, while it is probably a mistake to do so (having argued that lists of motives are almost certainly spurious), as a person with a foot in both the practitioner and academic camps I am going to give my list of motives or reasons for giving. However, let me emphasise that there is no research to back up this list: it should be used with caution, as it is nothing more than a starting point for a particular charity's consideration, and almost certainly the reasons that bring a person to the point of donation will be complex and interactive rather than singular. Moreover, this list is for the UK situation:

- ☐ Being asked.
- ☐ A sense of compassion.
- ☐ Habit or tradition.
- ☐ My religion encourages it.
- ☐ As a means of recognition by peers/superiors.
- ☐ Knowing someone alive or dead who was in that situation.
- ☐ Being, or having been, in that situation myself.
- ☐ Because the charity recognises me and keeps me involved.
- ☐ To receive benefits accorded to donors and their immediate family.
- ☐ Embarrassment (too embarrassed to say no).
- ☐ To get rid of the asker.

- ☐ Life has treated me well, I have a responsibility to help others less well off.
- ☐ Community expectation (e.g. new science block for the school).
- ☐ Feel good, feel better as a person.

I finish with the 'feel good' reason for giving, because if there were one over-arching reason for giving, I believe it is because they feel better as a person afterwards. The task of the charity fund-raiser is to establish what will make any individual or organisations 'feel better' afterwards.

The fund-raising product: mainly idea, sometimes service and physical good

Fund-raising products are essentially ideas

At its heart the fund-raising product is an idea. At first this seems strange because the money is required for very tangible activities, e.g. food for hungry people, education for disadvantaged groups, activity to stop whaling, etc. But in the vast majority of cases the donor will be relatively distant from the physical goods or services created by their donation. I emphasise 'relatively' distant because there are some situations in which a donor can experience the object of their donation, e.g. contributing towards saving a picture for the nation and then going to view it. However, this personal experience is still relatively distant in time and space from the donation. Normally the donor is 'purchasing' an idea which they will never see put into practice, or if they do, they will normally have no rights or control over it. Transferred into the commercial scene, this scenario would be either unbelievable or fraudulent!

Nevertheless, fund-raising idea product marketing has much to learn from service product marketing. Donating towards a fund-raising idea has major similarities with purchasing a service, but also some differences. it is *similar* in that:

- ☐ the idea product is intangible;
- ☐ ownership is not generally transferred;
- ☐ the idea product cannot be resold;
- ☐ the idea cannot be easily demonstrated before donation; and
- ☐ in most cases direct contact between the donor and the charity is necessary.

However, it is *different* to a service in that:

- ☐ the idea product can be stored (although it is questionable how meaningful this is);
- ☐ production and consumption do not really coincide;
- ☐ implementation of the idea is spatially and temporarily separate;

☐ the idea can be transported and even exported; and
☐ the donor takes no part in the production.

(This is a comparison with the list of attributes of services given by Baker 1991, p. 554.)

Constructing a fund-raising idea product is as simple or difficult as answering all the basic interrogatives. In other words, what is the proposition? Who is it going to benefit? How will it work, and what will be the outcome? However, selecting the proposition from the wide range of activities that the charity is undertaking must be in relation to whom the fund-raising idea product is being aimed at. In other words, the benefits of the idea product have to be selected and promoted according to the old marketing mnemonic of AIDA – attention, interest, desire, action.

In essence the fund-raiser takes the beneficiary service product and

☐ re-shapes it into an idea product;
☐ selects for featuring those of the beneficiary benefits which are most likely to appeal to the donor;
☐ makes the idea product as tangible as possible.

How does the fund-raiser re-shape the product? S/he examines the benefits it provides to the beneficiary and selects those which are most likely to appeal to the donor. For example, a visiting service to older people may have several effects including maintaining independence and relieving loneliness. The fund-raiser will be more effective as well as legitimate by choosing the attribute which is most attractive to the donor. What is illegitimate is to choose to feature an attribute which is not part of the beneficiary offering simply because it will appeal to the donor. Some fund-raisers in the disability and overseas aid fields have done just that, for example through inviting pity and showing pathetic images to donors when the benefits for beneficiaries are not ones of dependency but ones of empowerment.

Virtually all fund-raising experience suggests that the more specific the proposal can be, both in its description and outcomes, the better. An idea product of 'helping people overseas' is not nearly as attractive to the donor as '£15 will buy two hoes, two spades, a scythe and 25 kg of seeds to enable a family to plant and tend their land, providing them with enough food to be self-sufficient' (Oxfam 1993).

But however specific and concrete the idea is, it is still essentially intangible and the charity fund-raiser has to employ the techniques that goods and services marketers use to address this problem. They need to give evidence of tangibility both at the time of asking for money and subsequently by way of reassurance. Tangibility can be indicated through simple devices such as personalising individuals who are typical of the group of beneficiaries; providing photographs of the work in action; gaining testimonials from people who have been helped, through films and videos of the work; and even producing samples of the work. (For example, an overseas aid charity including a small packet of hydration salts in their direct mail letter, or a blind charity enclosing a sample of Braille, or Oxfam encouraging the general public at exhibitions to operate an appropriate technology water pump – see Figure 9.2. p. 208)

However, the 'after-sales service', as a service marketer would call it, is extremely important. If someone has purchased something as fragile as an idea, they will need subsequent reassurance to establish and maintain trust, which is perhaps the most vital aspect of the relationship between a charity and its donors. Wherever possible (and it is not always so), the fund-raising marketer will give progress reports to donors with either explicit or implicit opportunities to achieve continuing financial support. This formula, which is a product attribute, is applicable to every method of fund-raising apart from receipt of a legacy!

Service component of fund-raising products

Because idea products alone are so intangible, fund-raisers from time immemorial have introduced service components into their fund-raising, e.g. fund-raising dinners, sponsored walks, film premières, etc. There has to be an idea product at the core of any of these events, but the presenting product is effectively a service that encourages the exchange between the donor and the charity. Introducing the strong service component makes life very complicated for the charity marketer as described above in the section on different fund-raising methods and in the case study of the fund-raising dinner in Chapter 1. In the service component, the three extra 'Ps' of service marketing, i.e. people, physical evidence and processes, come into play. For example, the attitude and behaviour of charity staff in personal contact with donors become crucial to successful outcomes; similarly the effect of other participant donors is crucial. If 10 per cent of the participants of a sponsored walk are what might colloquially be called 'lager louts', what does that say to loyal family supporters about the charity? Will the latter continue to remain loyal?

Physical goods

The most concrete form of fund-raising products are physical goods and these were described in Chapter 6, and cover items such as Christmas cards, the contents of charity catalogues and so on, i.e. they are items that the purchaser donor would almost certainly have bought anyway, but they choose to buy them from the charity at roughly similar prices to what they would have paid commercially, with the added value of the charity branding.

Figure 9.2 Making the fund-raising *idea product* tangible – in its fund-raising drives, Oxfam aims to 'give people a better understanding of the reality of life in the developing world' (*Oxfam Review*, 1991/2) (Rob Davis/Oxfam)

Simultaneous multiple fund-raising products

Any marketer who has not by now gained a graphic picture of the complexity of managing charity work, as attested to by Drucker (1990, p. 83), is likely to do so under this section! For example, it is not unusual for charity fund-raisers to be marketing a fund-raising idea, a fund-raising service and fund-raising physical goods all at the same time. A very obvious example is the fund-raising dinner. Here the core fund-raising *idea* to, say, equip a new classroom, has to be established with a clear target sum, e.g. £5,000 to be raised from the dinner, and the idea has to be effectively communicated before, during and after the dinner to supporters. However, the *service* of the dinner itself has to be marketed, e.g. which aristocrats or dignitaries are going to be there and what opportunities will there be to meet them? Who will be your peers at the dinner and are these the kind of people you wish to meet? Can the answer to this last question be indicated by the prestigious venue, the price and the menu? Will there be entertainment provided at the dinner, and if so, do you declare who will be providing this in advance even though it may put some people off? On the evening itself, how do you staff it with sufficient charity representatives to provide specific back-up, but not so many as to make the diners feel that there are charity freeloaders? Given that many tables will be booked by one person on behalf of about a dozen other people, how do you get their names and addresses for follow-up work without appearing unduly nosy? These are just some of the service marketing challenges that have to be met and designed beforehand.

There will also be the obvious *physical goods* aspect of the service, such as the quality of the food, and in addition there will almost certainly be a raffle of donated items which is often the most profitable element of the event, exceeding profits on dinners paid for by tickets. This requires auction prizes that will appeal to those people attending, who in turn have to have enough money to purchase them, and who have to be advised in advance about what items are likely to be auctioned, but advised in such a way as not to scare them off!

And somehow in the middle of all this convivial and quite frequently inebriate enjoyment, the idea product of the equipment for the classroom has to be made as tangible as possible by the chairperson of the evening, because memories lapse and people are not there simply to have a good time – they came with the purpose of raising money for your core idea product.

Price – give choice

Some of the previous examples will begin to indicate how complex pricing decisions in the marketing mix are when it comes to charity fund-raising offerings.

Something as simple as a *price level* poses difficulties. The fund-raising idea can be defined in such a way as to get different price levels, and these are in part determined by the likely acceptability to potential donors. For example, Help the Aged's '£10 to make a blind person see' seems an incredible bargain. Is it actually too cheap to be believable? If it is, then the text of the appeal needs to explain why it is such a good bargain. Also such a low price might depress the total income level achieved for the idea. Therefore the charity has to consider upping the price by including the legitimate extra overhead costs, or by encouraging people to help restore the sight of 10 people or even 100 people.

Efficient fund-raisers will develop a portfolio of fund-raising products covering different aspects of the charity's work and different price levels from, say, £5 for a small item of physical goods for a charity beneficiary, right the way up to £1 million to build a new wing to a school.

Payment terms are complex even for the charity fund-raisers familiar with the field. These include a one-off payment, regular cash payments, standing orders, covenants, Gift Aid, special charity cheque accounts, payroll deductions, credit cards, sponsorship units, legacies, etc. Some of these payment methods allow the charity to reclaim tax that the donor has already paid (albeit only at the standard rate). As a general rule a charity will wish the donor to enter into a method of planned, continuous giving which will maximise a tax addition to a charity. However, deciding how to achieve this without scaring off the donor can be a complicated and sensitive process.

Promotion – the importance of personal selling

Advertising, *publicity* and *public relations* are the very stuff of charity marketing. However, publicity and public relations are considerably more difficult to achieve in the area of fund-raising than they are in the area of service giving. Television, radio and the press are far more hard-nosed about editorial coverage of fund-raising activity than they are about service-giving work. Perhaps the pleasant exception to this is the local press. Press, radio and/or TV support of fund-raising activity is very much an art rather than a science, and, in comparison to commercial products, suffers a chronic lack of under-funding. In part this is because the money simply is not there, and in part it is because the detailed causal link between the advertising of fund-raising activity and the final take has not been established.

Personal selling receives a very high profile in charity fund-raising. Although it only comes from estimates of experienced fund-raisers, I am inclined to believe the assertion that personal approaches to donors are five times more effective than telephone approaches, which in turn are five times more effective than written approaches – effective being described in terms of the numbers of donations and their total value. But what are the attributes of these 'personal sellers'? Bayley (1988, pp. 14–16) describes the key attributes as follows:

☐ proven leadership;
☐ involvement;
☐ commitment (to the charity, or at least to charity in general);
☐ community recognition (here community can be one of interest as well as geographic).

When we move into the field of *sales promotion* (or, as charity managers would call it, 'recognition and awards'), once again the commercial world of money-off initiatives and on-pack competitions seems relatively simple. Major donors, loyal donors and outstanding volunteers are all offered access to a range of incentives. These can be categorised in three main ways:

☐ status incentives;
☐ access incentives; and
☐ process incentives.

Status incentives are very varied, but they all provide the donor, or indeed volunteer, with enhanced status, certainly in the individual's mind and usually more widely among their peers. For example, powerful volunteer fund-raising leaders may be made vice-presidents of the charity – prestigious offices only offered to relatively few people, but sinecures, i.e. they do not allow the rewarded person significant involvement in decision-making, at least outside their own area of experience and expertise. Another form of status recognition is the naming of a classroom, lifeboat, residential block, etc., in a major donor's honour. Some charities create member grades depending on the length of donor service. Most charities invite major donors to receptions to hear about the charity's work. Some charities have a donor book where major donor names are recorded and some still list major donors in their annual reports, including people who have left a legacy.

Access incentives operate at the higher levels of donor (and, for that matter, volunteer) contribution level. For traditional, historical reasons charities have ready access to at least the aristocracy, and quite often to royalty. While royalty do not always wish to be associated with direct fund-raising, they are very happy to meet major supporters at receptions discreetly and decorously arranged. While I would not pretend that access opportunities are a sufficient incentive to secure extraordinary donor effort, they are certainly recognised informally as rewards which can provide peer group recognition on a fairly significant scale. At a 'lower' level, other access opportunities can be provided such as meeting the charity directors, chief executive, chairperson or committee chairperson. For the really interested and committed donor these meetings can be equally if not more satisfying because they learn more about the work and the impact their donations have. Big gift campaigns also provide access incentives in that, for example, business leaders know that they will meet business leaders from other sectors, and 'junior' business leaders will meet 'senior' ones.

Process recognition bears some relationship to status recognition in that it often involves appointing people to committees, but the appointments are working ones rather than sinecures, and generally have lower conventional status. However, they do provide opportunities for committed donors and volunteers to become more heavily involved in the work of the charity, on the basis of their knowledge and expertise, e.g. in certain forms of fund-raising or publicity committees, etc. Other forms of process recognition involve inviting loyal donors to service establishments or offices and meeting the workers involved in direct service delivery, but on a regular basis.

All the above incentives contribute to a relationship marketing approach. Charities are particularly well placed to be able to achieve such relationships, although they are often singularly oblivious and indifferent to these needs of their volunteers and donors. Many donors welcome the opportunity to become more involved in the charity, giving them personal development and the charity more effective advocates. Burnett (1992) develops comprehensive arguments on what he calls 'relationship fund-raising'.

Place/distribution of fund-raising ideas

In the selling of ideas, the distribution/delivery of those ideas becomes a much more dominant direct responsibility of the fund-raising marketer than their commercial FMCG counterpart. The 'medium is the method' of direct marketing fund-raising. Similarly the voluntary fund-raising committees, special events, fund-raising, retail shops, postal appeals, jumble sales, collecting boxes, etc., are all a part of the method of distribution of fund-raising, i.e. getting the fund-raising idea product out to the potential donor to purchase. *Location* of both the fund-raising idea product and the potential donor can be crucial. Most charities have strong and weak geographic areas of support which will have been determined over the years, e.g. through the presence of a stronger service delivery capacity, the strength of the fund-raising network in that area, the traditional strength of the fund-raising leadership, etc.

Accessibility of donating opportunities are crucial, as are *distribution* channels. In this respect charities connected with church networks achieve a massive competitive advantage because of their good geographic coverage. National charities spend a great deal of time and effort in extending and strengthening the distribution of their fund-raising arms across the United Kingdom.

Conclusion

Fund-raising has been the bridgehead through which marketing has increasingly established itself in the charity world. This has been achieved because commercial marketing is relatively easily and effectively translated into fund-raising, and because fund-raising and public relations have traditionally involved advertising agencies which have exported marketing concepts and practices.

However, charity fund-raisers have adopted these marketing principles and practices in sophisticated ways, often unique to the charity world. This is particularly true of price and promotion in the marketing mix, along with product as an idea.

In contrast with this sophisticated understanding and application of marketing techniques in the product mix, the understanding of donor behaviour in any scientific, objective fashion is in its very early stages. Arguably fund-raisers are selling nothing but ideas to donors for quite high prices and with virtually no understanding of donor behaviour! It works because donors trust charities to translate their donations into necessary and cost-effective action. Consequently donor trust of charity objectives and activities is one of the most precious and powerful attributes that the individual charity and the sector as a whole possess. Anything that substantially dents that trust will spell disaster.

Key points

Main fund-raising methods: legacies, trust donations, big gift campaigns, corporate giving (donations, gifts in kind, sponsorship, company-specific staff schemes, payroll deduction), special events, local fund-raising, direct marketing. Each requires a particular marketing approach.

Choosing the method
- [ ] Allow fund-raisers sufficient time for proper market and competitor analysis.
- [ ] Give priority to expanding existing donors and existing fund-raising products where these are successful.
- [ ] Diversify if existing methods are weak for some reason, e.g. under-utilisation of methods with short lead times, over-dependence on one form of support, market changes, increased competition.
- [ ] Remember that donor behaviour is complex, but quantitative research supported by careful qualitative research can be helpful.

The product
- [ ] Constructing the fund-raising product and promoting it is similar to a service. What is the proposition? Whom is it for? How will it work? What will be the outcome? Be as specific as possible.

☐ For the marketer, it is important to note that the fund-raising product can operate at a number of levels simultaneously – primarily an idea, but also a service and occasionally a physical good.

Price
☐ Develop a portfolio of fund-raising products at different price levels to attract as wide a group of donors as possible.
☐ Make complicated payment terms as straightforward as possible to avoid alienating potential donors.

Promotion
☐ Personal selling is probably the most effective means of promoting the product.
☐ Reward major and loyal donors or outstanding volunteers with incentives providing *status* or recognition, *access* and *process*.

Place
☐ Location of the product is crucial, as is ease of giving.

10

WHOLE CHARITY MARKETING: IDENTITY AND POSITIONING

Charity identity and charity positioning are inextricably linked. The charity identity has to reflect faithfully its role, and the role depends heavily on the positioning of the charity in the public's mind in relation to local and national statutory services, commercial organisations and particularly other charities. This chapter is the nearest that this book comes to strategic marketing planning. In the business world, *strategic marketing planning* has colonised (with some justification) the area known as *strategic planning* in the charity and statutory organisation worlds. In North America this colonisation has occurred also in the not-for-profit area. However, in the United Kingdom strategic planning in charities is well established and, provided that it assumes a marketing approach, seems to me to serve satisfactorily.

Public and beneficiary trust and confidence in the charity sector

Before looking at individual charities it is useful to look at the image or identity of the whole charity sector, as viewed by the public and beneficiaries. The Deakin Commission (NCVO 1996) on the future of the voluntary sector emphasises the importance of public confidence in charities for which there is conflicting evidence. That around 70 per cent of the public donate to charity and donate well in excess of £2 billion each year suggests a very high degree of trust and confidence. The Henley Centre has shown a decline over the years in trust and confidence in public institutions and, although not measured until 1996, we can assume charities are part of this trend. In 1996, 33 per cent of the public had a 'great deal or quite a lot of confidence' in charities as compared with 69 per cent in the Royal Mail, 46 per cent in the banks, 41 per cent in the BBC, 40 per cent in NHS, 35 per cent in schools, 25 per cent in the church, 14 per cent in the civil service and trade unions and 11 per cent in government (Henley Centre 1996). While our rank position is not too bad, a score of only 33 per cent is far from ideal.

More worrying is research (Fenton 1995) which reports a survey of 1000 members of the public in which donors (95 per cent of the sample) were asked about their trust in charities.

☐ 56 per cent do not believe that donations reach the people they are intended for;
☐ 52 per cent believe there is corruption in charities with people pocketing funds;
☐ 49 per cent believe that too many charities have plush offices, shops, etc.;
☐ 34 per cent believe too many charities do similar things;
☐ 17 per cent believe charities are run by disorganised amateurs.

Luckily there is some evidence that young people are not nearly so negative (Lynn and Davis Smith 1991; Gaskin, Vlaeminke and Fenton 1996).

Despite the encouraging views of young people one has to ask why the population of donors is so critical. Could it be unfair media portrayal, so often blamed for their standing by groups who feel they are underrated (e.g. politicians)? Deacon, Golding and Walker (1994) give us no hope here, having surveyed charity media coverage closely over a six month period, they concluded that 'there was a remarkable absence of reflective or negative commentary about voluntary activity in news coverage... '. So if journalists should choose to attack charities in the same way that they have attacked many other institutions we could be in for a rough ride.

This prompts the question: does it really matter? It could be argued that trust is important for any organisation with customers. But for charities it is much more important. As we have seen in pressure group/advocacy work and in fund-raising, the products are essentially ideas which have to be taken on trust. If a donor does not trust a charity then the donations are at risk. If voters, politicians and civil servants do not trust charities, will they embrace our campaigning ideas? Will new beneficiary customers come forward in large numbers?

So it is encumbent on charities, if they are to have a sympathetic audience, to put and keep their houses in order. Each charity that exhibits low standards is likely to fuel customer mistrust. Thus the way in which we develop (consciously or unconsciously) our individual charity identities is not only important to the particular charity, but to the whole sector.

Charity identity – brand and brand image

The charity identity is the very personality of the organisation as perceived by the target markets. It comes close to the term 'brand' used in commercial marketing where individual lines of physical goods have brands and brand names, e.g. Persil. Generally speaking, as far as services go, the brand is associated with the company, e.g. Forte hotels (for a discussion of commercial brands see de Chernatony and McDonald 1992). The term 'charity identity' is used here rather than 'charity brand' because of the commercial overtones of the term 'brand' which are unattractive to the charity world. Sometimes the term corporate identity is used.

It is useful in understanding the importance and value of a charity identity or brand to look at the commercial world where brand equity is the financial value of a brand and is based on such things as the extent of brand loyalty, name awareness, perceived quality, the strength of brand associations, other assets such as patents and trademarks, and communication and distribution channel relationships. You can see the financial value of brands when, in company takeovers, the purchaser appears to pay well over the odds for another company just because it has highly valued brands. For example, Nestlé paid far more than the strict value of Rowntree assets in order to purchase the Rowntree name and its various individual brands. While it may not appear on the balance sheet, a strong, well-supported brand can be said to be the most enduring asset a company has.

The charity brand and brand image, or what I would prefer to call the charity identity, is just as, if not more, valuable and has to be carefully nurtured to gain maximum success.

If the charity identity is the very personality of the organisation, what are its constituent parts? The most obvious constituent of the identity is the charity name, but other valuable elements are the logo or representative symbol, well-established slogans, publicly sited buildings especially shops, signs, vehicles, publications, staff (their presentation, attitudes and behaviour), supporters and beneficiaries. Indeed the whole representation of the charity to its target markets constructs the identity. The *physical representation* of the charity to the general public and potential beneficiaries (via name, logo, etc.) is capable of firm control by the charity. But because services are so dominant in the charity field, the *direct experiences* of the large numbers of supporters and beneficiaries are crucial in establishing the charity identity.

Why is charity identity so important?

If we learn from the commercial world of brands, it is because it *simplifies choice* for potential customers (in our case mainly beneficiaries and supporters). It guarantees *quality* and it allows *self-expression* (McNeal and Zeren 1981, p. 35). As a guarantee of quality it is important to all charity customers but especially for targeted decision-makers (Parminter 1997). More fundamentally it allows customers to distinguish between charities in general and between charities operating within specific fields (e.g. children).

It is more difficult for smaller charities to create strong identities because they have fewer resources and often an unsupportive organisational culture towards marketing. Nevertheless it is vital, and Dixon (1997) describes how

Crisis, a medium-sized UK charity for single homeless people, has achieved this using a marketing approach. Small local charities can boost the strength of their local identity by joining an appropriate national umbrella network, such as Age Concern, or MIND.

Charity customers face a bewildering choice with 180,000 or so registered charities, plus all the other not-for-profit organisations such as hospitals. A strong charity brand will be chosen more often, not only within the market sub-sector e.g. overseas aid or disability etc., but across the whole not-for-profit market. A strong charity identity will also give customers reassurance on the quality and effectiveness of the work undertaken, a tag to help customers instantly recall their favourable perceptions. A strong charity identity will also attract certain kinds of customer. GreenPeace supporters are very different from Age Concern supporters who in turn are very different from Royal Opera House supporters.

If that is why a strong brand is useful to customers, why is a strong charity identity so important to us? First, a strong brand gives us a high *awareness* which is obviously a necessary, but not sufficient, requirement for a large donor base and a large beneficiary take-up rate. Perhaps more importantly a strong charity brand gives us *customer loyalty*. Customer loyalty is crucial because it is estimated to be up to ten times more costly to recruit a new customer than it is to keep an existing one. And this is at the heart of the benefit of a strong charity identity, namely that the marketing spend is much more cost effective when a charity has a strong identity with its concomitant large customer base.

A final reason for our need for a strong charity identity is that it allows what the commercial marketers call brand extension, i.e. launching new products under the brand name. In essence this allows the charity with a strong identity to extend its work into a different but related area on the back of its good reputation. The extension could be into a new geographic area or it could be into a new work function. For example, following the remarkable success of Band Aid, through Live Aid, there have been a number of events and organisations launched with the word 'aid' in the title. Commercial marketers would argue, and I think they are right, that Wateraid's launch and present success will have been helped by the acquired communication strength of the word 'aid' and the generally good reputation of other events and activities under the 'aid' headline.

It is also important to be clear that charity identity or brand image is not what *we* think it is or want it to be, but rather how it is actually perceived out there by existing and potential customers. Of course, we must have aspirations for our charity identity, but they must be realistic aspirations and they must develop out of the reality of our current *perceived* charity identity.

In concise form, then, I would define a charity identity as '*the interaction of the target market's values with the received knowledge and experience of the charity'.*

Individual values are crucial. If a potential supporter does not believe that there is a role for charities and that such provision should be supplied by the state, then their reception of the messages coming from a charity will be considerably different from someone generally supportive of charitable endeavours. The distinction between knowledge and experience is also important. The charity can do much to control the information going out to target markets, and, all things being equal, potential customers will take the information at face value. However, once a potential customer (either beneficiary or supporter) has turned into an actual one, they will judge the charity identity to a greater extent on the basis of their experience, rather than on the more straightforward charity messages transmitted via advertising, publicity and public relations.

What are the charity target markets?

For analytical, planning and service delivery reasons, it is important to distinguish between various target markets. Chapter 3 lays out a typology of customers consisting of beneficiaries, supporters, stakeholders and regulators. That is not to say that on some occasions there will not be overlap between two or more of these groups which, for example in the case of mutual aid organisations, will come close to being complete, i.e. beneficiaries are supporters and vice versa. However, for the majority of charities, in most situations, these groups are distinct.

A further distinction which is extremely important is between *potential* customers and *actual* customers. As was described in the previous section, because charities are service dominated, actual direct experience of the charity has a powerful and distinct impact on how it is regarded.

As in the commercial world, charities spend a great deal of time, money and effort in addressing potential supporters, and often do much less with their existing supporters. This can not only be expensive (see pp. 201–3), it can also undermine charity identity.

On the other hand, charities are sometimes less assiduous in promoting to their potential beneficiaries. This is for a variety of reasons, not least the frequent difficulty of securing effective channels through which to reach them. However, an underlying inhibitor is that, in general, the more actual beneficiaries a charity recruits, the more money it 'loses' (i.e. the more it has to achieve through other forms of income generation). Thus there is not the same incentive for charities to reach out to potential beneficiaries as there is for commercial companies to reach more consumers.

These conclusions are particularly important in relation to charity identity because lost or undervalued supporters obviously do a great deal to undermine a positive charity image; and loss of opportunity among potential beneficiaries similarly reduces the charity's ability to promote its identity.

Why is charity identity development so difficult?

Commercial managers and academics have been open enough to acknowledge that in certain respects charity management, and charity marketing in particular, is very difficult because of our multiple customer groups (Drucker 1990, p. 83). Charity identity development, or what in commerce would be called brand development is perhaps *the* most difficult area. Why? Because in the charity brand one has to have a consistently presented identity which is acceptable to all four customer groups, i.e. beneficiaries, supporters, stakeholders and regulators. If one 'says' different things to different customer groups this will become obvious and the charity will put in jeopardy that most valuable charity asset – trust.

Why should we be tempted to say different things to different groups? The answers are not pleasant and represent a part of charity history we should like to forget. In this analysis I dwell only on beneficiaries and individual donor supporters. Beneficiaries often have no choice but to accept the charity offerings, but donors may go to any number of competitor charities and have their needs met. So for certain periods of their history some charities have sacrificed their overriding commitment to beneficiary needs and given priority to donor desires which undermine beneficiary needs. Examples of this were the emaciated children on the direct response adverts of overseas aid charities which left no dignity to the beneficiaries or the disability charities which used pathetic images of beneficiaries to gain more support.

So in developing their identities charities have to accept that they (a) cannot maximise their identity strength with all customer groups and (b), in my view, have to give priority to beneficiary needs and desires even though this could weaken the appeal to the supporter group. While this may seem morally obvious and legally required (by Charity Law) it is not infrequently challenged by fund-raisers. The most subtle challenge is to argue that supporter needs are 'equal' to those of beneficiaries. In my experience this results in messages which undermine beneficiaries.

It is reassuring that Tapp (1996), in an admittedly small survey, found that 'much of their day-to-day management is, however, concerned with such issues as maintaining a consistent style and tone of voice, and careful reviews of policies and actions to ensure they reflect their personality'. However, Pidgeon (1996) is not so sanguine about charities' ability to be professional in their approach to identity/brand development. He reports from his considerable experience in charity direct marketing that, unlike commercial organisation clients of his agency, charities clients were almost often unable to brief him in depth on 'the brand, the brand values and the position the brand holds in the market place'.

Both sets of evidence are reconcilable because in my experience charities have got better at ensuring 'consistent style and tone of voice' but seldom get to grips with (often unspoken) core values, what we stand for and what other relevant players stand for. These aspects need to be articulated, written down and formally agreed.

What constitutes the charity identity?

In discussing identity it is useful to distinguish between the *presented identity* (i.e. through one-way messages from charity to potential customer), *perceived identity and experienced identity* (i.e. where the customer and charity interact, normally in a support service setting or a beneficiary service setting).

Presented identity

Presented identity is the sum of the messages we send out to actual and potential customers: our purposes, values, activities and effectiveness. It is not just the consistent presentation of the name and logo. Pidgeon (1996) argues that while commercial organisations view their brands comprehensively and consistently, charities view their identities narrowly, simply as the graphic representation of their names and logos, normally consistently displayed. In my experience Pidgeon's view is correct.

Of the attributes that are presented to customers, the *name* though is clearly the most powerful element of the identity mix. The value to charity identity of names such as Save the Children, Help the Aged and Guide Dogs for the Blind is massive.

Berry and Parasuraman (1991, p. 120) propose four criteria for assessing the power of a brand name, which would seem equally relevant to a charity name. They are as follows:

1. Distinctiveness – the name immediately distinguishes the firm from competitors.
2. Relevance – the name conveys the nature or benefit.
3. Memorability – the name can be understood, used and recalled easily.
4. Flexibility – the name accommodates inevitable strategy changes in organisations.

The most dramatically successful names in the charity world fulfil all these criteria. Guide Dogs for the Blind fulfils the first three but is left with very little flexibility to do anything else but provide guide dogs for blind people.

The British Red Cross fulfils all the criteria except for relevance. It is very distinctive, memorable and flexible but the majority of people simply do not know what the Red Cross does in this country. What was the World Wildlife Fund (WWF) and is now the Worldwide Fund for Nature has had continuing challenges associated with its name. It has always been distinctive but not very memorable, and on occasions insufficiently flexible. It has solved the problem by using the initials WWF wherever possible, which works particularly well given their international remit.

However, it is important to point out that names can be very successful even when they do not fulfil every criterion. Greenpeace must be one of the most successful names and is certainly distinctive, memorable and flexible – but it does not convey, at least immediately, what the organisation does. However, the dramatic exploits of the organisation have more than overcome that problem.

Berry and Parasuraman (1991, p. 128) also argue that where a name has significant weaknesses as well as strengths, a decision to change the name should not be taken lightly. This is certainly the case with established charities which have a tremendous stock of awareness and goodwill built into their names, deriving in the main from decades, if not hundreds, of years of investment. In commercial marketing this is called brand equity and is sometimes valued on the balance sheet.

Also powerful in identity is the charity *logo*. WWF's panda, the Red Cross logo and so on are very powerful elements of the identity mix. In the case of WWF, the panda logo is probably better known than the name of the organisation and as such is extremely valuable – indeed so valuable that it is 'sold' on to commercial companies in joint promotional activity. Commercial exploitation of charity names and logos is a contentious area with passionate advocates on both sides. Some argue that the proper commercial exploitation of names and logos is not only valuable in income terms, but is also useful in spreading the message. Others argue that the purity of a charity identity is absolutely crucial in encouraging and maintaining the trust that supporters and beneficiaries place in it, and that commercial exploitation degrades the identity. As in most cases the true position is probably somewhere in the middle, i.e. commercial exploitation is beneficial providing that the criteria for acceptable use are strictly laid down and, even more importantly, strictly monitored. The Vegetarian Society has from time to time suffered because its 'licensing' of vegetarian products has not been sufficiently strictly monitored.

However, the rigorous and regular presentation of the name, logo and associated slogans is not enough to establish the strength of many charity identities. The content of *publicity and public relations* initiatives is crucial in establishing the identity. For example, powerful TV images of Oxfam workers giving practical help in disastrous situations of food shortage in a

Third World country, television reportage of feeding centres run by Crisis at Christmas, and the continuing powerful images surrounding Shelter, some 25 years since the TV film 'Cathy Come Home', all contribute significantly to charity identity.

However, you need to keep an eye on *all* your communications channels and not simply advertising, publicity and public relations. It never ceases to amaze me how charities use opportunities for branding poorly or lose them completely. For example, until 1986, RNIB had 60,000 talking book tape recording machines in people's homes – unbranded. Before you smile too broadly, make sure you check what invoices coming out of the finance department look like, check what the rogue publications which have not been through the publications department look like, check what the switch-boards in your organisations sound like to strangers, and so on.

The *physical expression* of the name and logo through signs, publications, advertisements, physical products, etc., often establishes the difference between the ordinary charity and the professional marketing one. The discipline required to have a common physical representation is great, especially in charities where individualism and dynamism are often a hallmark!

Perceived identity

Even if a person has little contact with a charity, the perceived identity can be different from the presented one. Individuals have many preconceived ideas about charities in general (e.g. 'I don't think they should exist'), groups of charities (e.g. 'We concern ourselves too much with animals and not enough with children') and individual charities (e.g. 'My mother collected for Barnardo's and I have always had a soft spot for them'). So charities have to devote considerable energy to finding out what their target groups think about them and must create their communications with this information in mind.

Experienced identity

Berry and Parasuraman (1991, p. 118) place much emphasis on the belief that in service companies it is the customers rather than the presented messages that are as important – if not more so – in the establishment of brand perception and organisation identity. They argue that an excellent branding strategy can make a strong service stronger, but it cannot rescue a weak one. If that is true of commercial services, it has to be true of charities and hence should go some way to reassuring cynics who regard promotion of charity identity as superficial misrepresentation.

Charities such as WWF, SCOPE and the RSPB have literally millions of supporters. If mass membership charities treat them with disdain by bombarding them with unwanted letters, triplicate or even quadruplicate mailings, addressing them as Mr when they are Miss, politely reprimanding them because they have not yet donated when they have, then no amount of presented advertising and publicity is going to convince any of these supporters that their charity identity is anything other than poor. The charities quoted above go to great lengths to care for their supporters which can turn them into a massive force of advocates in the population at large.

One cannot underestimate the positive advocacy powers of committed supporters in charities. Hinton (1993, p. 22) describes the motivating effect of supporter conferences in Save the Children and gives impressive anecdotal evidence of supporter commitment which these conferences and other volunteer support schemes encourage.

While the positive impact on charity identity of committed supporters and the negative effect of disaffected ones is great, so also can be the expressed views of particularly pleased or disaffected beneficiaries. The positive advocacy impact of newly blind elderly people enjoying reading novels which they felt they never could read again (via talking books) produces the most amazing amount of gratitude and positive commitment. Equally, however, a letter from an RNIB customer who has inadvertently been charged twice for a technical aid that broke within the warranty period and had to be replaced, has to be read to be believed!

Direct experiences and subsequent word-of-mouth recommendation from beneficiaries and supporters are crucial in establishing charity identity.

Research – crucial for identity maintenance and development

Marketing research and analysis are crucial in establishing, amending or repositioning a charity identity and position in the market. While it is possible to subdivide further, the views and commitment of four main groups of people need to be gained, namely beneficiaries, supporters, stakeholders (especially staff) and regulators.

Research among beneficiaries

Research among beneficiaries has been mentioned many times in this book. As far as the charity identity and position is concerned, it is vital to understand how actual and potential beneficiaries regard the charity, and particularly to obtain such basic information as what percentage has heard of the charity! Staff and trustees tend to imagine that the charity is very well known, particularly among beneficiaries. Market research often brings home uncomfortable truths. Research among beneficiaries is far less prevalent than one might imagine or hope. When RNIB published its major needs survey (Bruce *et al.* 1991) it was surprising how many other charities said that they wished they had similar research available for their own beneficiary groups and how they regard the charity. It is difficult to imagine how a charity can develop its identity and positioning, let alone provide core services, if it is unaware of the detailed needs of the actual and potential beneficiary groups. Penetration estimates, usage patterns and opinions among beneficiaries are fundamental inputs to charity identity and positioning.

Research among supporters

Research among supporters and potential supporters is more widespread. Once again this is probably because of the influence and involvement of advertising agencies in the fund-raising market. Virtually all the large charities undertake attitude research among their actual and potential supporters. This reveals strengths and weaknesses of the charity identity. On age profile, most charities have an older age skew among supporters, while a few (e.g. Oxfam) will have relatively more support among younger and middle-aged people. Some charities score particularly high in terms of honesty, efficiency and cost effectiveness. Others have stronger identity areas in the field of innovation and pioneering work (e.g. Greenpeace and Shelter). Whatever the results, research among supporters will tell the charity how it is regarded, how well it is getting its messages across and the extent to which it can or ought to shift supporter understanding of its identity.

Most of the larger, more marketing-orientated charities commission regular quantitative awareness and attitudinal surveys among the general public. Typically these surveys are undertaken by one of the large commercial survey companies, involve a sample of around 1,000 people and occur once or twice a year. The surveys cover prompted and unprompted awareness. The latter is sought by a question on the lines of 'Please tell me the names of ten charities that come to mind', the purpose being to identify the charities that are most prominent in the mind of the general public. Although all research will have inherent weaknesses, these regular awareness surveys provide a valuable tracking capability, e.g. if identical questions are asked among comparable samples at six-monthly intervals, then significant rises and falls of awareness (perhaps related to promotional activity) can be identified.

An example of *unprompted awareness* measurement is that commissioned by RNIB on a regular basis from the Harris Research Centre. Approximately 1,000 adults aged over 15 are interviewed at home via an omnibus survey. The question asked is as follows: 'Thinking now about charities, can you tell me the names of all charities or other fund-raising organisations you have ever heard of?' No names are read out to the respondents, but when they appear to 'dry up' the interviewer prompts with the question 'Any others?' three consecutive times. The results are then analysed and reported in total, and broken down by sex, age, social class and ITV regions. The national total results in 1997 were as follows:

Cancer Research Campaign	36%
Oxfam	33%
RSPCA	27%
NSPCC	23%
Barnardo's	19%
Help the Aged	17%
Save the Children	17%
British Heart Foundation	16%
Red Cross	16%
Age Concern	15%
SCOPE/Spastics Society	11%
Cancer Relief Macmillan	9%
RNLI	9%
RNIB	8%
MENCAP	8%
Salvation Army	8%
Christian Aid	7%
Marie Curie	7%
Guide Dogs for the Blind	4%
PDSA	3%
RSPB	3%
WWF	3%
Action for Blind People	2%
MS Society	2%
Shelter	2%
Action Aid	1%
MIND	1%
RNID	1%
Samaritans	1%
St John Ambulance	1%

Big promotional campaigns, especially advertising, can uplift awareness figures significantly. While Oxfam is the UK's consistently best known charity, on this occasion it was beaten by the Cancer Research Campaign who had just finished a major advertising campaign.

Prompted awareness, as the term implies, is where a list of charity names are read out and people are asked if they have heard of them. With this form of measurement much higher scores are achieved, e.g. Oxfam's awareness level rises to between 90 and 95 per cent.

Opinions differ on the usefulness of such general awareness tracking studies. My view is that unprompted awareness figures are a useful measurement of rising and declining popularity over time, and are especially useful when broken down into geographic areas, age, sex and socio-economic status. While one cannot guarantee that a spontaneous mention reflects a positive attitude towards the individual charity, given people's generally warm view towards charities this seems to me to be a fairly likely possibility. If that assumption is made, then charity unprompted awareness levels, over time, provide a useful relative measure of a charity's popularity. However, as with so many such measures, they give few clues as to *why* a charity's popularity is growing or declining; but they do prompt the charity marketer as to whether there is a general charity identity problem or not, and the extent of it.

Research among stakeholders

Charities are, rightly, increasing the amount of research they undertake among stakeholders. As the name implies, these are the people who have a particular stake in the effective running of the organisation (other than the broader groups of beneficiaries and supporters). Stakeholders consist particularly of staff and committee and council members, but also include the leaders of key external groups or organisations who work closely with the charity – for example, government ministers and civil servants, local authority representatives, very major funders, etc. It is particularly important to note that a welcome trend among charities is to include representative beneficiaries, or, even better, formal representatives of beneficiaries onto the charity councils and committees. This tendency sets charities apart from the vast majority of commercial organisations and provides a unique marketing opportunity. While the beneficiary representatives cannot be truly representative of every person that the charity is helping, they do provide quite a different kind of insight and input into trustee planning and evaluation of charity services. In terms of the commercial marketing rhetoric of 'involving customers' and the growing interest in relationship marketing, the commercial marketing sector has much to learn from these progressive charities.

Research among stakeholders commissioned from independent outside agencies, and undertaken with guarantees of confidentiality, can be of inestimable value in understanding how the charity is really regarded. For example, government ministers and civil servants will often, in public, give (superficial) accolades to an individual charity. However, in the privacy of their own offices, being interviewed with guarantees of anonymity, they will give quite a different story! It is important that these views, if they are widely held among stakeholders, are fed through to the charity.

Stakeholder research will also get under the surface of known differences between distinct groups of stakeholders. For example, disability charities founded by parents of disabled children (e.g. MENCAP and SCOPE) have real and understandable differences of opinion between parent representatives, the generation of disabled adults in committee leadership positions (who were originally their children) and stakeholders who believe that the remit of the organisation should be broadened outside the specific client group. Stakeholder research can begin to identify the extent of the opinion differences, likely areas of common ground, etc., in ways that are less easy to achieve in formal committee situations.

Staff are stakeholders and given the dominance of services in charities, staff views, attitudes and behaviour contribute significantly to charity identity and positioning. If charity senior managers do not understand the true views of staff at different levels as to the charity's operation, and in particular the projected identity and positioning, then, all too quickly, staff will be asked to project messages that they do not believe in.

Other-player analysis

Commercial marketers would call this competitor analysis, but in most situations such a term is inappropriate in the charity setting. I would define it as follows: 'The term "other player" signifies any organisation whose activities in supplying other similar products (goods, services or ideas) might have a significant impact on the charity's own activities'. Thus other players consist of other charities, commercial organisations, statutory organisations and, in some situations, what the Wolfenden Committee (Wolfenden 1977, pp. 22–27) calls the informal sector of family, friends and neighbours.

Macro environmental analysis

Before getting into detailed other-player analysis, especially if the review is a fundamental one, it is important to undertake a broader environmental analysis of likely trends that may impact on the charity. These are generally identified as either *social*, *political*, *technical* or *economic* impacts. Social changes would include such things as changing age structures (the ageing population); political changes (broadly defined) include such things as changing government policy to encompass greater purchasing of welfare state services from commercial organisations and charities, or new policies such as Care in the Community, etc. Technical changes might be the impact of more sophisticated, user-friendly and cheaper computers: for example, allowing disabled people to become more independent of personal helpers; or the impact of more sophisticated recording techniques on orchestral recordings, making them sound very different from live concerts. Changes in the economic environment might include the impact of a recession or a boom on the charity – moving into a recession may impact on charity income in some areas (e.g. individual giving); may be delayed in other areas (e.g. company donations that come out of previous years' profits); or may be relatively unaffected in other areas (e.g. legacies).

Other charities

For the relatively few charities that undertake other-player analysis, other charities tend to be the main focus of attention both in terms of service giving, fund-raising and pressure group work. As far as service giving to beneficiaries is concerned the particular charity subsector (e.g. charities concerned with old age, the dramatic arts, overseas aid or the environment) tend to be the most important for consideration.

When it comes to fund-raising, the net will inevitably be cast wider. Significant other charity players can be identified in a number of ways. For example, people leaving bequests tend to name several charities and the charities legacy department will be able to say who these are. Research among donors can provide similar evidence. Another way of identifying significant other players is to look at areas of a charity's fund-raising strength and identify any other rising star charities in this area. For example, if an individual charity has a great dependency on legacies, which are the other major bequest-receiving charities and which have grown the fastest over the years? Is it possible to identify why they have grown faster? Are they in your charity subsector?

Commercial organisations

At first sight, analysis of commercial organisations might seem irrelevant. However, this is far from the case, especially in the field of physical product and service product offerings. Most charities have implicit or explicit policies of cross-subsidy between various physical and service products offered. Some actually make profits for the charity, although these are best handled through a related charitable company. Commercial entrepreneurs are quick to spot market opportunities, creaming off profitable potential areas of charity activity and leaving the charity (perhaps correctly?) with the products that require heavy subsidy. For example the changes in social security payments for residential care for older people in the late 1970s and early 1980s provided commercial companies with significant profit opportunities in running old people's homes. The commercial sector of this market expanded dramatically while the charity residential homes sector remained sluggish. In the fields of technical aids for disabled people, certain government funding schemes have provided major market opportunities which have been taken up by commercial companies rather than charities, especially in the high technology field. This is not to argue that such commercial provision is wrong – far from it, because the charity sector alone is unlikely to be able to fulfil market need. It is unprofessional, however, when the charity is blissfully unaware of the marketing opportunity and the commercial organisation expansion until it is a *fait accompli*.

Statutory organisations

While lack of analysis of commercial other-players can result in missed opportunities, lack of analysis of statutory organisation other-players can be disastrous. Most charities are providing service products (and occasionally physical products) contiguously and in interaction with statutory providers and/or funders. With a few exceptions (e.g. the Royal National Lifeboat Institution), the charity provider is smaller and has to act in a complementary fashion to the statutory provider. For charities in the social welfare field, the reorganisation of social services departments in the early 1970s into generic providing arms (rather than specialist ones for the elderly, children, mental welfare, etc.) caught many charities on the hop. The transfer in 1990 of many Department of Employment programmes from national responsibility to the responsibility of local training and employment councils (TECs) had major impacts for NACRO (the National Association for the Care and Resettlement of Offenders). It resulted in NACRO reducing its centres from 70 to 41 and its places for unemployed people from 13,000 to 6,000, and making 600 staff redundant (Stern 1993, p. 61). The changing quantity of arts funding and the changing balance between national and regional distribution has had a major impact on many arts organisations. The dramatic shifts in health and social services away from virtually sole provider into a situation where the statutory authority is a commissioning agent asking other organisations to tender competitively for services caught many charities relatively unaware. Many social welfare charities had spent thirty years learning to embrace a new dogma which encouraged them to pioneer new services and pass them on to the state. They have had to relearn rapidly, and decide whether to compete with other charities and commercial organisations to win contracts, sometimes for the very services they had passed on to the state in the 1950s, 1960s and early 1970s. For example, local voluntary societies for the blind passed over their assessment and rehabilitation services to local government in the 1960s. Suddenly some social services departments were asking them to put in bids to take them back.

Positioning the charity

The preceding chapters have regularly looked at positioning for individual products, be they physical goods, services or ideas. However, here we are looking at the positioning of the organisation as a whole, and the reinforcement and development of the identity of the whole charity. To a great extent the overall identity and position is the sum of the decisions on the different individual charity products. Therefore there has to be overall guidance and decision-making in relation to individual activities. In addition, there are separate and 'whole organisation' decisions which have to be made on charity identity, e.g. in the selection or retention of the charity name, its logo, its unique contributions, etc.

Porter (1980) argues that commercial organisations should position themselves in one of three ways: through strong differentiation from competitors, through cost leadership (not necessarily the cheapest price but the price that sets the standard in the market) or through focus. Kotler and Andreasen (1991, pp. 206–12) argue that organisations should strive for any one of the following long-term market positions, namely market leader, market challenger, market follower or market nicher.

There is no doubt in my mind that if a charity can achieve it, the route of differentiation and distinctiveness is the one to take, providing that the cause is an acceptable or potentially acceptable one. For example, in the overseas aid field, the combination of name, reputation and activity are inherently stronger for Save the Children and Help the Aged than they are for Action Aid. In the UK volunteering market, the two major charities have sought differentiation. Both Community Service Volunteers and the Volunteer Centre UK (now the National Centre for Volunteering or NCV) exist to promote volunteering. Community Service Volunteers does it through the direct placement of (mainly) young people into volunteering situations, and using the experience gained to promote volunteering policy. The NCV was set up to provide an information, research and development resource on volunteering in general, and chose to be distinctive by deliberately not involving itself directly in volunteer recruitment and placement. This, it argued, ensured that its advice would not be skewed by involvement with a particular volunteer programme. In other words, Community Service Volunteers and the National Centre for Volunteering are differentiated from each other in a relatively narrow field.

Positioning of the largest charities providing a multiplicity of services at first looks straightforward. Across the whole charity sector, Barnardo's, RNIB and SCOPE are distinctly differentiated by the nature of the client group they are helping. Market positioning around a beneficiary group may be good differentiation and attractive to supporters. However, the vagaries of social policy changes mentioned above can cause problems for this positioning. For example, statutory services have increasingly preferred to work with generic groups of clients, e.g. disabled people rather than people with cerebral palsy. They would prefer to do business with generic charities rather than organisations dealing with what they see as narrow interest groups. Single-interest groups' response to this situation is to argue that such a positioning is important just because other people do not view the world from the position of the single interest.

However, trying to get across the very wide range of services that these charities provide for one beneficiary group and thus differentiate themselves from smaller charities operating in their subsector is very difficult. Emphasis on any one particular service, e.g. residential centres, talking books or employment rehabilitation, might differentiate the organisation, but it works against the charity by making it appear specialist and may restrict its room for social policy manoeuvre. For example, children's homes are no longer part of Barnardo's repertoire, and SCOPE no longer provides employment rehabilitation. For these large charities the only tactic open to them is that of market leader.

For smaller and medium-sized charities, niche marketing is attractive, e.g. the Macmillan nurses of Cancer Relief Macmillan against the giants of the Imperial Cancer Research Fund and Cancer Research Campaign, or Crisis at Christmas in relation to Shelter.

So the world of charity identity and positioning is nothing if not complicated! Steady evolution, if not on occasions revolution, of a charity's identity and position is required. It was only a matter of time before organisations with names and identities such as the Royal Home and Hospital for Incurables, the National Old People's Welfare Council and the Spastics Society had to update their identity and position.

Charity relaunch or repositioning

The charity world has been alive with launches, relaunches and repositionings, probably for as long as charities have existed. But the last thirty years have seen a great deal of activity. Among the trends that have encouraged this repositioning and relaunch activity have been the growing size and scope of statutory services (up to the 1980s) and their fundamental reorientation in the 1980s and 1990s; the accommodation of charities to these changes, initially through the handing over of services to the state, their partly consequentially increased role as critics of statutory services on behalf of disadvantaged groups (i.e. the rise of overt pressure group activity); the increasing adoption of commercial techniques, especially in fund-raising activities; the impact of a new breed of charity leaders who, partly personally, changed the whole dynamic of charity activities (e.g. Jackson Cole of Help the Aged, Des Wilson of Shelter, David Hobman of Age Concern, David Ennals and Tony Smythe of MIND); the increasing adoption of more professional management practice, initially in the 1970s from the statutory services, and in the 1980s and 1990s from commercial organisations; and the rapid rise in the number of charities.

To give comprehensive and detailed examples from these exciting years would make book in itself. What follows are a few short examples which indicate some of the aspects of a relaunch. However, these should not be taken to indicate that charity identity development, or brand development is common. Indeed Tapp (1996) argues that such development work is scarce.

Launch of Shelter: the national campaign for the homeless

The launch of Shelter in 1968, tied to the publicity rocket of the TV drama documentary 'Cathy Come Home', is already a legend. Des Wilson, as director, brought all the marketing and public relations skills that good journalists have, plus his public presentational skills. Reference is made earlier in the book to this launch, which essentially pioneered the way for charities to become overt pressure groups and campaigning bodies while retaining charitable status – even though the debate rumbles on.

National Old People's Welfare Council relaunched as Age Concern England

The National Old People's Welfare Council (NOPWC) was set up in the mid-1940s as a coordinating body of local old people's welfare committees – all under the arm of what has since become the National Council for Voluntary Organisations. In 1970 the NOPWC became independent of the National Council for Voluntary Organisations and appointed its first director, David Hobman. I joined at the same time, as Appeals and Public Relations Officer.

When a charity has such an indistinct, old-fashioned and unmemorable name as the National Old People's Welfare Council, there are no prizes for changing it! Nevertheless it felt quite difficult and brave at the time, with an organisation that was rather encrusted with tradition. However, the process of name selection was unusual. NOPWC got eight advertising agencies to bid for the charity account of a princely £1,000 per annum, with part of the pitch requirements being the proposal of up to ten new names for the charity. These 80 names were reduced to one, exclusively by market research, with the executive committee accepting the one recommendation – Age Concern. Then came the job of persuading the 200-plus local independent Old People's Welfare Committees to adopt the name, and this required a big selling job. Within a year one-third had done so; within five years, 90 per cent had done so. These local adoptions were crucial in the overall success.

However, it is important to point out that this name change coincided with other major repositioning activity, e.g. with the organisation becoming much more proactive in its development of national coordination work, becoming much more active as a pressure group and rejuvenating the network of local Old People's Welfare Committees.

As a result of this repositioning and relaunch the charity has moved from being small and completely unknown to becoming one of the largest and best known in the country. It is worth noting that it took three years (until 1974) for the new name even to register on unprompted awareness scales; and after nearly three decades, despite the fact that Age Concern has around 1,000 local groups, it still has a lower unprompted awareness rating than its competitor Help the Aged.

The first conclusion from this example is that relaunching a charity with a new name is a long-term undertaking which will take many years to achieve. (The Royal Society for Mentally Handicapped Children, relaunched as MENCAP, is another example of this.) The second conclusion from the Age Concern relaunch is that, with the benefit of hindsight, it was perhaps wrong to rely entirely on the market research conducted to reduce the options down to the final one. It was probably not coincidence that the name most preferred, Age Concern, sounds quite similar to Help the Aged which was already a well-known and established charity at that time. However, because the two names are relatively similar, this makes market differentiation for both charities difficult.

Royal National Institute for the Blind

In the mid-1980s RNIB undertook a major strategic review of its aims, activities and resources. One of the major conclusions drawn was to concentrate more resources and activities on indirect services. Until that point RNIB, as one of the largest UK charities, had concentrated almost entirely on direct services to blind and partially sighted people. The review concluded that the major challenges that blind and partially sighted people faced were largely caused by insufficient attention from statutory organisations such as health services, social services and education, and from commercial organisations such as national utilities, supermarket chains, etc. So one of the major planks of the RNIB strategy of 1987, entitled 'Meeting the Needs of Visually Handicapped People', was a major expansion of indirect service activity to influence other organisations dealing directly with blind and partially sighted people. Eleven new indirect services were launched, including separate units offering training, advice and consultancy for the health services, social services and other local voluntary agencies working with blind and partially sighted people. More generally, campaigning and pressure group work was expanded dramatically.

It was decided that this repositioning should not be signalled by a name change although there were (and are) reasons for so doing. For example, the ponderous title did not reflect the wide range of over sixty services being delivered, nor did it reflect the exciting range of new physical and service products such as electronic newspapers, TV audio description and the indirect services described above. Also research among supporters revealed that, while the charity was seen to be doing a good job efficiently and effectively, it was felt to be rather old fashioned. Superficially this seemed to indicate an ideal opportunity and definite need for a name change. However, an umprompted awareness level of 8 per cent was not to be discarded lightly. It would take many years to rebuild to that level. Furthermore the 'establishment' quasi-academic ring to the title is helpful to pressure group work. Also very importantly, the current name was highly acceptable to organisations representing beneficiaries. (Over two-thirds of RNIB committee members are visually impaired, and the majority of these are elected by organisations of blind and partially sighted people.) Their leaders were against a name change and even argued against the addition of the word 'people' as subsequently adopted by RNID (becoming the Royal National Institute for Deaf People).

The preferred marketing solution was not to change the name but to move to the second most important physical indication of charity identity, the logo. After extensive market testing of options created by a design agency, the testing taking place among visually impaired as well as sighted customers and staff, a new identity was drawn up in the autumn of 1993.

However, as Berry and Parasuraman (1991, pp. 171–2) conclude, it is vital in a service organisation to have staff enthusiastic about the company. Charities are service dominated and it is essential to enthuse staff about a relaunch as it is they who carry the tangible product to customers. However, in charities there is an additional reason, namely that we do not have the money to devote to a relaunch that a commercial organisation would have available, and so staff and volunteers well disposed towards the new identity form a disproportionately large part of the promotional mix. The market testing of the new identity for the RNIB was undertaken among staff as well as beneficiaries and supporters, to ensure acceptability. The new identity was taken out personally to each of the 47 service locations across the United Kingdom by the five senior directors and the chief executive, and a short video was made, describing the reasons for the changes. The reaction to this internal promotional exercise was extremely positive.

The relaunch gained extensive TV, radio and press editorial coverage and was supported by press and poster advertising and a commercial link with BT phone cards. Heavy personal involvement of well-known figures such as Stevie Wonder, the Prime Minister and Anneka Rice provided the catalyst for media interest.

Royal Commonwealth Society for the Blind

An example of a relaunch which almost 'just happened' was the adoption by the Royal Commonwealth Society for the Blind of the cover name SightSavers. RCSB had successfully achieved a Blue Peter children's TV appeal for their work. This programme is one of the most influential on a charity's fund-raising, image and awareness strength among young people. However, the programme-makers were worried that the rather ponderous title of the charity would be difficult to get across to the young audience who were to be enthused to raise millions of pounds. They came up with the name of SightSavers which the charity has subsequently adopted as its public cover name. This is perhaps an example of what one might call serendipity marketing!

Barnardo's

Barnardo's had a similar image problem to RNIB. Market research showed that the image of the then Dr Barnardo's was still too Victorian. But with an unprompted awareness level of 20 per cent, Barnardo's would have been foolish to seek modern anonymity as a replacement to Victorian fame! The brilliant marketing solution it came up with was to drop the 'Dr', thus losing an element of its name that over-contributed to the formality of the image and referred people automatically back to the Victorian founder. In addition it developed a new logo, using all the market research activity described above.

While Barnardo's has recently reported that its identity among the general public has not shifted as much as it would have wished, it still seems to me to be one of the most thoughtful examples of a major national charity relaunch that we have seen so far.

Conclusion

Charity positioning and charity identity (brand) are fundamental considerations in a marketing approach. With around 12,000 new charities being registered each year and resources scarce, competition for attention from all customer target markets is intense. Consequently launches and relaunches are frequent, but only exceptionally reach the public eye. Such relaunches require a fundamental marketing approach, rather than action on the whim of the advertising agency, chief executive or chairperson. The charity identity ideally has to be memorable, distinctive, descriptive and flexible, but above all it has to reflect a reality rather than an advertising agency's dream. Relaunches have to reflect real advances in the charity's work if they are to be fundamentally sound.

Above all there are no quick fixes. Charities do not have, and in any event should not spend, the millions of pounds that a commercial company would devote to a relaunch of one of its major brands. Charity identities are built up slowly, methodically and painstakingly over decades. Managers with a marketing view will be more than conscious of the heritage of their charity. Changes are likely to be incremental rather than revolutionary. They will certainly need to take account of the changing social, political, technological and economic environment in which we work. They will also have to take account of the needs and wishes of supporters. But if charity is to mean anything, and if marketing is to mean anything in the charity world, it will be the needs and wishes of the end beneficiaries that will drive us forward.

Key points

Identity

☐ The physical representation of the charity (logo, name, the 'brand') should be firmly controlled.
☐ The charity name should be:
  – distinctive;
  – relevant;
  – memorable;
  – flexible.
  But do not risk sacrificing existing goodwill and awareness by changing what might seem to be a weak name without proper consideration.
☐ Be aware of the commercial value of the logo, but control its use carefully.
☐ Take particular care over the physical expression of the name and logo – in advertisements, publications and signs.
☐ The message given to and perceived by supporters and beneficiaries is crucial in establishing identity. Make sure that their direct experiences are positive.
☐ Research among beneficiaries, supporters, stakeholders and staff is crucial in establishing, amending or repositioning identity and market positioning.

Positioning

☐ If possible, build market position by distinctiveness and strong differentiation.

11

MARKETING: THE WAY FORWARD

Charities face a dilemma. The need for them is acute – arguably greater than any time over the last 50 years. But coincidentally their role has become much more complicated, even muddled, and probably will not become clear for another five or ten years.

Our niche markets of pioneering and pressure group activity remain. However, the statutory authorities, far from wanting to take on new, proven services, are busy contracting out traditional mainstream provision; not simply to charities but also to quasi-governmental organisations (e.g. hospital trusts and opted-out schools) and commercial companies. Often this contracting-out is under competitive tender. Charities are unsure when and where to compete, or even whether and from what perspective to engage in the debate about the rules that should govern this rapidly evolving mixed economy of welfare. In short, charities are being buffeted by much larger political and economic forces. Traditional strategic positions and operational techniques are not guiding us through this storm.

I hope that this book has shown how marketing as a philosophy, as well as a strategic and operational tool, can help and provide us with a means of steering successfully through these rough seas of change; and, more fundamentally, help to keep our course true to our reason for existing.

While financial and production disciplines are as important as they have ever been, on their own, or even in combination, they are not enough. Commercial organisations, let alone charities, are not successful in anything but the short term when they are finance led or production led. The increasingly dominant ethos in the commercial world is to be marketing led.

The applicability to the charity sector of the marketing ethos, of starting with the needs and wants of the customer, is strikingly obvious. Indeed critics might say that this is what we have always done. I think that position is arguable, but would need to write another book of a more historical nature! What is important is that charities, like marketing, have at their heart the needs of customers, whether they are called clients, students, patients, users, audience or patrons; and so we have a philosophical fit between marketing and charities.

Marketing is also well suited to cope with the increasingly competitive and rapidly changing world of the mixed economy of welfare, since marketing was developed as a means of coping with an increasingly competitive commercial and production environment of the 1950s and 1960s. It defines its product offerings of goods, services and ideas not only in terms of the customer, but also in relation to other providers. So it is particularly good at helping in situations where the boundaries between services and sectors are changing – a challenge now crucial to charities.

Such a philosophy is also well suited to the growth of consumerism in the charity world. It is an approach that concentrates on customer needs and uses techniques such as marketing research. It sits well with a model that sees customers as having rights, and with a reality of rising charity customer expectations.

For charity workers still worried about its origins, it is important to emphasise that marketing as a practice is value-neutral. It can be used for good or ill – to promote smoking or to discourage it. As a philosophy it is not value-neutral. It is bad marketing to promote harmful products which clearly do not meet the needs of customers.

Last, it is important to emphasise that marketing is not some wonder ingredient – not just icing on the cake. It is a holistic operational approach which enables charities to adapt their goods, services and ideas in ways that fundamentally take account of the needs of their end customers, but which also takes account of what other providers are doing. As the previous chapters have shown, its key analytical tools are as follows:

- [ ] marketing research;
- [ ] customer segmentation;
- [ ] positioning of offerings (in relation to other providers); and
- [ ] other-player analysis.

Crucial to the success of the offering are the eight 'Ps' of the charity marketing mix:

- [ ] philosophy;
- [ ] product;
- [ ] price;
- [ ] promotion;
- [ ] place;
- [ ] people;
- [ ] physical evidence; and
- [ ] process.

Using a marketing philosophy and marketing techniques in charities will not in itself redefine the boundaries between the various sectors of the evolving mixed economy, nor will it, in itself, redefine the role of charity. What it will do is help individual charities to operate successfully during and after this period of turbulence in a way that will be true to the people and causes to which they are committed. In short, marketing in charities is a powerful philosophical and practical force for positive development and progress.

APPENDIX 1

Johns Hopkins structural operational definition of the broad voluntary sector. Kendall and Knapp (1996) pp. 18–19

"Organisations appearing to meet all of the following criteria were regarded as voluntary bodies for the purposes of cross-national comparison.

Formal. Only structural entities with constitutions or formal sets of rules, perhaps (but not necessarily) registered with a public authority or voluntary intermediary body, were included. This ruled out the large set of informal household and neighbourhood support activities, which are particularly important in the community development and social welfare fields.

Independent of government and self-governing. Groups were required to be constitutionally or institutionally independent of government, and self-governing – that is, with their own internal decision-making structures, and not directly controlled by a private (for-profit) entity or by the state. This criterion does *not* exclude from the sector constitutionally independent organisations heavily dependent on the private market or the government for their resources.

Not-profit-distributing and primarily non-business. Organisations were ruled out if they were empowered to distribute net earnings to controlling persons (even if on solidaristic principles) or had a commercial orientation which made them indistinguishable from for-profit firms. Cooperatives, financial and other mutuals (including building societies, most friendly societies and motoring organisations) were among the exclusions.

Voluntary. A meaningful degree of voluntarism in terms of money or time through philanthropy or voluntary citizen involvement was required to qualify an agency as belonging to the sector.

Two further criteria were adopted for the purposes of statistical mapping only. *Party political* organisations were excluded. And *sacramental activities*, taken to include places of worship and the central infrastructure and support bodies of the churches, were omitted – although they are recognised in the classification scheme."

APPENDIX 2

Office of National Statistics definition of general charities within the UK voluntary sector (Hems and Passey 1996, p. 10)

"General charities are defined in national accounting terms as 'private, non-profit-making bodies serving persons' (PNPMBs). The four key criteria are:

1. *Independent governance*
   General charities are separate from government and business. This criterion excludes the folowing types of organisation:

   ☐ Those bodies allocated in national accounts terms to general government, such as:
      – registered charities which are also non-departmental public bodies or quasi non-governmental organisations including the British Council and the British Museum;
      – educational establishments, including universities and voluntary aided schools, which are recognised as exempt or excepted charities and are predominantly funded by government.
   ☐ financial institutions which are allocated to the corporate sector in national accounts, e.g. Charities Official Investment Fund (COIF).

2. *Non-profit distributing*
   General charities do not distribute profits to shareholders. This criterion excludes cooperatives.

3. *Objects have a wider public benefit*
   General charities provide a wider public benefit that goes beyond any membership. This criterion excludes:

   ☐ Mutual types of non-profit organisation which are solely for the benefit of their members, such as:
      – friendly societies and building societies (which may also be seen as financial institutions);
      – housing associations;
      – sports and social clubs;
      – independent schools; and
      – trade unions.

4. *Non-sacramental religious bodies/places of worship*
This criterion excludes organisations which are predominantly sacra-mental religious bodies or places of worship from a general charities definition.

The definition of general charities within the UK voluntary sector therefore includes:

☐ The household-name, national charities, such as:
- Shelter, Save the Children Fund, Action Aid, Royal National Insti-tute for the Deaf, Royal National Institute for the Blind.
☐ Local charities."

REFERENCES

Age Concern England (1974), *The Attitudes of the Retired and Elderly*, Age Concern: London.

Ali, M. (1996), *The DIY Guide to Marketing*, Directory of Social Change: London.

American Marketing Association (1985), *Marketing News*, 1 March.

Ansoff, H.I. (1965), *Corporate Strategy*, McGraw-Hill: Toronto.

Arbuthnot, S. and S. Horne (1997), The Marketing Activities of UK Charities, *Journal of Non-profit and Public Sector Marketing*, 5.1, 63–79.

Baker, M.J. (ed.) (1987), *The Marketing Book*, Heinemann: London.

Baker, M.J. (1991), *Marketing*, 5th edn, Macmillan: Basingstoke.

Barclays/NGO Finance 100 Charity Index, *NGO Finance Magazine*, Vol. 76, Plaza Publications: London.

Bayley, T.D. (1988), *The Fundraiser's Guide to Successful Campaigns*, McGraw-Hill: New York.

Berry, L.L. and A. Parasuraman (1991), *Marketing Services: Competing through quality*, The Free Press/Macmillan: New York.

Blois, K.J. (1987), Marketing for Non-profit Organisations, in M.J. Baker (ed.), *The Marketing Book*, Heinemann: London.

Blyth, B. (1989), Marketing Research, in N.J. Thomas (ed.), *Marketing Handbook*, 3rd edn, Gower: Aldershot.

Booms, B.H. and M.J. Bitner (1981), Marketing Strategies and Organisation Structures for Service Firms, in J. Donnelly and W.R. George (eds), *Marketing of Services*, American Marketing Association: Chicago, 47–51.

Borden, N.H. (1964), The Concept of the Marketing Mix, *Journal of Advertising Research*, 4(2), 2–7.

Brophy, M. (1992), Foreword, in J. McQuillan, *Charity Trends 1992*, CAF: Tonbridge.

Bruce, I. (1973), How to Use Public Relations in the Social Services, in *Report of a Working Group on Public Relations in the Social Services*, United Nations: New York.

Bruce, I. (1985), Policy Guidelines for a Development Programme, *New Beacon*, January, RNIB: London.

Bruce, I. (1991), Employment of People with Disabilities, in G. Dalley (ed.), *Disability and Social Policy*, Policy Studies Institute: London.

Bruce, I. (1992), Using Market Research as a Tool in National Campaigning, *Review of the European Blind*, 3(LXXVII), Berlin.

Bruce, I. (1993), Social Marketing, in I. Bruce (ed.), *Charity Talks on Successful Development*, VOLPROF, Centre for Voluntary Sector and Not-for-Profit Management, City University: London.

Bruce, I. (1994), *Meeting Need – Successful Charity Marketing*, ICSA: Hemel Hempstead.

Bruce, I. (1995), Do not-for-profits value their customers and their needs?, *International Marketing Review* 12.4, 77–84.

Bruce, I., D. Castillejo, C. Cornford, C. Gosford and F. Routh (1974), *Patronage of the Creative Artist*, Artists Now: London.

Bruce, I., A. McKennell and E. Walker (1991), *Blind and Partially Sighted Adults in Britain: The RNIB survey*, HMSO: London.

Bruce, I. and A. Raymer (1992), *Managing and Staffing Britain's Largest Charities*, VOLPROF, Centre for Voluntary Sector and Not-for-Profit Management, City University Business School: London.

Burnett, K. (1992), *Relationship Fundraising*, White Lion Press: London.

Burnett, K. (1996), *Friends for Life – Relationship Fund-raising in Practice*, White Lion Press: London.

CAF (1991), *Directory of Grant-Making Trusts*, 12th edn, CAF: Tonbridge.

CAF (1992), *Charity Trends*, 15th edn, CAF: Tonbridge.

Chamberlin, E.H. (1938), *The Theory of Monopolistic Competition*, Harvard University Press.

Chase, R.B. (1978), Where Does the Customer Fit into a Service Organisation?, *Harvard Business Review*, Nov./Dec., 137–42.

Conway, T. (1997), Strategy versus Tactics in the Not-for-profit Sector: A Role for Relationship Marketing, *Journal for Non-profit and Voluntary Sector Marketing*, 2.1, 42–51.

Corporate Intelligence on Retailing (1992), *Charity Shops in the UK*, Corporate Intelligence Research: London.

Cowell, D. (1984), *The Marketing of Services*, Heinemann: Oxford.

Coxall, W.N. (1985), 2nd edn, *Parties and Pressure Groups*, Longman: London.

Crosier, K. (1975), What Exactly is Marketing?, *Quarterly Review of Marketing*, Winter.

de Chernatony, L. and M.H.B. McDonald (1992), *Creative Powerful Brands*, Butterworth Heinemann: Oxford.

Deacon, D., P. Golding and B. Walker (1994), Voluntary Activity in a Changing Communications Environment, *ESRC Fund Report*, Loughborough University: Loughborough.

Deacon, D., N. Fenton and B. Walker (1995), Communicating Philanthropy: The Media and the Voluntary Sector in Britain, *VOLUNTAS*, 6.2, 119–139.

Dibb, S., L. Simkin, W. Price and O.C. Ferrell (1991), *Marketing: Concepts and strategies*, Houghton Mifflin: Boston.

Dibb, S., L. Simkin, W.M. Price and O.C. Ferrell (1994), *Marketing Concepts and Strategies*, Houghton Mifflin Company: Boston and London.

Dixon, M. (1997), Small and Medium Sized Charities Need a Strong Brand Too, *Journal of Non-profit and Voluntary Sector Marketing*, 2.1, 52–57.

Doyle, P. (1991), Managing the Marketing Mix, in M.J. Baker (ed.), *The Marketing Book*, 2nd edn, Heinemann: London.

Drucker, P. (1990), *Managing the Non-Profit Organisation*, Butterworth Heinemann: Oxford.

Eiglier, P. and E. Langeard (1977), *A New Approach to Services: New Insights*, Report 77/115, Marketing Science Institute: Boston.

Embley, L.L. (1993), *Doing Well While Doing Good*, Prentice Hall: Englewood Cliffs, NJ.

Espy, S. (1993) *Marketing Strategies for Nonprofit Organisations*, Lyceum Books: Chicago.

Eurostat (1988), Commission of the European Community (no further details).

Evans, K.R. and R.J. Schultz (1996), Towards an Understanding of Public Purchaser and Salespersons Interaction Activities, *Journal of Non-profit and Public Sector Marketing*, 4.4, 55–75.

Fenton, N. (1995), Charities, Media and Public Opinion: The Ideology of Welfare, in *Researching the UK Voluntary Sector*, NCVO: London.

Field, F. (1982), *Poverty and Politics*, Heinemann: London.

Fine, S.F. (1990), *Social Marketing: Promoting the causes of public and non profit agencies*, Allyn and Bacon: Needham Heights.

FitzHerbert, L. and L. Rhoades (1997), *The National Lottery Year Book*, Directory of Social Change: London.

Ford, D. (1996), Obtaining Legacies Face to Face, *Journal of Non-profit and Voluntary Sector Marketing*, 1.3, 203–212.

Foxall, G.R. (1987), Consumer Behaviour, in M.J. Baker (ed.), *The Marketing Book*, Heinemann: London.

Gabor, A. (1980), *Pricing Principles & Practices*, Heinemann: London.

Gaskin, K., M. Vlaeminke and N. Fenton (1996), *Young People's Attitudes to the Voluntary Sector*, Loughborough University: Loughborough.

George, W.R., J. Patrick Kelly and Claudia E. Marshall (1983), Personal Selling of Services, in L.L. Berry, G. Lynn Shostack and G.D. Upah (eds), *Emerging Perspectives on Services Marketing*, American Marketing Association: Chicago.

Greengross, S. (1993), Accountability, in I. Bruce (ed.), *Charity Talks on Successful Development*, VOLPROF, Centre for Voluntary Sector and Not-for-Profit Management, City University Business School: London.

Gronroos, C. (1980), *An Applied Service Marketing Theory*, Working Paper No. 57, Swedish School of Economics and Business Administration: Helsinki.

Gwin, J.M. (1991), Constituent Analysis, *European Journal of Marketing*, 24.7, 43–48.

Halfpenny, P. and S. Saxon-Harrold (1991), *Charity Household Survey 1989/90*, CAF: Tonbridge.

Harker, D. (1993), The NGO Finance Annual Survey of Charity Shops, in *NGO Finance*, **3**(1), London.

Harrison, T. (1987), *A Handbook of Advertising Techniques*, Kogan Page: London.

Hems, L. and A. Passey (1996), *The UK Voluntary Sector Statistical Almanac 1996*, NCVO: London.

Henley Centre (1996), *Survey of Public Attitudes*, Henley Centre/NCVO: Henley.

Hibbert, S. and S. Horne (1996), Giving to Charity: Questioning the donor decision process, *Journal of Consumer Marketing*, Vol. 13, No. 2, 4–13.

Hill, E., C. O'Sullivan and T. O'Sullivan (1995), *Creative Arts Marketing*, Butterworth Heinemann: Oxford.

Hinton, N. (1993), Planning for Growth, in I. Bruce (ed.), *Charity Talks on Successful Development*, VOLPROF, Centre for Voluntary Sector and Not-for-Profit Management, City University Business School: London.

Hiscock, H.E. (1991), *Trading by Charities*, Charities Advisory Trust: London.

Holwegger, K. (1996), The RNID's Customer Care Initiative, *Journal of Non-profit and Voluntary Sector Marketing*, 1.2, 105–120.

Horne, S. and M. Moss (1995), Box Collection Schemes: Analysis of Box Performance and Site Locations, *Journal of Non-profit and Public Sector Marketing*, 3.2, 47–62.

Horne, S. and M. Moss (1996), Charity Box Collection Schemes, *Journal of Non-profit and Voluntary Sector Marketing*, 1.3, 263–273.

Johne, A. (1996), Succeeding at Product Development Involves More than Avoiding Failure, *European Management Journal*, Vol. 14, No. 2, April 1996.

Joseph, K. (1971), Speech to Age Concern England AGM, in *Introducing Age Concern*, Age Concern: London.

Kay, J.A. (1993), *Foundations of Corporate Success*, Oxford University Press: Oxford.

Kendall, J. and M. Knapp (1996), *The Voluntary Sector in the UK*, Manchester University Press: Manchester.

Kotler, P. and A. Andreasen (1991), *Strategic Marketing for Non-Profit Organisations*, 4th edn, Prentice Hall: Englewood Cliffs, NJ.

Kotler, P. and A. Andreasen (1995), *Strategic Marketing for Non-Profit Organisations*, 5th edn, Prentice Hall: Englewood Cliffs, NJ.

Kotler, P., G. Armstrong, J. Saunders and V. Wong (1996), *Principles of Marketing: The European Edition*, Prentice Hall: Hemel Hempstead.

Kotler, P. and K.F.A. Fox (1985) *Strategic Marketing for Educational Institutions*, Prentice Hall: Englewood Cliffs, NJ.

Kotler, P. and E.L. Roberts (1989), *Social Marketing: Strategies for changing public behaviour*, The Free Press/Macmillan: New York.

Leat, D. (1993), *Managing Across Sectors*, VOLPROF, Centre for Voluntary Sector and Not-for-Profit Management, City University Business School: London.

Lindsay, G. and A. Murphy (1996), A Systemic Approach to the Application of Marketing Theory for Charitable Organisations, *Journal of Non-profit and Voluntary Sector Marketing*, 1.3, 252–262.

Lovelock, C.H. and C.B. Weinberg (1984), *Marketing for Public and Non-Profit Managers*, John Wiley: New York.

Lovelock, C.H. and C.B. Weinberg (1989), 2nd edn, *Public and Non-profit Marketing*, The Scientific Press: Redwood City, CA.

Lynn, P. and J. Davis Smith (1991), *The 1991 National Survey of Volunteering in the UK*, The Volunteer Centre: Berkhamsted.

Martin, J., A. White and H. Meltzer (1989), *Disabled Adults: Services, transport and employment*, OPCS Survey Report 4, HMSO: London.

Maslow, A. (1943), *Motivation and Personality*, Harper & Row: New York.

McCarthy, E.J. (1981), *Basic Marketing*, 7th edn, Richard D. Irwin: Homewood, IL.

McKechnie, S. (1993), Pressure Group Work, in I. Bruce (ed.), *Charity Talks on Successful Development*, VOLPROF, Centre for Voluntary Sector and Not-for-Profit Management, City University Business School: London.

McNeal, J.U. and L. Zeren (1981), Brand Name Selection for Consumer Products, *MSU Business Topics*, Spring.

Miller, C. (1991), Lobbying: The development of the consultation culture, in G. Jordan (ed.), *The Commercial Lobbyists*, Aberdeen University Press.

NCVO (1996), Meeting the Challenge of Change, *Report of the Commission on the Future of the Voluntary Sector*, Chaired by N. Deakin, NCVO: London.

NCVO (1997), *Charitable Giving by the General Public and the National Lottery*, NCVO Research Department: London.

O'Sullivan, C. and T. O'Sullivan (1996), Naivety and Relationship Marketing in Non-profit Organisations, *Journal of Non-profit and Voluntary Sector Marketing*, 1.1, 32–40.

Oxfam (1992), *The Oxfam Review 91/2*, Oxfam: Oxford.

Oxfam (1993), Newspaper Fundraising, insert leaflet, September, Oxford.

Parminter, K. (1997), Successful Campaigning: Winning Friends and Influencing People, *Journal of Non-profit and Voluntary Sector Marketing*, 2.1, 18–22.

Passey, A., and L. Hems (1997), *Charitable Giving in Great Britain 1996*, NCVO: London.

Paton, R. (1996), What's Different About Non-profit and Voluntary Sector Marketing? A Research Agenda, *Journal of Non-profit and Voluntary Sector Marketing*, 1.1, 23–31.

Pentreath, R. (1994), Yorkshire Bitter Can Seriously Improve Your Skydiving, *Sport Parachutist*, Journal of the British Parachute Association, December 1993/January 1994, 9.

Pharoah, C. and R. Welchman (1997), *Keeping Posted – A survey of current approaches to public communication in the voluntary sector*, CAF: West Malling.

Pidgeon, S. (1996) *Stand By Your Brand, If You Are Aware Of It*, Third Sector 27/06/96.

Pigou, A.C. (1932), *The Economics of Welfare*, Macmillan: London.

Porter, M.E. (1980), *Competitive Strategy: Techniques for analysing industries and competitors*, The Free Press/Macmillan: New York.

Porter, M.E. (1985), *Competitive Advantage: Creating and sustaining superior performances*, Collier Macmillan: London

Posnett, J. (1992), Income and Expenditure in Charities in England and Wales, in *Charity Trends 1992*, CAF: Tonbridge.

Pyne, A.E. and D.R. Robertson (1997), Charity Marketing – More Focus on the Beneficiary, *Journal of Non-profit and Voluntary Sector Marketing*, 2.2, 154–162.

Rados, D.L. (1981), *Marketing for Non-Profit Organisations*, Auburn House: Dover, MA.

Reichheld, F.F. and W.E. Sasser Jr (1990), Zero Defections: Quality comes to services, *Harvard Business Review*, Sep.–Oct., 301–7.

Rodger, L.W. (1987), *Marketing the Visual Arts*, Scottish Arts Council: Edinburgh.

Sargeant, A. and H. Stephenson (1997), Corporate giving: Targeting the Likely Donor, *Journal of Non-profit and Voluntary Sector Marketing*, 2.1, 64–79.

Saxton, J. (1996a), Strategies for Competitive Advantages in Non-profit Organisations, *Journal of Non-profit and Voluntary Sector Marketing*, 1.1, 50–62.

Saxton, J. (1996b), Five Direct Marketing Strategies for Non-profit Organisations, *Journal of Non-profit and Voluntary Sector Marketing*, 1.4, 299–306.

Scott, D. (1993), Fighting Cancer with More than Medicine, in the *Annual Review* of Cancer Relief Macmillan Fund, London.

Sewell, C. and P.B. Brown (1990), *Customers for Life*, Doubleday: New York.

Shenfield, B. and I. Allen (1972), *The Organisation of Voluntary Service*, PEP: London.

Shostack, G.L. (1977), Breaking Free from Product Marketing, *Journal of Marketing*, **41**(2), American Marketing Association: Chicago.

Shostack, G.L. (1982), How to Design a Service, *European Journal of Marketing*, **16**(2).

Simon, H. (1989), *Price Management*, Elsevier: Amsterdam.

Spillard, P. (1987), Organisation for Marketing, in M.J. Baker (ed.), *The Marketing Book*, Heinemann: London.

Stern, V. (1993), The Influence of Rapidly Changing Government Policy, in I.

Bruce (ed.), *Charity Talks on Successful Development*, VOLPROF, Centre for Voluntary Sector and Not-for-Profit Management, City University Business School: London.

Tapp, A. (1996), Charity Brands: A Qualitative Study of Current Practice, *Journal of Non-profit and Voluntary Sector Marketing*, 1.4, 327–336.

Thomas, M. (1980), Market 'Segmentation', *Quarterly Review of Marketing*, **6**(1).

Walker, E., M. Tobin and A. McKennell (192), *Blind and Partially Sighted Children in Britain: The RNIB survey*, HMSO: London.

Wilson, A. (1984), *Practice Development for Professional Firms*, McGraw-Hill: Maidenhead.

Wilson, D. (1984), *Pressure: The A–Z of campaigning in Britain*, Heinemann: London.

Wolfenden, J. (1977), *The Future of Voluntary Organisations*, Croom Helm: London.

Zeithaml, Valarie A., A. Parasuraman and Leonard L. Berry (1985), Problems and Strategies in Services Marketing, *Journal of Marketing*, Spring, 33/146, American Marketing Association: Chicago.

INDEX